# *Irvin S. Cobb*

# Irvin S. Cobb

Anita Lawson

Bowling Green State University Popular Press
Bowling Green, Ohio 43403

Library of Congress Catalogue Card No.: 83-73108

ISBN: 0-87972-275-4 Clothbound

**For my father**

**William Lawrence Saffels**

**1911-1982**

# Contents

# Acknowledgments

Many individuals and institutions have given me help and encouragement in the preparation of this book. Irvin Cobb's grandchildren, Buff Cobb and Thomas Brody, have been generous with their time, their recollections, and their hospitality. Nelson Buhler, the trustee of the Cobb estate, has given both professional and personal assistance. The support of the Cobb family has been invaluable.

The Murray State University Committee on Institutional Studies and Research has provided funds to support my research, and Murray State has provided me released time from teaching. Murray State librarians, especially Keith Heim and Betty Hornsby, have provided excellent professional assistance and personal encouragement.

Many other librarians in Kentucky and elsewhere have provided me with excellent service. A few who have been especially helpful are Doris Simon of the Paducah Public Library; Riley Handy and Elaine Harrison of the Kentucky Library at Western Kentucky University; Sharon McConnell, Curator of the Townsend Room of the Crabbe Library of Eastern Kentucky University; Jacquelyn Bull of the University of Kentucky Library; and Paul Rugen of the New York Public Library.

More persons than I can list here have graciously provided me with information and insights. Especially helpful were John Pearce Campbell, Catherine Adams, Mary Dorian, Hardin Pettit, and E.J. Paxton, Jr., all of Paducah; Carol Sutton of the Louisville *Courier-Journal;* and James C. Bowling of New York City.

In preparing the manuscript I was aided by an excellent typist, Jamie Helton. Among those who read the manuscript in various stages of completion and offered valuable suggestions were Charles Roland, Margaret Trevathan, Berry Craig, Robert Burdette, Richard Steiger, and Delbert and Edith Wylder. The book's flaws should be attributed to my occasional failure to follow their advice.

I am grateful to all of those who have helped so much. I am especially grateful to Hughie Lawson, who was my chief adviser throughout and who never let me down.

# Acknowledgments

# Foreword

A full-page picture of Irvin Shrewsbury Cobb, then forty years old, appeared in the May, 1917, issue of *American Magazine* with the caption, "This man is a national institution." Cobb remained a national institution for two more decades, but the nature of his reputation changed, and those changes perhaps tell almost as much about the moods and needs of the American public in those decades as they do about Cobb himself.

In 1917 Cobb's reputation was mainly based on his humorous articles and stories in newspapers and *The Saturday Evening Post* and on his personalized war reporting from Europe in 1915. His public image was the crack reporter with a heart and a funnybone, a man concerned equally with reinforcing human values and deflating human pomposity. His pride in his hometown of Paducah, Kentucky, became his trademark, especially after he began to write the Judge Priest tales based on his own childhood. This small town connection, however, did nothing to diminish his authority. Perhaps because such a large portion of the reading public viewed themselves as small town dwellers, perhaps because other writers such as Sut Lovingood and George Ade had popularized its virtues, the small town viewpoint seemed the proper one from which to expose the absurdities of New York politics, to parody the anxieties of a hospital patient, and to deplore the plight of occupied Belgium. While Cobb's Southern origins led his readers to expect an accent and colorful anecdotes with Southern settings, these features do not seem to have been an important part of his appeal.

In the twenties and thirties Cobb's appeal broadened as he moved into other areas. His public speaking engagements to describe the war soon led to routine lecture tours on general topics. His short stories, especially the Judge Priest tales, found an audience as large as that for his humorous sketches. He appeared on radio shows, wrote syndicated columns, talked with and about celebrities, became a movie star, and was asked to deliver an opinion on every popular issue of the day from the length of hemlines to the presence of communists in Hollywood. But, while he remained a national institution, his function changed. He ceased to be the spokesman for the dignity of the ordinary man in events both ridiculous and awesome and became instead a museum exhibit, the professional Southerner. By the late thirties Irvin Cobb was still a national figure, but few of his readers besides those in his native Kentucky identified with his viewpoint any more. He became an outsider.

The transformation is especially interesting because it was by no means a sinking back into an earlier identity. Although Cobb in his later years was welcomed to Kentucky as the favored son who had represented Kentucky to the world, Cobb as the country perceived him in the thirties was only a caricature of the Kentuckian he had tried to present earlier. In the "Preface" to *Back Home*, 1912, the first collection of the Judge Priest tales, he spells out his aim in these stories: to present a true picture of the Southerner. Although the rest of the country viewed Southerners as either plantation aristocrats or poor white trash, the typical Southerner was actually a small town man of some property whose principles and humanity made him kin to small town dwellers all over the country. By the late thirties the man who had made this distinction was appearing in a weekly radio show entitled "Paducah Plantation" and serving as Hollywood consultant for Southern authenticity in movies, with special attention to accents, Spanish moss and mint juleps.

Cobb himself contributed to the narrowing of the public's image of him. After the crash of 1929 his attitudes turned increasingly conservative, and the man who had campaigned enthusiastically for Al Smith in hostile Kentucky warned his friends about the dangers of Franklin Roosevelt. His early humorous writing had been an irreverent and up-to-date investigation of the absurdities of human conventions and attitudes, with the author himself frequently the butt of the jokes. In the thirties his humor became forced and even sour because too frequently it called on the conventions and attitudes of an earlier decade. Rather than exploding cliches, Cobb in his later years embalmed them. His jibes at himself were no longer wry and uninhibited, but were constricted to certain narrow areas: Cobb as fat man, Cobb as bemused male in a female household, Cobb as clumsy bull in the china shops of grand opera and literary salons.

In part Cobb's transformation from Everyman to professional Southerner was the result of his own doubts about his abilities. During the late teens while he was being hailed as the new great

American writer by authorities as diverse as Bob Davis and Sinclair Lewis, he felt safe only to call himself a good reporter. He was always confident of his ability to tell a story, but less secure about his abilities in the areas of characterization, theme and tone with which he experimented during the teens and early twenties. When his reading public seemed more interested in the plots and the Southern bric-a-brac, Cobb stopped experimenting with literary technique and turned out work that became more wooden as the years went by.

Cobb's insecurity about his own abilities was due in part to a revolution that took place in American literature in the teens and twenties. Cobb's literary ideal was Mark Twain, and in many ways his career parallels that of Mark Twain. Both were reporters, humorists, fiction writers and lecturers. At the turn of the century Mark Twain's type of literature was eminently respectable and the numerous other journalists turned fiction writers (Stephen Crane, Harold Frederic, O. Henry) assumed their works were as deserving of the title of literature as any other. Ironically, it was another journalist, H.L. Mencken, whose championing of such unlikely highbrows as Theodore Dreiser and Sinclair Lewis relegated Cobb, along with most of the other writers who published in *Munsey's, The Saturday Evening Post* or *Cosmopolitan*, to the low-brow category forever. Cobb's chief pattern in fiction, to demonstrate a possibility for reconciliation and brotherhood in a basically corrupt world, appeared old-fashioned and sentimental when juxtaposed with the new Lewis-Dreiser pattern: to reveal the corruption behind the facade of an apparently well-ordered and benevolent world. So in the same years that Cobb was being hailed by some literary lions as the writer of the decade, another faction was formulating a new definition of literature that would practically shut him out. The small town viewpoint, once accepted as an appropriate standard for moral and political judgments, became instead an object of attack in the new literature. Yet for every reader that Cobb lost to the new literature, he gained ten who could not stomach the naturalists but who found Cobb both safe and comfortable. His reading audience thus grew larger and narrower at the same time. Cobb, whether performing on stage or on paper, always had the storyteller's sensitivity to the audience's expectations and interests, and he gave his new audience what they wanted. As his writing narrowed in scope, the public persona that he presented narrowed also.

There is no doubt that Cobb enjoyed both his celebrity and the money it brought. From his childhood he had enjoyed an audience, and the crowds that flocked to hear him were probably a sufficient balm to heal more wounds than H.L. Mencken could inflict. The anxieties about money in his childhood home and his earnest desire to do well by the five women in his care made it impossible for him to adopt a bohemian nonchalance toward money; instead, most of his career decisions were made on immediate economic considerations. Various events in Cobb's career show his willingness to go to extremes both to please an audience and to earn a dollar. Since Cobb had never overestimated his abilities, the enthusiastic audience for his work and the money he made were probably worth more to him than a chance at literary greatness would have been.

Although Cobb made friends easily and always welcomed new acquaintances, after 1920 he became increasingly more comfortable among his cronies in the low-brow group than among the more self-consciously literary. Theodore Dreiser, Sinclair Lewis, Ring Lardner and the Algonquin crowd were friends of Cobb when he was more famous than they, but after they became prima donnas he preferred to lose touch with them. Years as a reporter had made Cobb comfortable within the bounds of respectability and cautious originality demanded by the middle-class magazines, and the insistance on individualism and horror of censorship that the high-brow writers professed seemed to Cobb the whining of spoiled children. Instead, he relied on the company of more congenial, less prickly types, such as Bob Davis, O.O. McIntyre, and Cobb's closest friend, Will Rogers. In many ways the role of popular writer, in which success is gauged by book sales and cheering crowds, suited Irvin Cobb perfectly.

Yet in his tailoring of his career to the demands of his "low brow audience" Cobb lost something else that was very important to him: his role as trustworthy authority on public issues. In his early career he had managed a balance between the funny business and the editorializing so that the former attracted an audience for the latter without diluting its authority. Somewhere in the late twenties he lost this balance and his serious pronouncements were more frequently treated as part of the joke. Here again it is difficult to separate audience pressures from the gradual decay in Cobb's own abilities. At any rate, at the beginning of Cobb's career as a short story writer, the unattractive characters are the ones who talk bombast, while Judge Priest is the mild mannered, gentle soul who can win cases with simple descriptions and homey appeals to decency. When Cobb began his career as a lecturer, he took pains to explain that he was not a rhetorician, just a storyteller. Cobb's writing style in the teens was as taut and journalistic as any editor could wish. By the thirties, however, both Cobb and Judge Priest had become as flamboyant and overripe in their rhetoric as a W.C. Fields imitation. Cobb's public image had become not the early Judge Priest figure of Southerner-as-Everyman, but one of his own bad examples. And the public pronouncements of such a figure, no matter how entertaining he is, are not to be taken seriously.

Another factor in the trivializing of Irwin S. Cobb was the increasingly impersonality of his contacts with his audience. As columnist and lecturer, and even as short story writer, he had spoken to his audiences in his own voice. Although that voice may have been inhibited or narrowed by the demands of his medium and the wishes of his audience, a real human being always lay behind the work. When he went from lecturing into radio broadcasting, his role changed. Seldom did he solo on radio; more frequently he participated in a group discussion in which he was expected not to offer insights but to play the role of Comic Southerner. He played the same role in the movies and his identity became completely submerged in the role. His newspaper columns, which in the teens had been marvelous comic essays reflecting his wry point of view, reappeared in the thirties as lists of old and seldom funny jokes with no unifying point of view at all.

Whether Irvin Cobb as comic Southerner was more a self-creation or a public product, by the late thirties the public didn't want it any more. The end of Cobb's life was not happy. He was living in Hollywood, the worst place to be unpopular, his movie offers dwindled, he became too ill to lecture, and, in an especially devastating blow, his syndicated column was cancelled. When his audience faltered, so did his faith in himself, and he found he could no longer write fiction. Instead, he turned to memoirs and in 1941 produced *Exit Laughing*, a series of autobiographical sketches that contained his best writing in a decade. The book was well received by both reviewers and purchasers, but Cobb was too bitter and ill for this good news to be of much help. The last few years of his life were in agonizing contrast to what had gone before. At times he lashed out with pettiness and even bigotry. The public seemed scarcely to notice, however, and preserved its image of Cobb as the jolly Southerner, devoted to the traditional values, until that view was severely damaged by the publication of Cobb's last letter dictating his funeral services. In this letter Cobb had his say about established religion, described heaven as dubious and dull, praised Jesus Christ as "the greatest gentleman that ever lived" and compared the Old Testament God to Hitler and Stalin. Cobb's antipathy to established religion began in his childhood, but he had never before made it so public. The public which had prompted him to take quite another role reacted in disgust, and letters to the editor poured in across the country scalding his memory with libellous fury. Whether that was his intention or not, Irvin Cobb left the world his own man.

The story of Irvin Cobb is a fascinating one for many reasons. His life was true to a traditional Horatio Alger pattern: poor boy makes good through hard work and lucky breaks. If he was never accepted by the literary elite, he was at the right place at the right time in many other areas: the New York newspaper world in the first decade of this century, behind the German lines in World War I, in the Broadway world of the twenties, in Hollywood during the thirties. His personal magnetism drew others to him, and his association with the many celebrities who became his friends, from Woodrow Wilson to Flo Ziegfeld give valuable insights in themselves. Giving focus to the richness of his experiences and associations, however, is the complicated figure of the man Irvin Cobb: harsh to himself, yet generous to others; opposed to restrictions, yet comfortable with conventions; willing to give everything to please an audience, yet frustrated when they refused to accept him as he was.

# Chapter One

"I *was* Tom Sawyer," Irvin Cobb liked to say, and Paducah, Kentucky, during his childhood was a robust, brawling river town like those described by Mark Twain. The settlement had been established only fifty years before Cobb's birth in 1876, but its position at the point where the Tennessee River flows into the Ohio provided a prosperity only slightly affected by the uncertainties of the Civil War years. By the seventies the town had a population of nine thousand, black and white, over one third of whom were directly dependent upon the river for a livelihood. Sidewheelers, sternwheelers and wharf boats vied for space at the landing to load the tobacco, cotton and peanuts grown on the Western Kentucky farmlands and the whiskey produced in the Paducah distilleries. Ferryboats, tugboats, transfer boats and skiffs crowded the waterways, and the air was full of black coal smoke and the noise of rasping chains and shouting rivermen. Farther inland the growing railroad lines which ultimately would take over much of the river trade loaded timber and mules. Between the river front and the railroads rushed drays, wagons and buggies, sending up clouds of dust on the Paducah streets.[1] In spite of its bustle of industry, Paducah was in many ways a frontier town in the seventies. The Chickasaw Indians who had originally claimed the land had withdrawn peaceably decades earlier, but there was still a feeling of being on the edge of the civilized world. The river and the men it brought gave Paducah residents a heightened awareness of the possibility of both failure and success. Physical danger was always present in a world of knife-toting, hard-drinking rivermen, of uneasy race relations, of swift currents and spring floods. But the river also brought constant reminders of a wider world of multiple opportunities; a boy growing up in Paducah learned both to be careful and to dream.

Both Cobb's grandfathers had come to Paducah from farther east in Kentucky: Reuben Saunders came from Frankfort in 1847, and Robert Livingstone Cobb from Eddyville in 1870.[2] The Cobbs had been prominent citizens before the Civil War, but the Saunders provided Irvin Cobb with whatever sense of social position he had as a boy.

The Cobbs came from Irish stock that had settled in Vermont, where Irvin Cobb's great grandfather Gideon Cobb married Modena Clark, the granddaughter of Vermont's first governor. Around 1800 Gideon and Modena led a band of families to settle in the vicinity of Eddyville, at that time the westernmost border of the Chickasaw territory. There Gideon Cobb erected the first foundry in Kentucky. Their son, Robert Livingston Cobb, enlarged the family holdings so that just before the Civil War he owned a bank, a tobacco warehouse, two large farms, and a part interest in two steamship lines. His home, White Hall, was the most elegant of the lower Cumberland Valley.[3] His sons, Robert and Joshua, were given excellent educations at boarding schools and at Georgetown College. This comfortable life was destroyed by the Civil War. Robert Livingstone Cobb was an ardent secessionist in a neutral state; he sold some of his holdings to invest in Confederate bonds, and lost much of the rest through failures brought on by the War. His eldest son, Robert, became a Confederate hero; Joshua, Irvin's father, who had enlisted as a Georgetown student, lost the sight of one eye in the War and returned to a home far different from the one he had left. Joshua Cobb had worked in the tobacco business with his father, and in 1867 he took the first of several traveling jobs in the steamboat or tobacco trades. His travels took him as far west as Paducah and as far south as New Orleans.[4] Probably by the time Robert Livingstone Cobb moved to Paducah in 1870, Joshua Cobb had come to think of Paducah as his home; in 1872 he married Manie Saunders and settled there in his father-in-law's house.

The Saunders were more colorful than the Cobbs. While Gideon Cobb had come as the leader of a caravan to found an industry, James Saunders had come a decade or so earlier from Virginia with a young wife, a pack and a tomahawk to homestead in a territory still occupied by Indians. James Saunders' Welsh-Scottish father had served in the Revolutionary War. One of his older brothers had married an Indian woman and their son, according to Saunders family legend, ran away from West Point to Mexico, where he became the legendary Santa Ana.[5]

James Saunders, whose laconic manner of speaking earned him the nickname "Jimmy Dry," was famous for his prowess as a volunteer rifleman against the Indians. The fertile soil and rolling hills of the wilderness where he had settled attracted many others, and by the time Reuben Saunders, one of the youngest of his children, was born in 1808, the growing town of Frankfort, Kentucky, had spread almost to his door. Reuben worked two years for a Frankfort newspaper as a teenager, but he would probably have become a farmer like his father had he not caught the eye of Ira Julian, a moderately wealthy citizen of Frankfort. Perhaps Julian heard about Reuben Saunders' knack for curing sick or injured animals; perhaps he saw some other signs of promise in the boy. At any rate, he agreed to loan the money for Reuben's tuition at medical school.[6] After attending schools in Alabama and South Carolina, Reuben Saunders received his degree at Jefferson Medical College in Philadelphia in 1836. He practiced first in Alabama, then returned to Kentucky and finally settled in Paducah in 1847.

Although Reuben Saunders soon became one of Paducah's prominent citizens, there was nothing refined about the conditions of his practice. The sick and injured of Paducah presented themselves at his house, where he prescribed for them as best he could from the medicines available. Dr. Saunders was a tall, gaunt, silent man who retained many of the mannerisms of his frontiersmen forebears; he never wore an overcoat, but draped himself in a bright blue Indian blanket in cold weather. Paducah itself presented several problems with medical implications: the Ohio River flooded to some extent every spring, with severe floods every five to ten years. Fires swept the city on occasion, most severely in 1852, when only two houses were left standing. And, most distressing of all, the town was subject to cholera epidemics spread by transients from other river ports. There had been several mild outbreaks before Dr. Saunders' arrival. In 1851 he tended the victims of another epidemic and saw ten of them die. The worst outbreak, however, was in 1873, when a worldwide epidemic claimed lives in India, Europe, New York, Philadelphia, and all over the South. Hundreds lay ill in Paducah, and, as the exhausted Dr. Saunders went from bed to bed, through accident or inspiration he tried an injection of belladonna. It seemed to have a beneficial effect, so Dr. Saunders telegraphed his medical school, which then sent the formula all over the world. The formula was named for Dr. Saunders, and, although its actual medical benefits must have been slight, several foreign countries decorated him for the discovery. Later that year when Ira Julian lay fatally ill, Reuben Saunders took the medals and ribbons and presented them to the old man. Julian died soon after, and by his request the medals were buried with him.[7]

The cholera treatment was a year in the future when Dr. Saunders' daughter Manie married Joshua Cobb in 1872, but if her father's fame had not yet spread round the world it was certainly solid in Paducah. Dr. Saunders was not only a successful doctor but a beloved figure in his adopted town, and Irvin Cobb claimed that over a hundred young people in Paducah and McCracken County were named Reuben or Reubie after his grandfather. The two story frame house on Third Street where the Saunders lived was one of the most pretentious in the city, and both the house and its owner were renowned because of an incident in the Civil War. Although Kentucky remained a neutral state, the sentiments of Paducah and western Kentucky were with the Confederates, feelings that were only intensified when Ulysses S. Grant arrived to occupy the city in September, 1861, announcing "I am here to defend you against this enemy."

Paducah became an important hospital station and Dr. Saunders volunteered his services throughout the War, treating both Union soldiers and Confederate prisoners alike. After Lee's surrender, the commandant of the Paducah garrison issued a petty order to humiliate the town whose silent hatred he had felt for three and a half years: he required that every house in town be illuminated in honor of the Union victory. All of the citizens complied except Dr. Saunders. He and his four daughters waited inside the totally dark house until ten o'clock in the evening, when a company of soldiers came to enforce the order, threatening to burn the house if it were not followed. According to family legend, the doctor, whose two sons were with the Confederate Army, refused to capitulate, saying, "I will not go through with this mockery." The Union lieutenant then called the doctor aside and whispered that he would spare the house because the doctor had saved his brother's life, but explained that he must order the soldiers to set the fires. The doctor and his family retired and the next morning saw the charred evidence on the outside of the frame house where fire had been repeatedly set and then put out. This story of defiance and reconciliation, so like the plot of an Irving Cobb narrative, was told to young Irvin over and over during his childhood in his grandfather's house. Neither of Dr. Saunders' sons returned to Paducah: the elder, a surgeon, went to the Sandwich Islands, where he had attained the romantic-sounding post of Court Physician to the King of Hawaii by the time Irvin Cobb reached manhood. The younger son went West for a life equally romantic in its appeal to his nephew, that of a gambler and

Dr. Reuben Saunders' house in Paducah where Irvin Cobb was born in 1876. This picture was made in 1930; the house has since been torn down.
Photo reprinted by permission of Louisville Courier Journal and Times

gunslinger.

Irvin Cobb grew up in a household of ghosts and legends, and the heroic, glamorous past was in some ways more real for him than the present. Cobb absorbed more from the tales of his grandfathers and their brothers and sons than a taste for adventure: all his life he felt it was his duty to be strong and resolute and his responsibility to protect those who were weaker than he.[8] This sense of duty and responsibility had for him a particular urgency because of the peculiar and, to the children, frightening use made of the stories in his childhood home: they were counters in a struggle between his parents in which his father was always defeated because he failed to live up to the Saunders' expectations.

The potential for strain is obvious in the personalities and situations of the three adults in Cobb's childhood home. Reuben Saunders, strong, resourceful and compassionate, never met a situation he could not handle. His daughter, Manie, who was fiercely devoted to her father, was apparently as strong minded as he, but, perhaps because her sex limited her chances for personal achievement, the sense of service and sacrifice in his character became in hers a tendency to manipulate and to point out to others their duty. To Manie, Joshua Cobb's duty to emulate the standard of her father was unquestionable and his failure to measure up was obvious. His wealthy and heroic ancestors had been attractive to her once, but now the tales with which he matched her own did nothing to improve her assessment of him or his own self-esteeem.

Irvin Cobb's sense of duty and responsibility was thus very similar to the one his mother found lacking in his father. There is no evidence that Cobb ever resented her imposition of such a stern standard on him. Manie Cobb was an attractive woman in many ways, sociable and even flirtatious, lively and quick-witted, a skilled hostess and a careful dresser. Her oldest son was solicitious of her and anxious to please her until her death in 1932. Cobb's daughter insisted after his death, however, that he never felt that he had won her approval. If this is true, the problem was too deep for him to discuss in his autobiography, *Exit Laughing*, in which he praises his mother for the energy with which she met both joy and grief, for her outspokenness, for her fine complexion and for her lack of religious prejudice. The two faults Cobb finds in her are her social and sectional snobbery.[9]

Cobb's discussion of his father in *Exit Laughing* is much more candid. Joshua Cobb lacked the steely strength of his wife and father-in-law. While they were adored by young Irvin, he reports feeling frequently ashamed of his father. Cobb describes his father as a "perky little red bantam"; he was small and delicately built, with red hair and a pink, freckled complexion. He was vain and opinionated, but without the force to put his opinions across. When he and Manie were first married, Joshua Cobb worked as an appraiser and grader of tobacco, a job that apparently suited him well. In 1878, the needs of a growing family and Manie's notions of what was suitable for her station forced him to leave that job and go to work for the steamboat and wharfboat business run by the Fowlers. Manie's elder sister had married a Fowler, and, although her husband had been dead for ten years, Joshua Cobb was taken into the business as a relation. Working on the river did not suit him as well as grading tobacco, and, although he made the switch without complaining, Irvin Cobb traces his father's eventual decline into alcoholism to this change. The Fowler concern was headed by Captain Joseph Fowler, another of the many forceful, successful men so different from Joshua Cobb whose acquaintance was important to young Irvin. Joshua Cobb was very much a subordinate in the Fowler business. He ran the boat store, did various clerking jobs, and filled in for others. In addition to its other holdings, the firm operated a daily packet ship from Paducah to Cairo, Illinois. Joshua Cobb captained this ship when the regular captain was ill and was teased for putting it to shore whenever it looked like rain. So frequently, in fact, did the men with whom he worked make fun of Joshua Cobb's timidity that Irvin was amazed and gratified to learn—from someone else—that he once singlehandedly quelled a riot that broke out among black passengers on the packet ship.[10]

Perhaps because he was so much happier in his own childhood, perhaps because they did not lecture him on his shortcomings, Joshua loved children. Irvin Cobb later gave to a fictional character (also a red headed failure) Joshua Cobb's most attractive hobby: gathering up a group of children who could not have gone otherwise and taking them to the circus, spending a week's salary on tickets and popcorn and peanuts. After depositing them at their doorways, Cobb's father would go, all alone, to the Palmer House and systematically get drunk, even though at that time drunkenness was not customary with him.

Joshua and Manie's first child was a daughter named Reubie Fowler Cobb after Manie's father and brother-in-law. She later dropped the "Fowler." Irvin Shrewsbury was second. He was originally to have been named his father's choice, Joshua

8

Shrewsbury, after his father and his father's best friend, Joel Shrewsbury. The baby's aunts objected, however, that such a choice was too old-fashioned,and insisted on a more romantic name like "Irvin." The recipient never appreciated this attention. As a boy he found that having a romantic name was not at all desirable, and as a man he complained facetiously that his aunts had robbed him of the world's most perfect name for a humorist: Josh Cobb! Eventually there were four children. John was a few years younger than Irvin, and Manie, her mother's namesake, was almost ten years younger. The Cobbs moved out of Dr. Saunders' house at Manie's birth and into another house that the doctor owned and had deeded to his daughter.

Irvin inherited his father's wide-set eyes and bushy eyebrows and his grandfather Saunders' height. His hair was black, stiff and straight. Reubie was pretty and dainty and bright, as was Manie later. Perhaps Irvin and John suffered by comparison, or perhaps their mother had had enough of Cobb men and their ways. For whatever reasons, the girls were pampered and petted by their mother, while the boys were strictly disciplined and perhaps even neglected. Reuben Saunders favored Irvin and spoke up for him, sometimes without too much success. Cobb's daughter attests that Christmas made him extremely uncomfortable all of his life because of his memories of unequal treatment in his childhood. One Christmas after they were no longer living in Dr. Saunders' house the unmusical Irvin was given a cheap fiddle for Christmas while Reubie was given a diamond ring. Dr. Saunders dropped by for a Christmas visit, found Irvin in tears, and went out and bought him a pony. When Manie Cobb thanked him for the nice gift for the children, Dr. Saunders answered, "It is not for the children. It is for Irvin. Only for Irvin. Remember that, Manie." But the doctor was a busy man, and Reubie was soon riding the pony at her mother's insistence.[11]

## Notes

[1]Fred Gus Neuman, *The Story of Paducah* (Paducah: Young, 1927), p. 115; p. 97.

[2]J.H. Battle, et al., *Kentucky: A History of the State* (Louisville: F.A. Bulley Publishing Co., 1885), Part II, pp. 320; 291; G.W. Hawes, *Commercial Gazetteer and Business Directory of the Ohio River* (Indianapolis: Hawes, 1861), p. 148.

[3]Letter, Irvin S. Cobb to John Wilson Townsend, Sept. 20, 1921, John Grant Crabbe Library, Eastern Kentucky University.

[4]Battle, p. 291; Fred Gus Neuman, *Irvin S. Cobb* (Paducah: Young, 1924), p. 13.

[5]Cobb later said that he was always careful not to investigate this implausible story too closely for fear of disproving it; his grandchildren say he believed it completely.

[6]Robert H. Davis, *Over My Left Shoulder* (New York: D. Appleton & Co., 1926), pp. 222-226; Fred Gus Neuman, *Irvin Cobb: His Life and Achievements* (Paducah: Young, 1934), p. 23. In *Exit Laughing*, p. 30, Julian's first name is given as "Charles"; Cobb's memory was probably better when he gave information to Davis and Neuman.

[7]Battle, p. 320.

[8]Elisabeth Cobb, *My Wayward Parent* (Indianapolis: Bobbs-Merrill, 1945), p. 24, passim.

[9]Cobb, *Exit Laughing*, (Indianapolis: Bobbs-Merrill, 1941), pp. 547-549.

[10]Cobb, *Exit Laughing*, pp. 340-343; letter, Fred Neuman to John Wilson Townsend, Feb. 8, 1922, John Grant Crabbe Library, Eastern Kentucky University.

[11]E. Cobb, *Wayward Parent*, pp. 25-26.

# Chapter Two

Irvin Cobb's childhood became the material for hundreds of short stories and humorous sketches; for many of his readers, growing up in Paducah was the pattern of a Southern childhood. Cobb was selective in his use of his past, however; the tense situation in Dr. Saunders' household is omitted. His serious tales, in fact, are remarkable in that they so seldom deal with family situations. Judge Priest, the idealized moral arbiter of so many of his stories, has no wife or children, only servants, and the problems that he solves are more frequently among individuals or social factions than among family members.

In his semi-autobiographical humorous sketches Cobb's parents appear as shadowy authority figures, his brother sometimes joins in the mischief, his sisters tattle and cry—but they are not individualized, only presented as the standard threats of exposure and punishment confronting any lively boy. Like Tom Sawyer, the boy of Cobb's sketches equates happiness with escape from the constraints of home, church and family. Cobb doesn't picture for us a Paducah made up of houses: its locales are streets, wharves, yards and barns. Cobb's favorite place as a boy seems to have been his father's boat store, where Civil War veterans and river men met to swap stories, chew tobacco and relax outside the constraints of female interference and the Presbyterian Church. Cobb's humorous portrait of himself as urchin is eternally barefoot, a slingshot in one pocket, a dime novel in the other, barely recovered from his last caning and already into his next bit of mischief. When Cobb later spoke of his fond memories of Paducah, it was not his home he was thinking of, but the many opportunities the river town afforded him to escape from that home.

On Sundays there was no escape. Manie Cobb marched her children to the gloomy old building that housed the First Presbyterian Church, where they were lectured on predestination and damnation in sermons that stretched out interminably. Cobb could later joke about the theology of his childhood:

> Heaven was a place which went unanimously democratic every fall, because all the Republicans had gone elsewhere. Hell was a place full of red-hot coals and clinkered sinners and unbaptized babies and a smell like somebody cooking ham ....[1]

But his revulsion was no joke. He states in *Exit Laughing* that he was probably no more than eight years old when "some vague adolescent sense of the plain fitness and fairness of things" made him secretly reject the stern theology he had been inculcated with. He remained a freethinker from that point on, never joining a church or accepting a creed.[2] In the letter left after his death giving instructions for his funeral, he digresses with a description of what to him would be an ideal religion: a combination of some of the more tolerant and ethical qualities of Unitarianism, Reformed Judaism, Mormonism and the Salvation Army, devoted to the social morality of Jesus Christ. Even if such a religion existed, however, he doesn't see himself as a member, just a supporter.[3] What disturbed Cobb in religion was not theological problems but the human element, and from his childhood he felt that organized religion brought out the worst in people, not the best.

The ordeal of Sunday did not end with the sermon. After the pleasures of an enormous Southern noon-time meal, the afternoon, in which all games, all noise, and even all pleasureable books were forbidden, seemed almost as hard to endure as the morning. Only an excursion with his father, who was reared in a less rigid Episcopal tradition, or his grandfather, who was a law unto himself, rescued the Cobb children from the afternoon routine of reading improving books or staring listlessly into space. Because of Reuben Saunders' duties and Joshua Cobb's timidity, these respites came very seldom.

On weekdays there were on the Saunders property two places of refuge for the children. One was the kitchen, presided over by Amanda Given, the strong-minded and loyal cook, nurse and housekeeper to Dr. Saunders' household. An unlikely tale by Hal Corbett claims that Mandy consulted a judge to find out if she was legally obligated to nurse a baby as ugly as Irvin proved to be; actually, she mothered and defended all four Cobb children, plus others before and after them. "Right now," said Cobb sixty years later, "I can shut my eyes and see her, all gnarled and painfully kinked, and so bossy and loudmouthed and competent." Children who attempted to pester or tease her were chased out of the kitchen with a brandished skillet, but hurt or lonely children received snacks—biscuits and jelly, baked sweet potatoes or apples, fried pies—and affection.

Another black servant, Uncle Rufus, also welcomed the company of the Cobb children. An ex-slave who remembered his mother as a proud African princess, Rufus was aloof and serious. When not running errands, he remained inside the one room shack that was all that remained of Dr. Saunders' slave quarters. Like Mandy, he fed and entertained the children who visited him, offering them sweet potatoes and hoe cakes. But visits to Rufus were most thrilling because of the tales he told of "hoodoos," ghosts, devils and "ha'nts." After an evening visit the children would be afraid to go from his cabin to the main house unless Mandy lighted the way with a lantern from the porch. Rufus' stories were so frightening that Cobb claimed to be a grown man before he could enter a darkened room without tensing in expectation of "Old Raw Haid and Bloody Bones" or some other gruesome phantasm, but the excitement was so enjoyable that the children always went back for more.[4]

By the time Irvin Cobb entered public school in 1883 his world was wider than Dr. Saunders' yard. Not only had Paducah become his playground, but townspeople were beginning to notice the tall funny kid of Josh Cobb's. Early friends and teachers attest to the impression his distinctive personality made even as a boy. Not only was he lively and fun-loving; he was genuinely funny and pleasant to be around as well, and most adults forgave his pranks because they enjoyed his company. A statement by Miss Mary Dodson, Irvin's ninth and tenth grade teacher, shows this remarkable situation:

> For Irvin's good and for my own peace of mind I had early in the previous year given him a desk immediately in front of mine. I do not know that Irvin enjoyed this very much, but I did. He was so well-informed, so keenly alive to what was going on in the world, so appreciative of things going on in our work that we often exchanged remarks *sotto voce* across my desk.[5]

Manie Cobb was always certain that Irvin inherited his intelligence from Reuben Saunders; the skill at repartee may have been from Manie herself. Cobb's mother and both his sisters were renowned for their lively table talk, and if the Cobb household was sometimes tense, it was always noisy, frequently with laughter. There was probably an element of showing-off or defending himself from attack in Cobb's non-stop fun-making. In the main, however, Cobb just loved an easy atmosphere in which people seemed to be enjoying themselves and took upon himself the job of creating it. As an old, sick man he came to resent this self-imposed duty of entertaining the world, but as a boy he embraced it.

Cobb's teachers were not all as tolerant of his restlessness as Miss Dodson, but for the most part Cobb was very successful in school. He stayed in the public schools until 1886, studying under Miss Nannie Clark, who was only sixteen when he first entered. She remembered Irvin as "one of my bright pupils."[6] Then his parents enrolled him in a private school run by Dr. Lewis Schuck, the minister of the First Baptist Church. Dr. Schuck's credentials in literature and culture were very impressive by Paducah standards, but his attempts to deal with ten or twelve small boys were not successful, and Cobb was relieved to get away from the stuffy church parlor and go back to public school in 1888, when he encountered Mss Dodson. In school he loved history and literature and anything that his mind could transform into romantic heroics; mathematics was a bore to him and he did poorly in it. Later he claimed not to know the higher multiplication tables: "At the grammar school I got through *Ray's Higher Arithmetic* on the simple expedient of doing their Latin for certain of my classmates while they did my problems for me."[7]

He continued to be difficult to manage; Cobb wrote in a private letter in 1921 that he was "chucked out . . . for general cussedness" in 1890. The circumstances are not clear; at any rate, that year Irvin was enrolled in a private school run by William A. Cade in the tiny suburb of Arcadia.[8] Reuben Saunders picked out the school as especially beneficial for Irvin; he also bought him a gun to give him something to do on the long walks back and forth to school. Irvin loved the walks, the gun and Professor Cade. He stayed in the school until financial problems in 1892 forced him to quit school altogether.

Cobb later described Cade as "one of the most lovable and most impractical men I ever knew." He loved boys and literature equally, and frequently called his pupils out on Saturday to go on picnics and fishing expeditions with him. He was strict in demanding diligence and respect for learning from his pupils. His favorite punishment for talking during lessons or turning in insufficient work was the assignment of Latin verses or Shakespeare quotations to memorize. Cobb found this punishment to his liking. He could memorize a passage by reading it over several times, and he soon discovered that memorizing the penalty verses took him less time than translating the original Latin assignment. When Cobb once mastered seventy verses of Shakespeare in less than two hours,

Cade began to look for other ways of punishing him. Cade appreciated Cobb's facility with language, however, and probably did much to develop it. One of his students reports that Cade emphasized the development of graceful, idiomatic English and even had the students report after recess any awkward or ungrammatical statements they had heard other students make.

One of Cobb's school friends described him this way during his years at Cade's school:

> He was a long, lean, lanky boy with big feet. A pretty good baseball player, an indifferent fighter. Usually able to pacify things with his high-sounding talk, poor in mathematics, keen in literature, gifted with the photographic eye.[9]

Cobb was very talented at making sketches from real life, and as a boy he hoped to be a painter when he grew up. Others of his schoolmates remember his drawing portraits of the pupils, the teacher, or the people walking past the windows when he should have been studying. When he first became a reporter he planned to be a newspaper cartoonist some day, but writing opportunities came sooner and he eventually lost his knack for drawing. In 1891, however, the dream was very real, and when a low-budget magazine called *Texas Siftings* published four of his drawings his happiness was only slightly deflated by its neglecting to pay him for them.

While some of the books Cobb encountered in school thrilled and delighted him, he reserved his greatest devotion for the books considered unimproving and even detrimental in his day. Mark Twain and Robert Louis Stevenson were his greatest enthusiasms. Later he said, "The day when I got hold of *Treasure Island* is marked in my mind with a red asterisk the size of a sunset, and there is another blazing star for *Huck*." Other literature he enjoyed as a child includes *Robinson Crusoe,* Dickens, Cooper, *Don Quixote, Swiss Family Robinson*, Stanley's *Adventures in Africa*, George W. Harris, *Sut Lovingood's Yarns*, De Maupassant, *Fables in Slang* and Kipling. In addition to these works, most of which could be read in front of the family at least on weekdays, he developed a passion for the dime novels that were strictly forbidden. In 1921 he wrote a whimsical tribute to these books called *A Plea for Old Cap Collier*. In this book he tells of a time during Spring housecleaning when one of these novels was discovered under his mattress, causing him to be "paddled until I had the feelings of a slice of hot, buttered toast somewhat scorched on the underside." He claims his mother informed him that boys who read books like that "always came to a bad end, growing up to be criminals or Republicans or something equally abhorrent."[10]

Cobb was punished for many other lapses besides reading dime novels; as he puts it, "that was when nearly everything a normal, active boy craved to do was wrong and, therefore, held to be a spankable offense." He did seem to have a genius for getting into trouble. He tells of taking his golden-haired young niece to the barber shop to test the clippers on her ringlets and of doing unpardonable things with frogs to maiden aunts. Probably his worst escapade was the adventure he later wrote up as "The Thrill of a Lifetime." According to this account, he and three other boys tied a coffee can to a dog's tail to see what would happen. The results were sensational: the dog in his frenzy ran into the path of a funeral procession, knocking the coffin over and spilling the corpse out on the street. Later in New Orleans Cobb ran into one of his fellow malefactors, who reported that up until he enlisted in the Spanish-American War his father had whipped him for the incident every time he saw him.[11]

Paducah offered many opportunities for an adventure-minded young boy. Cobb and his friends played on the Indian mounds in the vicinity, pretending to be braves and picking up arrowheads, beads, pottery and old bones for their collections. Cobb remained a collector of Indian artifacts all his life, and in his collection at his death among the more exotic items which he had acquired as an adult were some of the pieces he had picked up as a boy in the fields around Paducah.

The river was a playground in itself. The boys made rafts or borrowed boats to get to the swimming area on the sandbar where the two rivers met. A frightening experience when he stepped into a cross current and almost drowned limited Irvin's interest in swimming somewhat, but he always loved the water's edge and the noisy, smelly business of ships and cargo. Periodically the river invaded the town. While adults viewed the Spring floods as events of terror and destruction, children remembered them for their almost festive excitement. The great flood came in 1884, when Irvin was eight. Dr. Saunders' house was in the small area of Paducah on ground higher than the reach of the water, but many houses were totally covered. Cobb later remembered:

> We kids thought that was the greatest thing that ever happened. The schools closed, of course, and we spent all day paddling around town in boats, or going into stores, downtown, in skiffs. I still remember rowing over to see my cousins, and finding them

sitting on the roof of the front porch sailing boats.[12]

Most remarkable in Cobb's childhood was the number of men who took an interest in him and welcomed him into their conversations. Among those whose influence were Captain Fowler, Professor Cade and Judge Bishop, who gave many of his characteristics to the fictional Judge Priest. Most important among these father-figures was Cobb's namesake, Joel Shrewsbury. Shrewsbury had no family: he never married and had renounced his relatives because they had sided with the North while he had fought for the South. So he adopted the family of Joshua Cobb, his best friend. To the children he was "Uncle Jo," eccentric, demanding, tempestuous and completely adored. He had a small income from property and an informal association with the local newspaper, but mostly he sat at Soule's Drugstore or on the boat shore porch and talked. His dedication to the Southern cause was total, while his idea of the Southern gentleman seems to have drawn largely on Sir Walter Scott. He insisted that Irvin must study horsemanship, dancing, and the violin in order to qualify, although Irvin's talents in those areas proved downright ungentlemanly and the lessons, which Shrewsbury had paid for, were soon discontinued. Shrewsbury's hot temper and pugilistic notions of protecting one's honor were tempered by his charity and quick wit, and to a romantic, adventurous boy he was perfection. Cobb says:

> From my sixth birthday on until my thirteenth I was by day his faithful tagging shadow, and by night I dreamed dreams about him, wherein he did large heroic deeds and I went along and held his coat and helped bury the unregrettable dead.[13]

Shrewsbury was extremely well-read and a local fount of information. If a questioner ever doubted the answer Shrewsbury gave him, he would go check the answer in the encyclopedia for him. But he never answered another question put by that person. Shrewsbury encouraged Cobb's early artistic ambitions and also shared with him his fascination with the newspaper business. When Cobb had to find a job in his teens, he remembered Shrewsbury's suggestion that he become a reporter. Shrewsbury's notions of the Southern gentleman may have been of little use to Cobb, but the viewpoint of ambitious self-improvement that accompanied it proved more effective than the dancing lessons and served Cobb very well.

# Notes

[1]Irvin S. Cobb, *A Plea for Old Cap Collier* (New York: George H. Doran, 1921), p. 11.

[2]Cobb, *Exit Laughing*, p. 49.

[3]The letter is reproduced in E. Cobb, *Wayward Parent,* pp. 252-253.

[4]John Wilson Townsend, *Concerning Irvin S. Cobb (1876-1922)* (unpub. mss., Townsend Collection, Univ. of Kentucky Library), pp. 6D-6H.

[5]Fred Gus Neuman, *Paducahans in History* (Paducah: Young, 1922), p. 87.

[6]Neuman, *Paducahans in History*, p. 82.

[7]Irvin S. Cobb, *Myself to Date* (New York: Review of Reviews, 1923), p. 18.

[8]Letter, Irvin S. Cobb to John Wilson Townsend, Sept. 27, 1921, Crabbe Library, Eastern Kentucky University.

[9]Neuman, *Paducahans in History*, p. 93.

[10]Cobb, *Cap Collier*, pp. 13-15.

[11]Irvin S. Cobb, *Prose and Cons* (New York: George H. Doran, 1926), pp. 279-293.

[12]Interview published in Houston *Post*, Jan. 28. 1937; clipping in Paducah Public Library.

[13]Cobb, *Exit Laughing*, pp. 83-86.

# Chapter Three

After the Cobbs moved in 1885 to the house Dr. Saunders had deeded to Manie the family situation became even worse. Joshua Cobb had never made enough money to satisfy Manie, and now she had difficulty maintaining a separate establishment without Dr. Saunders' contributions. The problem is clear even in Cobb's tribute to his mother: he praises her for managing on so small an income, especially since the importance she placed on family station and on "keeping up with" their comparatively wealthy relatives required a lot of expenditure on dress and furnishings. She managed, Cobb says in *Exit Laughing*, by thrift and cleverness, and by denying herself the trinkets and decorations so important to this lady who had once been the belle of Paducah. Undoubtedly she frequently informed her husband of her sacrifices.

Also during these years in the late eighties Reubie made a decision which affected her younger brothers and sister profoundly. Presumably she was reacting to some shocking experience, although she never told even her mother what it was. For whatever reason, she decided never to leave the house again and demanded that the blinds be drawn day and night and no company admitted. Cobb's mother was devoted to her eldest daughter, and her requests were carried out. Inside the house Reubie remained as cheerful and as caustically witty as ever, peering out from the blinds to spy on her neighbors going by and to make belitting remarks about their dress and character. Irvin, John and Manie were never permitted during their adolescent years to bring any friends to the house and were given no explanation other than that Reubie wanted it that way.[1]

When Reubie entered her twenties she loosened her self-imposed isolation somewhat. Friends were once more invited to the house, where Reubie and her mother reigned at the dinner table. Reubie was courted by a young banker, Richard Rudy, and she permitted him to take her for a weekly evening buggy ride. The courtship lasted for forty years, and she seldom left the house except for those buggy rides. Three days after Manie Cobb died in 1932, Reubie and Richard Rudy were married. Both of them died the next year.

The problems of the eighties were followed by a series of disasters in the nineties. In 1891 Reuben Saunders died. Manie was named in his will as a chief beneficiary, but lengthy litigation tied up her inheritance for almost five years. The eye condition brought on by a Civil War injury which had impaired Joshua Cobb's vision for years suddenly grew worse: the eyelids became swollen, infected and very painful. Then early in 1892, the steamboat company changed hands and Joshua Cobb was fired. The Cobbs had planned for Irvin to leave Professor Cade's in 1892 to go to military school and eventually to college; instead, he quit school and took the job on the newspaper that Joel Shrewsbury's friendship made possible. Joshua Cobb, useless and almost blind, spent the remaining years of his life drunk.

In *Exit Laughing* Cobb calls the memories of the last four years of his father's life "like a scar burnt in my brain." During those years in which he was supporting the family while his father toured the saloons he grew very bitter toward his father and perhaps very protective of his mother, whose pretensions of gentility were crumbling around her. Only many years later, his daughter says, was he able to think of his father without rancor, and then it was because he formulated the hardly credible but very touching explanation of his father's behavior that he presents in *Exit Laughing*[2]. There he suggests that, having found himself with nothing to give his family but an insurance policy with a suicide clause, Joshua Cobb set out deliberately and resolutely to drink himself to death. Whether his death was self-willed or not, it was long and painful both for himself and his family. They buried him on Christmas Eve, 1895.

Whatever Cobb's disappointment at interrupting his education to become the family breadwinner, he loved the newspaper business from the start. In the autobiographical volume *Stickfuls* which describes his career in journalism he paints a warm portrait of the establishment that produced the ***Paducah Evening News***. "Boss Jim" Thompson was the chief owner and head of the shop, his brother, "Colonel Henry," was the editor, and several other brothers and cousins held positions of one sort or another. Several Civil War veterans held the kind of indeterminate editorships that Joel Shrewsbury had filled, writing if and when they felt like it. Until Cobb joined the staff there was only one reporter—a man of enormous energy at gathering stories but little skill at writing them. There were also numerous others with no pretense of a position who hung around the shop, talking, joking and waiting for a new subscription to be paid in. By shop tradition, half of the two dollar subscription fees went in the drawer, half went to buy drinks all around at Uncle John's Saloon next door for anyone in the shop at the time. Cobb was too young to join in these convivial processions the first one and one half years he worked on the newspaper.

The *Evening News* also had a busy print shop, running jobs for the local businessmen and the shipping industry. Here Cobb first met that perennial feature of the newspaper business, the tramp printer. Scruffy, usually alcoholic romantics, these characters toured from place to place, carrying gossip and tales of the outside world to the steadier employees who lacked their wanderlust. Tramps and regulars, friends and employees, the population of the shop was the kind of group Cobb felt most comfortable with all his life: story-loving, poker-playing, hard drinking, convivial and all male.

The *Evening News*, which also had a Sunday morning edition and a weekly edition, was a prosperous newspaper. It was stoutly Democratic in its editorial policy, vociferously supporting any Democratic candidate faced with a Republican opponent. The Democratic primaries, however, were a different matter, and the editorials supported whichever candidate offered the highest price for that support. This policy was open and uncriticized, and the *Evening News* staff were proud of their occasional triumphs in electing a man supported by no other newspaper. Cobb was thus initiated early and rather painlessly into the code that proved so difficult for some other newspapermen of the time to accept: editorial policy is one thing and a reporter's opinions are another, quite separate, and totally unimportant consideration.

When the sixteen year old Irvin Cobb presented himself as an apprentice at the *Evening News*, on January 16, 1892, the editor gave him a pencil and a pad and told him to go find some items. He wandered apprehensively in the suddenly empty streets until finally he came to the Market Square, usually bustling in the warmer months but almost deserted in January. He did manage to pick up one item there, however, and that evening the *Evening News* carried the following story, unsigned:

> Cal Evitts, the efficient and popular market master, says there were more rabbits brought to the local market this week than any week this winter. Molly Cottontails sold this morning for ten cents dressed or five cents undressed.[3]

Irvin Cobb had broken into print. He soon found other sources of news not on the regular reporter's beat—the railroad shops, the packet-ships, the local hotels. Soon he realized the importance of personals, since subscribers like to see their names in the paper. Cobb learned to get four items out of a trip planned by a local businessman: one would announce the trip, one would say he had departed, one would announce his expected return, and the last would rejoice at his safe arrival. Cobb learned the trade rapidly, and by the end of his third week Boss Jim judged him ready for a salary: a dollar seventy-five a week. By the end of two months he was writing more than half of the copy and drawing four dollars a week. The regular reporter gladly shared his duties, and Cobb covered crimes, weddings, revival meetings, trials, political speeches and the county fair. He stopped doing the chalk sketches that had at first accompanied some of his stories and his earlier ambition to switch to a cartoonist career was forgotten. He was working hard and doing well at a job he loved, and his youth made it seem easy. He later recalled:

> I could work at high-pressure fifteen hours at a stretch, play dime-limit draw poker all night, drink my share of the drinks, and come to work next morning, blear-eyed perhaps and a trifle drowsy, but without a twitching nerve in my body. Until I was beyond voting age I didn't know there was such a thing as a hangover.[4]

Cobb later assessed the influences, good and bad, that his early newspaper experience had on his literary development. He was given enormous freedom in the composition of his stories: none of them were ever cut or corrected, but went straight into the paper with misspellings, poor syntax and overblown phrasing intact. Thus while he learned early the joy of putting words on paper and had plenty of opportunity for self-improvement, he had no disciplining hand to make him polish his sentences or cut down on his adolescent enthusiasms. He learned rather painfully the importance of self-discipline when he became for a short time the managing editor of the paper.

When Cobb had become a nationally recognized newspaperman much was made of the fact that he had been the country's only nineteen-year-old managing editor, but Cobb himself was always candid in admitting to the stroke of chance which got him the position and the poor judgment which lost it for him. In 1896

The staff of the *Paducah Evening News*, November, 1896. Irvin Cobb, Managing Editor, is seated at left front. The other two men at the front table are the owners.
Photo reprinted by permission of Mrs. Catherine Adams

Col. Henry Thompson died and Boss Jim sold out his share of the newspaper to go into another business. Many of the other regulars had died or quit also, so the new owners offered the job of managing editor to Cobb. Cobb had talent, ambition and energy, but these qualities did not compensate for his immaturity, for Cobb describes himself as being "as careless and nearly as dangerous as a two-year-old child playing with a box of matches in an oil warehouse." He published unflattering remarks about local citizens and flamboyant, opinionated editorials. Over them he tacked smart-alecky headlines. (Once he headed a straight story about a commission the governer had named with the headline "A Good Joke Will Be Found at the Extreme Southern End of this Dispatch." The last name in the story was that of a Paducah lawyer known as a wind-bag.) There was no moral or political conviction behind his sensational journalism: he was simply a reckless nineteen-year-old who had been given too much responsibility. After a few citizens had brought libel suits against the paper and a few more citizens had threatened Cobb's life, both he and the owners reconsidered the situation, and by the next year Cobb was just a reporter again.

Some of the stories Cobb covered for the paper also had a sobering quality. In 1896 he had to write up for the *Evening News* the hanging for murder of a black man who had worked with him several summers earlier making ice deliveries. Cobb sat up all night with reporters from rival papers, playing poker and waiting for the call to the jail at an hour before daybreak. They arrived at the jail to find the condemned man, dressed in an ill-fitting suit and white cotton gloves, delivering a sermon on repentance to the other prisoners, who were raptly attentive, shouting out responses and snatches of song. Their admiration turned to fear, however, when he promised to return from glory that evening to haunt the wicked, and it was through a clamor of groans and screams that the man was escorted to the gallows outside. The sheriff became nauseated at that point and could not go through the required formality of reading the death warrant, so that job was given to Cobb, who was feeling rather weak himself. Cobb read the stern words to his old companion, who answered, "Young Cap'n, I always knowed that if ever you could do ol' George a favor you certainly would. Thank you sir, kindly." George's confidence failed him at the gallows, and the rope proved too long, so his death promised to be a miserable drawn-out strangulation. Cobb and another reporter joined to pick up his feet and kick away the gravel so that death could come more quickly.

Then they returned to their newspaper offices to recover and to turn in their copy.

Cobb later wondered if it would have been possible in 1896 to write up that experience as he had felt it that day. He didn't; the four columns that appeared in the paper that evening followed the traditional formula for a hanging, reviewing the crime, the trial and the witnesses of the execution, with a final summary of past hangings in the county. He decided in retrospect that a more dramatic and personal writeup would probably have offended the subscribers, to whom his own feelings might have been incomprehensible.[5]

By 1896 Cobb's skills as a reporter had increased considerably, and in addition to his duties at the *Evening News* (for which he now was paid twelve dollars a week) he was a resident correspondent for several city newspapers, including the Chicago *Tribune*, then edited by the legendary Joseph Medill. Being resident correspondent involved no regular salary; reporters were paid according to the length of any local story which they had telegraphed in to the city newspaper and which was subsequently printed. It was because of this association with the Chicago *Tribune* that Cobb became the only cub reporter so far as he knew to follow the Hollywood formula of filing the big scoop. Cobb attributed this success to neither his ability nor his shrewdness, but to "raw, crude luck from beginning to end."

In 1897 a gruesome murder in Chicago caught the attention of the whole country. Two burglars, Merry and Smith, had killed Merry's wife through slow torture, wrapped up her body in a carpet, and buried it at a crossroads outside Chicago. Some accomplices confessed, but Merry and Smith escaped the police trap that was set for them. The descriptions of the men were telegraphed to all points, and alert citizens all over the country started reporting suspicious transients who might have been the culprits but proved not to be.

The actual Merry and Smith eluded the police until they got to Kentucky. Merry's feet were frostbitten, making walking difficult, so they tried to stick to the railroads. They made the mistake of bragging about their identity to a tramp they met on a box car, showing him a clipping describing their crime and waving their revolvers at him. When he left the train near Mayfield, Kentucky, he took the clipping with him and showed it at a house where he stopped for food. He was taken to the house of the town marshall, who believed the story and set out on the trail of Merry and Smith, catching up with them at Fredonia. After he locked them up at

Princeton, the county seat, he wired Chicago that Merry and Smith were safely apprehended.

The Chicago police, who were receiving reports of Merry and Smith from every state in the union, did not move quickly to confirm the report. By the time Chicago had started taking the report seriously and the *Tribune* had decided to send a reporter down to get the story, the last train had left with representatives of all the other Chicago dailies on board. The *Tribune* then wired Cobb and all the other local representatives in Kentucky and told them to go to Princeton and send in what they could.

Cobb arrived in Princeton to find the town full of reporters. The jailer was taking his job very seriously, standing at the door with a rifle and swearing that the Twelve Apostles could not get in that jail to talk to the prisoners. Cobb wandered around for a while and then went to see the only person he knew in town, an old Confederate Army friend of his father's who was now mayor. On hearing his plight, the mayor took him straight to the jail, where he was taken past the mob back to an exclusive interview with Merry and Smith, who were apparently a little disgruntled at having to miss all the excitement they had created. They made fun of the nervous, gangling kid in front of them, bragged about their prowess in eluding the Chicago police for a whole month, and then settled down to tell him the whole story of their escape, drawing maps in his notebook to demonstrate the route they took out of Chicago. Cobb then collected some more information from the Mayfield town marshall and started organizing his story.

Cobb's problems were not over yet. When he went to the Western Union office to wire his story to the *Tribune*, he discovered a lone operator already snowed under with lengthy stories submitted by the regular Chicago reporters. Even without interviewing the prisoners they had found lots to say, and some of them kindly supplied this timid newcomer who claimed to be representing the *Tribune* with the early facts of the case. None asked him if he knew anything they didn't, and he volunteered no information. But the Western Union lines were all tied up.

After supper, Cobb went to the railroad station to talk to the train dispatcher, who agreed to send a quick synopsis to the *Tribune* for Cobb right then and perhaps to send some more later when he finished the railroad business. The *Tribune* realized what a bonanza it had as soon as the synopsis came through, and wired back for the whole story as soon as possible. Cobb started writing his story in anticipation of getting wire space and was astonished as the pages started piling up—thousands and thousands of words. Finally the train dispatcher not only started sending in the story himself, but called his day relief back to help on an auxiliary wire. The telegraphers would stop from time to time for an encouraging message to come through from the *Tribune*, "Let it all come. Spread yourself and keep sending until we say stop." The other Chicago reporters became aware that something was going on, but Cobb held his wires. Finally, at two in the morning the message came through, "That's enough. Good stuff! Good boy! Good night!" Cobb took the late train to Paducah, sleeping all the way. The next day he waited impatiently for the Chicago *Tribune*, which reached Paducah in the evening. It was a glorious sight. One whole column on the first page and five columns on the second were his words. His space rates on the story came to almost fifty dollars. In addition, a letter came in the mail which read:

> Dear sir: You did excellent work in covering the Merry story for this paper, and I wish to thank you.
>
> I have instructed the cashier to send you a check for fifty dollars as a bonus.
>
> Yours truly
> Joseph Medill[6]

Because of his naivete, Cobb wasn't as impressed with the signature as he should have been—he knew Medill was the editor of the *Tribune*, but he assumed that even on city newspapers the editor was the proper person to praise a cub reporter for a job well done. He was very impressed with the bonus, however, for it brought his pay for the story to almost a hundred dollars. He had never had so much money at one time before, and for the first time he began to dream of working some day for a city newspaper where money like this was handed out, preferably before their "mad extravagance plunged them into bankruptcy."

## Notes

[1]E. Cobb, *Wayward Parent*, p. 34.
[2]E. Cobb, *Wayward Parent*, p. 25.
[3]*Stickfuls,* as reprinted in Cobb, *Myself to Date*, p. 29.
[4]Cobb, *Exit Laughing*, p. 96.
[5]Cobb, *Myself to Date*, p. 48.
[6]Cobb, *Exit Laughing*, pp. 107-109.

## Chapter Four

Cobb's first experience on a city newspaper was a disillusioning one. Probably on the strength of his Merry-Smith story for the Chicago *Tribune* he was offered a trial job on the Cincinnati *Post*. Cincinnati was a city of almost a quarter of a million people in 1898, and the opportunity seemed to be what Cobb had been waiting for. The Paducah *Evening News* accepted Cobb's resignation reluctantly but took pride in his elevation to an "important and lucrative position with the metropolitan press," as it was described in the *News* column announcing his departure.

The position turned out to be neither lucrative nor important. The *Post* was not locally owned but belonged to a syndicate that published newspapers in several towns across the Middle West and Southwest. In 1898 the *Post* was plagued with a series of turnovers, promotions and dismissals as the outside owners attempted to reorganize the newspaper and improve its circulation. At that time the policy of the newspapers was to cover all national and international news that came in over the telegraph wires in addition to all the local stories turned in by the city room reporters. The resulting space problems were solved by cutting all stories to the bare bones.

When Cobb arrived at the *Post* in early October of 1898, he was assigned, not to the city staff where his talents would have been most useful, but to the telegraph room, a dark, dirty crowded space where reporters like Cobb were expected to sit all day among the clattering telegraph operators and reduce the stories that came in over the wires. After a few weeks in this environment Cobb felt he had had enough, and he sent out inquiries to the newspapers in Louisville, one hundred miles to the southwest, in an attempt to move. He still had no positive offer from a Louisville newspaper when, at the end of his fourth week on the Cincinnati *Post*, he received a notice that the managing editor (the third occupant of that position since Cobb had arrived) was pleased with his work and was giving him a pay increase of three dollars a week. Cobb had almost decided to endure another month or two of the smoke when, the next morning, the managing editor called him in and fired him. He had received a telegram from a syndicate supervisor ordering the immediate reduction of the staff by about eight positions. Several months later Cobb ran into the editor who had fired him when they were covering the same story—he had been reduced to a reporter on the *Post* by that time.

There was nothing for Cobb to do at that point but go back to Paducah and try to explain to everyone what had happened to his big chance. That embarrassment was minor compared to his disgust with the Cincinnati *Post*, however, and when, two days after his arrival in Paducah, he received a telegram from Cincinnati asking him to come back and take a position on the city staff, he considered several blistering replies and finally let the offer go unanswered. Instead he pursued a Louisville job and was hired as a reporter on the Louisville *Evening Post* in November of 1898.

The *Evening Post* did not have the national attention that Col. Henry Watterson had gained for his morning paper, the Louisville *Courier-Journal*, but it was a reputable paper run by more sensible and businesslike methods than the Cincinnati *Post*. Cobb settled in at a rooming house run by Miss Eliza Overton, whose table was famous, found a congenial roommate in D.D. Smith, who later became mayor of Frankfort, and set out to make a name for himself on the paper.[1] In 1899 he was assigned to cover the campaign of William Goebel for the Democratic nomination for governor. He also covered the Democratic convention at which Goebel was nominated and his campaign against the Republican candidate, which ended in a contested election. Cobb was on the scene when Goebel was assassinated on January 30, 1900. Thus he was the most likely reporter to cover the arrests and trials of the various Republican conspirators charged with the murder. William Goebel and his assassination therefore dominated most of Cobb's three years on the Louisville *Post*.

William Goebel the man is a figure as controversial after his death as before. He has found his apologists, especially Urey Woodson, an aide to Goebel who in 1901 bought a Paducah newspaper and hired Cobb as its editor. Woodson wrote a book in the thirties in which he describes Goebel with admiration as the first New Dealer and insists that had he lived his accomplishments would have been as great as those of Robert La Follette, Louis Brandeis and even Franklin D. Roosevelt.[2] Cobb was as impressed with Goebel's talent and determination as Woodson, but he saw the potential of his drive in quite another way, as he described him later:

> Since he passed, I have met a good many of the distinguished men of this country, but I have yet to meet one who impressed me as being mentally superior to William Goebel, that son of a Pennsylvania German, whose ambitions and whose death—and the manner of it—practically plunged Kentucky into civil war. He was a Napoleon of politics if one ever lived. He had audacity, ruthlessness, a genius of leadership, an instinct for absolute despotism, a gift for reorganization, a perfect disregard for other men's rights or lives where his own wishes were concerned; the brain to plan and the will to execute. He had devoted followers by the thousands, and hundreds called him their friend, but I do not believe any living creature ever read the inside of that dark and lonely soul of his. Had he lived, I am firmly convinced he either would have ruled the Democratic Party in the nation or he would have wrecked it. He loved power as drunkards love their bottle and he would have waded through blood up to his armpits to have his way .... Even so, there is no doubt but that Goebel aimed at the ultimate betterment of plain people; the trouble was that his good motives were tinctured by the lust for authority which gnawed at the man day and night, making him a malignant and an alien force. In Southern public life he loomed as a curious and an alien pinnacle.[3]

Cobb later compared Goebel to Huey Long, and both were similar in their appeal to populist sentiments, in their victory over a hostile establishment, and of course in their violent deaths on the capitol grounds. But Goebel had none of Long's love of and power over crowds; he had no skill at oratory and no personal warmth. He preferred to work behind the scenes, manipulating and gaining power behind the screen of a band of lieutenants. His portraits show an erect, neatly groomed figure with dark hair and piercing eyes. To Cobb his appearance was reptilian:

> He had a curious yellowish cast to his skin as though stale suet rather than live flesh lay beneath it.... His eyes were glazy, shallow, coal black; except when he was stirred an ophidian film was on them. His throat was disfiguringly swollen, with loose folds of skin overlappng the collar line. It was very like the throats of certain lizards. In repose he would put you in mind of a coiled snake, in action, of the snake about to strike, and when he did strike, lashing out viciously, you almost could see the spattered venom fly.[4]

Goebel was not a newcomer to Democratic politics when he

announced his campaign for the nomination. He had already served several terms in the State Senate, where he was conspicuous for his populist stands against the railroads and the corporations. He was instrumental in calling a Constitutional Convention in 1890 with Cassius Clay, Jr., as its President. The leadership of Clay and Goebel at this convention produced a Constitution, ratified in 1891, which imposed stricter regulations on the actions of the railroads. Goebel supported William Jennings Bryan and the free silver movement in the national election of 1896, and in a reaction to Bryan's defeat he formulated what came to be called the "Goebel Law," passed by the General Assembly in 1898. According to this law, officers who would prevent election abuses at local precints would be named by County Election Commissioners, themselves named by three State Election Commissioners to be elected by the legislature. The General Assembly in 1898 was largely Democratic, and the three State Commissioners named were all Democrats also. The Republicans attacked the law during the 1899 campaign, insisting that it was a blatant attempt by the Democratic Party to control the election process and put in a Democratic administration.[5]

This charge was not the laughing matter it would have been a few years earlier, when a Democratic victory required no underhanded efforts. In 1899 the Democratic Party in Kentucky was in disarray. Until 1895 Kentucky had gone regularly and automatically Democratic, and the unquestioned party loyalty Cobb had been exposed to as a boy in Paducah permeated most of the state. Only the mountain dwellers of eastern Kentucky and the blacks were assumed to hold any Republican sentiments, and keeping them in check presented no problem to the Democratic establishment. Such a state-wide Republican Party as existed in Kentucky was held together largely out of a desire for Federal patronage jobs, and the slate of largely unsuitable candidates for state jobs it proposed in 1895 had been compiled and submitted in as perfunctory a manner as earlier Republican slates. Dissatisfaction with the conservative state Democratic leadership and support for the national issues of free silver and the agrarian movement led several important Democratic figures to repudiate the Democratic slate, however, and, when the smoke had cleared, the Republicans in Kentucky had done the impossible: elected the entire Republican slate for state-wide offices.[6] By 1899 the Democrats had had four years of Republican rule under which to blame each other, form new alliances, and plot their return to power. William Goebel saw this confusion as a perfect opportunity for his own advancement and announced his campaign for the Democratic gubernatorial nomination.

The owners of the Louisville *Post*—with Henry Watterson, the "silver-tongued" W.C.P. Breckenridge and many bankers and businessmen—had been among those leading the revolts from the Democratic party, so they had little desire to return the power to the aristocratic but feeble Civil War colonels and plantation squires who had proved so undesirable earlier. They wanted a new, updated leadership and they sent out reporters to cover anyone who might fill the bill. William Goebel proved to be the man with the strength to take the party nomination, but the party he led after the convention was as disunited and rancorous as before. The oldline Party members were disgusted by his "poor white trash" origins and his populist sentiments; the more dynamic free silver Democrats were not sure of their place in Goebel's scheme. Goebel had to fight the Democrats in order to fight the Republicans, and in those days the fighting was sometimes done with guns. Cobb says that from his vantage place in the press stand at the Music Hall in Louisville where the convention was held he saw six-shooters drawn and fired "half a dozen times." After Goebel's nomination many of the reform elements in the Democratic Party supported him. The Louisville *Post* endorsed him, so Cobb kept his uneasiness to himself. But one group of Democrats seceded from the party and campaigned against Goebel. The fiery Kentucky politician and orator Theodore Hallam was one of the chief spokesmen for this group, and a retort he made on one occasion when he was speaking against Goebel became one of Cobb's favorite stories. A member of the audience called out, "Didn't you say at the Louisville convention not four weeks ago that if the Democrats nominated a yaller dog for governor you would vote for him?"

In Cobb's version, Hallem answered calmly, "I admit that I said then what I now repeat, namely, that when the Democratic Party of Kentucky, in convention assembled, sees fit in its wisdom to nominate a yaller dog for the governorship of this great state, I will support him—*but lower than that ye shall not drag me!*"[7]

Goebel's Republican opponent in the election was the attorney general of the state, William Sylvester Taylor, called "Hawg Jaw" by his neighbors because of his unfortunate appearance. Cobb says that in profile he looked like an "ungroomed and dandruffy Hapsburg—perhaps a seedy uncle of King Alfonso of Spain." More was weak about Taylor than his chin: his position on the slate was determined by party bosses who were thinking of other factors than Taylor's fitness to be governor and who largely repudiated him after the assassination investigation exposed his cowardice and made many suspect that he was implicated.

The Democrats who campaigned against Goebel were successful in convincing large numbers of their party members to vote for Taylor, and the November election returns showed that Taylor had won by a margin of 2300 votes. While preparations were being made for Taylor's December inauguration, the Goebel Democrats called the returns into question and appealed to the General Assembly to study the matter. In spite of—or even because of—such efforts as the "Goebel Law," elections were notoriously easy to tamper with in the years of written votes and ballot boxes, and it is impossible to determine today who actually won the election.[8] Cobb later stated, however, that, judging by the anti-Goebel feelings in the state, he felt that Taylor definitely won the election and that any falsification of the returns that occurred was probably in Goebel's favor.[9] While the largely Democratic legislature was considering Goebel's appeal, he was shot on January 30, 1900. On February 1 the legislature declared Goebel the winner of the election and he was sworn in. On February 3 he died of his wounds, leaving the lieutenant governor, J.C.W. Beckham, to take his place.

The Republicans had not ignored Goebel's appeal to the legislature and the threat it raised that they would be deprived of their offices. Charles Finley, the Secretary of State under the previous administration, and Caleb Powers, whom Taylor had just named his Secretary of State, arranged to fill seventeen boxcars with irate Republicans from the eastern Kentucky mountains, whose illiterate inhabitants were feared for their trigger-happy ways, and to bring them to Frankfort for a meeting. Kentucky's capital city had a population of fewer than 10,000 in 1890, and these whiskery, stolid giants toting their rifles—Powers claimed there were 1200 of them—created an awesome spectale. A meeting was held on the State House grounds at which the group approved a resolution "to respect the verdict of the people as counted at the polls." Then the mountain men wandered through the government buildings, glowering at the largely Democratic legislators. That night they built camp fires and slept on the State House grounds. The next day most of them went home. Two hundred stayed, however, and with their presence the tensions did not diminish.

It was unusual that when William Goebel appeared at the front gate of the capitol grounds on January 30, with the bodyguards Eph Lilliard in front of him and Jack Chinn behind him, there was not a mountaineer in sight. When Goebel's party was still about forty feet from the entrance a shot rang out from the direction of the windows of the Executive Office Building. It passed through Goebel's body and burrowed in the trunk of a hackberry tree.

According to his own accounts, Irvin Cobb was in the restroom of the State House washing his hands when the shot rang out. He ran out the side door and down the alley, reaching the street as the bodyguards had started to carry Goebel away. Cobb, who knew the guards because of his coverage of the Goebel campaign, shared their burden. During the tortuous three block trip back to the Capitol Hotel—Goebel fainted at one point and they thought him dead—Lillard and Chinn told Cobb their version of what had happened. Cobb says he later met a police officer who had been at the back of the alley and who claimed that he had almost fired at a dark-haired, long-legged man—an accurate description of Cobb—who came running suspiciously fast out of the State House door seconds after the shot, but had held back when others ran out between them.

By the time Cobb had left Goebel in the care of a doctor at the hotel and gone back to the State House to get some more information so that he could wire the complete story to the *Post*, Gov. Taylor had already summoned a body of militia from the armory to fight back the mob of Democratic sympathizers who threatened to storm the capitol buildings. The militia cleared the grounds and surrounded the Executive Office Building and the Executive Mansion. A contingent was also dispatched to march back and forth in front of the Capitol Hotel where Goebel lay.

Soon more than 1900 members of the State Guard had arrived in Frankfort under the command of the Republican administration. The sessions of the House and Senate were adjourned immediately after the shooting, and the committee considering Goebel's election appeal, which attempted to meet at the State House, was turned away. They met at the Opera House and declared Goebel the winner of the November election.

A majority vote of the legislature was needed to accept the committee report, so the militia prevented it from convening in the State House, the County Court House or the Opera House. On January 31 a number of Democratic legislators equivalent to a majority met secretly in the Capitol Hotel and accepted the committee report. That night William Goebel was administered the oath of office and signed a document naming some of the members of his administration. The next day, fearing an objection, the legislature accepted the report again and Goebel was sworn in for the second time. J.C.W. Beckham was sworn in as lieutenant governor and took the position of Acting Governor because of Goebel's condition.[10]

After the legislature had created a Democratic administration for the state, the tense situation in Frankfort only missed becoming a civil war. The two thousand troops that Taylor had called in remained under the command of the Republican Adjutant General. Acting Governor Beckham brought in another company from Lexington, who remained under Democratic command, and sent an order to Springfield, Massachusetts for large quantities of guns and ammunition. Volunteers to fight for the Democrats came from all over Kentucky. It is startling to read accounts of Frankfort during this period that describe the movements and encampments of "the Republican army" and "the Democratic army," but this is the only way to describe the state of affairs for over two months.

Irvin Cobb spent the tense winter weeks chasing down rumors and filing stories. The most persistent rumor was that Goebel had died on the day he had been shot and had never been sworn in. Other rumors suggested that he had been shot by one of his own men or by an irate Democrat. These rumors were not stilled by Goebel's actual death on February 3; in fact, a mythology grew up about the deathbed scene. When Goebel's noble and stirring last words were delivered to the press, Cobb, suspecting that the oratorical phrases were hardly Goebel's style, convinced a witness to tell him of the real events at Goebel's deathbed. According to this candid version the dying man had requested oysters to eat and, when he had gagged on one, he wheezed, "Doc, that was a damned bad oyster!" fell back and died. Cobb recognizing that such a story was outside journalistic decorum, filed the elaborate farewell and kept the oyster story to himself. Goebel's body lay in state for several days. After his funeral Beckham was sworn in as governor.

During the period of unrest Governor Taylor and members of his Cabinet and staff remained holed up in the capitol buildings afraid to leave. The Republican militia would allow no one into the area. Occasionally Taylor would issue proclamations, such as the one on January 30 adjourning the legislature until February 6, but any order not immediately enforceable by the militia was ignored. Taylor's sanctuary became his prison, and the Democrats slowly took command of the situation. Because of some investigations in eastern Kentucky by Thomas Cromwell, a reporter from the

Cincinnati *Enquirer*, Beckham decided that the assassination had been planned in London, Kentucky, by some of the Republican office holders several days before Goebel was shot. On March 9 warrants were issued for Caleb Powers and his brother John, Charles Finley, William H. Culton, a clerk in the State Auditor's office, and John Davis, a Frankfort policeman. Beckham also suspected Henry Youtsey, another clerk in the State Auditor's Office, of involvement in the plot, but did not include him in the warrant in an attempt to get him off his guard. He was arrested later. Culton was arrested on March 9, but the others were not to be found and were assumed to be shut up in the Executive Office Building.

On March 10 Beckham got word that a group of suspects disguised as ordinary soldiers was being secretly escorted to the train station, presumably to take a train for the eastern mountains. He wired Cromwell at Lexington, who met the train with local authorities and a posse of a thousand. They arrested Caleb Powers and John Davis, both carrying pardons from Taylor in their hands which the Lexington authorities refused to accept. John Powers and Charles Finley were not found; it is not known when they escaped but they managed at some point to leave the state.

Gov. Taylor remained in the state buildings behind his guard for several more days. He issued a statement that he was not involved in the assassination in any way: "... I am not a criminal, neither shall I ever be a fugitive from justice ...."[11] Since Taylor was not named in the first warrant, he then was allowed to go to Louisville but was ordered not to leave the state. In the meantime the Republicans had appealed the legislative decision favorable to Goebel to the United States Supreme Court. On May 21, Taylor waited for the results of that decision at the Louisville Custom House, knowing that on federal property he would be safe from immediate arrest if the decision were against him.

Cobb had returned to Louisville in pursuit of Taylor, and in *Exit Laughing* he claimed that he was the only reporter to find out that Taylor was at the Custom House. He gained admittance to the postmaster's office, from which he watched for several hours as Taylor paced the floor, cursing his luck but insisting he would face whatever came in the name of dignity and honor. Honor lost out, however, when a closed carriage was sent by friends, and he sneaked out the back way unknown to Cobb or the officers waiting for him. He was taken to the ferry to Indiana as the annoucement came over the wires that the Supreme Court had upheld the General Assembly decision and that Beckham was the legitimate governor of the state. Taylor settled in Indianapolis, where Charles Finley had already arrived. Although both were indicted for conspiracy, all attempts to extradict them failed, and Taylor practiced law in Indianapolis until his death in 1928. After the Supreme Court decision, the siege was over and the Democrats moved their newly sanctioned administration into the State House and the Executive Office Building.

There were nine trials and retrials for the Goebel assassination, the last one eight years after the shooting. Irvin Cobb covered the trials until he returned to Paducah in 1901. Because the suspects contradicted one another—and even changed their own stories from one trial to another—no clear picture of who was involved in the conspiracy or even who pulled the trigger has emerged, and the exact truth of the matter will probably never be known. Arthur Goebel, the governor's brother, testified that before Henry Youtsey came to trial Youtsey gave the following explanation of the conspiracy. (Youtsey at times denied the confession and at times accepted it.) According to this explanation, Caleb Powers set up the plot and turned over his private office to Youtsey and Jim Howard, one of the eastern Kentucky riflemen. Powers then left town on the train. Youtsey stayed with Howard until he saw Goebel approaching, pointed him out to Howard, and left as Howard was firing his gun. When he heard the shot from the hallway, Youtsey ran to Taylor's office to tell him Goebel had been shot. When Youtsey came to trial in October of 1900, he insisted on his innocence. Youtsey proved to be an unreliable but entertaining courtroom actor: during his own trial he yelled out remarks about Goebel and statements of his own innocence. Several times he appeared to fall unconscious. Youtsey was convicted and given a life sentence. In 1903 Youtsey was brought back to the courtroom to testify in Caleb Powers' second trial. At this point he admitted to all the actions described in the Arthur Goebel testimony and cheerfully stated that his earlier fainting fits had been a sham to try to sway the jury.

Caleb Powers was tried four times. He appealed two verdicts of life imprisonment and one for the death penalty and had them all reversed. The fourth trial resulted in a hung jury; a fifth trial in 1908 never took place because Powers received a pardon from then Governor Willson.

A deposition from ex-Governor Taylor was read at Powers' first trial. Taylor admitted to complicity in the scheme to bring the mountaineers to Frankfort, but denied any knowledge of the assassination plans or any acquaintance with Jim Howard. He had taken refuge in Indiana, he said, because he feared he could not get a fair trial in Kentucky. Like Taylor, Powers admitted to the mountaineer scheme but insisted that he had no foreknowledge of the plot to shoot Goebel from his office window. While in jail awaiting trial Powers wrote a book protesting his innocence, *My Own Story*, which brought him a great deal of sympathy. After his pardon his largely Republican district elected him to the United States House of Representatives for four terms. In Congress Kentucky Democrats and their sympathizers refused to serve on committees with Powers.

Jim Howard was a stolid, handsome man who admitted to some feud killings in eastern Kentucky but insisted he had not even been inside the Executive Office Building on the day of the assassination. He was a Democrat who had supported Goebel in the election, but his case was damaged not only by Youtsey's testimony, but also because the companions he named as his alibi refused to fully corroborate his story. He was tried three times and finally given a life sentence. Governor Willson pardoned him at the same time he pardoned Powers, issuing a statement that he thought Youtsey had fired the shot. Youtsey served eighteen years of his life sentence and was finally pardoned in 1918. He continued to insist on the guilt of Powers and Howard after his release. Cobb was still discussing the case in correspondence with his Kentucky friend John Wilson Townsend in 1941, and both agreed in the judgment that Howard was innocent and that Youtsey had fired the short. Cobb expresses pity for Youtsey, however, whom he describes as "the cat's-paw for desperate bloody men."[12] Whether or not he felt Taylor was one of those men he does not say.

During the Goebel assassination trials Cobb developed the skills at recording trial testimony which later helped make him one of the top trial reporters in New York City. He also made some life-long friendships with other reporters who covered the Goebel stories. Keats Speed was a rookie reporter for Cobb's own newspaper who later, as managing editor of the New York *Sun*, fondly remembered carrying copy for Cobb at the 1899 Democratic convention.[13] Opie Read, travelling through Louisville, spent an evening in Cobb's company, drinking a French wine reputed to "inspire eloquence and promote statesmanship." As always Read and Cobb were more eloquent than statesmanlike.[14] Graham Vreeland of the *Courier Journal* and Jack Stewart of the Cincinnati *Enquirer* also remembered with pleasure the time they spent in

Cobb's company in Frankfort.[15] Cobb's closest friendships begun during the Goebel period were those with Kent Cooper, later the head of the Associated Press, and Ray Long, later Cobb's editor at *Cosmopolitan.* Cooper and Long worked on two rival Indianapolis newspapers in 1900. According to Cooper's autobiography, at the time Taylor was expected to produce a deposition for the Powers trial they gained access to Taylor's office and found the discarded carbons of the deposition in the waste basket. They immediately published the text without explaining where they had got it. Taylor accused them of tampering with the U.S. mail, which gave Long and Cooper another story. The Louisville *Post* sent Cobb up to check out the situation, and the three reporters became close friends.[16]

## Notes

[1]Willard Rouse Jillson, *Irvin S. Cobb at Frankfort, Kentucky* (Carrollton, Ky.: News Democrat Press, 1944), pp. 3-4.

[2]Urey Woodson, *The First New Dealer: William Goebel: His Origin, Ambition, Achievements: His Assassination: Loss to the State and Nation: The Story of a Great Crime* (Louisville, Ky.: The Standard Press, 1939), pp. xii-xiv. A much more balanced view is found in James C. Klotter, *William Goebel: The Politics of Wrath* (Lexington: The University Press of Kentucky, 1977).

[3]Cobb, *Myself to Date,* p. 90.

[4]Cobb, *Exit Laughing,* p. 201.

[5]Woodson, p. 24; pp. 46-47.

[6]Klotter, p. 24; pp. 30-31.

[7]Cobb, *Exit Laughing,* p. 208.

[8]The election returns are discussed in Woodson, p. 203, and Klotter, pp. 86-91.

[9]Cobb, *Exit Laughing,* p. 203.

[10]Klotter, p. 104.

[11]Woodson, p. 76.

[12]Cobb papers, University of Kentucky Library.

[13]Letter from Keats Speed, *Louisville Courier-Journal,* 10 March, 1940.

[14]Opie Read, *I Remember* New York: Richard R. Smith, Inc. (1930), p. 49.

[15]Jillson, p. 6.

[16]Kent Cooper, *Kent Cooper and the Associated Press: An Autobiography* (New York: Random House, 1959), p. 15.

# Chapter Five

In June of 1900 the trial of Caleb Powers was recessed in order to move it from Frankfort to Georgetown, and Irvin Cobb took advantage of the break to go to Savannah, Georgia, and marry Laura Spencer Baker, whom he had met during a visit she made to friends in Paducah several years earlier. Laura's family enjoyed the glorious past and inconspicuous present typical of many Southern families; it included heroes of both the Revolutionary War and the Civil War. Laura's father worked as a receiver of tax returns,[1] and with careful economy he and his wife managed to provide their two daughters and their son with good schools and social advantages.

In *My Wayward Parent* Elisabeth Cobb contrasts the childhood experiences of her parents. Unlike the tensions in the Cobb household, the atmosphere at the Baker's was warm and loving. Laura's parents were strict but gentle—Laura was once removed in disgrace from a theater where she had laughed out loud, but the only punishment in the Baker home was being prayed for. To Laura's daughter the greatest difference in the two homes was in the attitude of the two sets of parents toward money. Laura's parents were incredibly generous toward their children—not only with money, but also with time and household arrangements:

> So the Baker girls had house parties and picnics and friends in for supper. Laura says she can never remember an evening when the place wasn't full of young folks. They played the guitar and the piano, and made lemonade and sandwiches, and danced and gave barbeques, and had twelve in for the weekend, and the dressmaker in twice a year to sew—only the dresses, though, for their mama made all their exquisite underclothes herself by hand, yards and yards of hand-embroidered ruffles for their petticoats, miles of rolling and whipping and hem stitching on their nighties and wrappers and corset covers.[2]

The Baker girls were sent to Belmont College in Nashville in the mid-nineties, and during a long vacation in 1896 they went to spend several weeks in Paducah with their classmate Nell Thornbury and her sister. Nashville and especially Belmont possessed a gentility in those days similar to that of Savannah, and Laura was not prepared for the muddy streets and frontier atmosphere of Paducah or for the brash friendliness of its citizens. The Thornbury girls were very popular, and the teen-aged boys of the town—including the reporter Irvin Cobb, whose occasional feelings that as a school dropout he no longer was a suitable member of the young social set were not shared by any of his friends—decided to give the sisters and their guests a royal welcome. Cobb's friend Will Gilbert, the musician of the group, had organized a brass band in which he generously allowed the tone-deaf Cobb to play the drum. To carry the girls from the train station to the Thornbury home the boys had decorated an open carriage with bunting and banners. They pulled the carriage through the streets to the loud accompaniment of the band, frightening horses and attracting barking dogs. Laura was shocked, terrified and not at all pleased. She privately vowed to get away from that awful place as soon as possible.[3]

The loud music and raucous good humor at the dance held in her honor that night was equally unpleasant. Remembering the experience in 1964 she said, "I would not sing. I would not dance. I would have nothing of it." But the boys were funny, and Laura was good-humored and high-spirited, and soon she decided not to worry about the frontier manners but to join in the fun. Only Irvin Cobb seemed to her to be too crude to bear, although he was the funniest of the lot. She made up her mind never to laugh at him. Then during one party when the company was making fun of Irvin's new mustache, which was incongruously red and refused to lie flat, she joined in the criticism. He replied, "Now, Miss Laura, don't jump on something when it's *down*," and she laughed, but she still refused to like him.[4]

Irvin, on the other hand, was thoroughly entranced. Laura was tiny—at barely five feet tall she was a foot shorter than the lanky Cobb—and very pretty, with brunette coloring and dark hair. Cobb was twenty years old at the time they met; she was a few years younger. In the following years he pursued her with talk, letters and presents (with some of the money he was paid for the Merry-Smith story by the Chicago *Tribune* he sent her "the handsomest box of superior mixed bonbon chocolates to be had at Gilbert Brothers' Drugstore—large bow of lilac ribbon on the cover and pair of stylish embossed tin tongs inside") and gradually she became interested enough to ask her parents to invite him to the Baker's annual house party in Savannah.

That first trip to Savannah must have been an anxious time for

Irvin Cobb. To him Laura and Savannah were everything that he was not—refined, graceful, with traditional customs and manners that he didn't even know about. He packed his pitifully small wardrobe and boarded the train for the first trip he had ever made that far away from Paducah. He need not have worried—the Baker hospitality enveloped him and he soon found himself popular with the Bakers, the other houseguests and Laura herself. And he discovered that the ways of Savannah were in some respects not all that different from those of Paducah. Years later Laura's father liked to tell of one incident during Cobb's first visit. The Savannah boys, who prided themselves on their capacity for liquor, decided to take Cobb on a tour of the local watering holes and show him a thing or two. Mr. Baker awoke at four A.M. to find a reasonably sober Cobb just coming in. When asked where he had been, Cobb replied, "I've been having a fine time, putting all those boys to bed."[5]

Cobb continued his long-distance courtship after his return, and finally Laura discarded her Savannah beau and agreed to an engagement. Elisabeth Cobb was never able to get a satisfactory explanation of her mother's decision to marry this homely reporter from a frontier state with three other women to support and dubious prospects:

> She grows very coy and confused when pressed on this subject, and babbles a lot about the other beau, and how attractive he was, and what a sweet person, and then she sighs and says, "Dear Harry! But that was before I met your father."
>
> "But that's what I want to know. Why did you get engaged to my father?"
>
> "I can't seem to remember. He wanted me to be."[6]

To a reporter in 1964 Laura Cobb explained, "He was cute. Of all the people I've known—and I've known lots—he was the cutest. Kipling was almost as cute."[7]

The Cobbs' marriage was successful by any but the most idealistic standard. There is no record of there ever being any woman in Cobb's life at any time besides Laura, and he always mentioned her with affection and even awe. Even later when he wrote partially autobiographical humor and Laura appears as the determined, whimsical and bewildering female the genre seems to call for, his treatment of her is gentle and respectful. They didn't always understand each other, and their natures were quite different. Elisabeth Cobb describes her mother as "merry and literal-minded and conservative and easily shocked—enthusiastic, very impatient, quicksilver to move, passionately loyal, and about as non-literary as a literate person can be." She lacked Cobb's incredible imagination and his fascination with words. She loved clothes and flowers and elegant surroundings; Cobb was happiest in a messy newspaper office or at the bar of a men's club or sitting by a campfire. But Cobb loved Laura for her cool elegance and probably appreciated her willingness to participate in only part of his life. Later in their marriage their social lives were almost totally separate; their daughter explains, "he took to fishing and she took to bridge, and when they did meet, between rubbers and trout seasons, wherever it was, they instantly bought a house. Out of pure nervousness, I sometimes think ...."[8] But this life apparently suited them both very well, and each retained a deep respect for the other.

The wedding, on June 12, 1900, at Laura's house in Savannah, was a beautiful one. Laura's friends helped to decorate the house with smilax and sweet peas and her uncles mixed the Artillery punch for the menfolks. It was made in twelve gallon batches and contained six different types of wines and liquors with only enough fruit juice for flavoring. When time came for the wedding party to assemble it was discovered that the groom had no gloves, but he tried on a pair of the bride's and they fit perfectly; Cobb, in spite of his height, had tiny hands and feet. Cobb describes his memory of the ceremony this way:

> When we stood up before the minister and I repeated after him the words, "with all my worldly goods I thee endow," I could not help grinning inwardly. All my worldly goods, as nearly as I could recall at the moment, consisted of two suits of clothes, a set of Redpath's *History of the World*, and a collection of postage stamps. My salary was eighteen dollars a week.[9]

Most of Cobb's salary went to his mother and sisters in Paducah, and the ninety dollars Cobb had managed to save for his marriage was all spent on the wedding trip to Washington, D.C. Irvin and Laura were delighted with each other, but the honeymoon was hardly a total success. The train ride was hot and Washington was even hotter. Cobb arranged for supper—stuffed tomatoes and champagne—to be served in their hotel room. In keeping with Southern custom, Laura had barely tasted alcohol in her life, but Cobb told her to try the champagne, that it would make her forget the heat and her exhaustion. She was reluctant, but Cobb always insisted that after one glass she exclaimed, "Why this is better than any lemonade I ever had in my life! I don't want this little old glass—I want a tumblerful!" On the third glass she passed out, and Cobb was sure he had killed her. He frantically called the hotel doctor, who said, "Dead my foot! She's drunk as hell!"[10]

When after several days the heat continued and the money had gone, the Cobbs left Washington earlier than they had planned and went to Georgetown, Kentucky, where Laura joined her husband at the press table for six weeks while he covered Caleb Powers' first trial. They then went to Louisville for a brief period before they returned to Georgetown in early October to cover the trial of Henry Youtsey.[11]

At some point during the Youtsey trial Cobb played hookey during an apparently slack period to take Laura on an overnight trip to Cincinnati, only to miss one of the high points of the trial and to put himself in danger of being fired, had he not been helped by a sympathetic telegraph operator. The story was one of Cobb's favorites, and some of the facts probably became fuzzy over the years. In *Exit Laughing* Cobb connects the trip with Arthur Goebel's first surprise visit to the stand, when the insistence of the younger brother of the victim that he had heard Youtsey confess his complicity in the murder caused an uproar in the courtroom. Youtsey met the accusation with shouts, first of his innocence, and then, most provocatively, with the statement, "Goebel is not dead and all the devils in hell couldn't kill him." Cobb may have missed this scene, but it is unlikely he was out of town during this outburst, for it occurred on October 9, the second day of testimony. More likely dates for the Cobb trip are October 15-16, for Youtsey's outburst was followed by catatonia, which suspended the trial for several days and left Cobb with little to do. When the trial was abruptly recontinued on October 15, Arthur Goebel took the stand again. If it was this later testimony that Cobb missed, it was quite important to the subsequent conviction of Youtsey, even if Youtsey was still in a trance and unable to disrupt the courtroom. Goebel with icy calm recalled Youtsey's description of the murder, with Governor Taylor as mastermind, Jim Howard as gunman, and Youtsey as go-between. The accuracy of Goebel's testimony is still as uncertain today as the authenticity of Youtsey's catatonia.[12]

Cobb enjoyed showing his bride the sights of Cincinnati, but the morning paper he grabbed in the train station the next morning destroyed his mood. On the slow train to Georgetown he counted the minutes and the miles. The *Post* was an afternoon paper and Cobb hoped to make the 11:10 AM deadline. The train, due in at 10:30, was thirty minutes late, so Cobb deserted Laura at the station and ran as fast as he could to the Western Union office. The telegraph operator, a friend, was glad to see him because the *Post* had been sending urgent requests for copy all morning. "So," Cobb quotes the friend, "Not knowing what else to do ... I took a chance. I went up to the hotel and got a dupe of Clarence Walker's [official court] transcript of what happened last night, and about three quarters of an hour ago I put it on the wire." Someone at the Louisville *Post* added a 200 word introduction to the 4,000 words the telegraph operator had sent out. Cobb later claimed that, not only had his escapade not been discovered, but that the editor even sent him a telegram congratulating him for having invented a new way to report a trial.[13]

Although the Goebel stories dominated Cobb's years on the Louisville *Evening Post*, there were slack periods when he was assigned to other news and feature stories. His bent for humorous writing, which had been first encouraged on the Paducah *Evening News*, was known in Louisville as well, and not long after his arrival at the *Post* Cobb was given a humorous column entitled "Kentucky Sour Mash" which continued to appear in the *Post* on no regular schedule as long as he was a reporter on the paper. The subject matter was Kentucky politics and public figures, and the tone was whimsical to sarcastic. Occasionally the column included verses, sometimes humorous and sometimes sentimental. Cobb later abandoned writing poetry; of his early efforts he says, "My poetry was so wooden that it fairly creaked at the joints, but I could turn it out by the yard."[14] "Kentucky Sour Mash" was very popular, and Kentucky residents who had forgotten Cobb's serious reporting when he became a national figure remembered the column.

In May of 1901 Urey Woodson, a former Goebel aide who was Cobb's friend in spite of their disagreements about Goebel, made plans to start a new paper in Paducah, the *Democrat*. He offered Cobb a higher salary than he was making in Louisville to come be the managing editor. After careful consideration and attempts to convince the reluctant Laura that it was a wise decision, Cobb accepted the job and returned to his native town. The *Democrat* succeeded, the older *News* floundered, and several months later Woodson worked out a consolidation of the two papers, published as the Paducah *News-Democrat*, with Cobb as editor. The Louisville *Post* made several offers to Cobb to come back at a higher salary, but he stayed with Woodson in Paducah until he left for New York in 1904.

One of Cobb's reasons for returning to Paducah was economic. He felt that if both of the households he was supporting were in the same city, some of the expenses could be cut. He and Laura moved into a separate small apartment of their own, but they took most of their meals at Manie Cobb's with Irvin paying all the expenses. Thus Laura met with her in-laws two or three times a day, almost every day. The situation was a strained one.

Elisabeth Cobb writes that her father once told her, "with the bitterest, hurt, lost, young look on his face," that Manie Cobb never forgave him for marrying and thus forsaking part of his responsibility to her and to his sisters. Laura, with her education and her assured sense of social position, was probably an ideal to Manie in some ways—an example of what Manie's daughters could have become had their father been more dependable. But jealousy drove out any admiration Manie might have felt for her daughter-in-law, and her behavior toward Irvin's bride was cool and formal. Elisabeth Cobb says that years later her grandmother's rare compliments to Laura were prefaced with, "Well, I'll say this much for you, Laura." The example she gives, however, shows a begrudging admiration: "Well, I'll say this much for you, Laura, you could make a home out of a desert waste, and find friends there before sundown."[15] There may have been some ways that Laura could have won over her mother-in-law, but she did not know or use them, and, beneath a surface of polite conversation, Irvin Cobb's women disliked and mistrusted each other.

Cobb's brother John was still at home at this time and, in fact, worked at the *News-Democrat* as a reporter. He soon left Paducah for newspaper work in Louisville and then in Memphis.[16] The two brothers at some time had a difference of opinion so heated that they apparently never saw or spoke to each other again. Cobb never mentions his brother except in references to their childhood experiences. Until his mother's death he made at least one trip a year to Paducah to visit her, but no mention is ever made of John's being present at those visits or returning to Paducah at any other time. John obviously did not share Irvin's strong sense of responsibility toward their mother and sisters, and that in itself may explain Irvin's disgust with him. There were also rumors that John was an alcoholic. He was a good newspaperman, though, and liked by his colleagues.[17] He died in Memphis, leaving no children.

Reubie Cobb was still in her self-imposed isolation when Irvin and Laura returned to Paducah—one of the reasons, no doubt, that the young couple took separate quarters instead of moving into the family house. Reubie was her usual caustically gay self, laughing at the world outside her window in such a manner that Laura was sure she was being attacked too. Young Manie, who was barely fifteen, was probably more willing to accept Laura—Manie resented her mother's favoritism toward Reubie and probably welcomed the disruption this new family member made. But both Reubie and Manie were as jealous as their mother of the attentions which Irvin devoted to this interloper. Both seemed to feel that the money he earned belonged to them. Laura has told her grandchildren several stories of their selfishness. Christmas seemed to be an especial ordeal, with the sisters never being satisfied with the gifts Laura picked out and Irvin paid for.[18]

But Laura's in-laws took up only part of her day, and in general her life in Paducah was happy. She was delighted to get out of the Louisville boarding house and into a tiny apartment where she could arrange her elegant—and unused—wedding presents and even purchase a few new decorations and a rubber plant. She made friends to help her pass the long days while Cobb got out the paper, many of them sisters and wives of Cobb's boyhood friends. The Paducah humor was still as bizarre as before, and late in the evening when Cobb got in from work, bringing a snack—"oyster loaf, and wonderful sandwiches, and the biggest, briniest dill pickles in the world"—which they would sit on the bed to eat, each would have funny stories to share of what the Corbetts or the Gilberts or the men at the newspaper office had said that day. Laura remembers those sessions as the best part of her life in Paducah—she so seldom saw her husband at any other time.

Cobb's position as editor required long hours with almost no slack periods. He put out eight papers a week, one every afternoon Monday through Saturday, a Sunday morning issue, and a weekly edition. The machines ran all the time—when the afternoon paper was off the press a night shift started setting up the type for the next day's edition. Cobb had continual difficulties with both his staff and his machinery. Even with a full complement of two reporters and an apprentice Cobb planned and wrote much of the copy; at times he wrote almost all of it. Cobb was concerned with the quality of the paper; he proofread almost every item that went in and tried to use original features in the Sunday edition, not syndicate articles. The weekends were the most difficult—Cobb tells of going to work at 7:30 A.M. on Saturday, getting the Saturday paper out of the way and moving immediately to the Sunday morning edition. Sometimes that was not ready for the press until 5 A.M. Sunday morning. He staggered home then to sleep till noon, but after lunch he'd be back at the office, finding or writing material for the night shift to set up for the Monday paper. Cobb remembers his attitude toward the job this way:

> It was drudgery—manual and mental labor of the most exacting sort—but I was proud of my job and proud of the paper we turned out. I was fairly young to be in sole editorial management of a paper of such pretensions, and I was drawing a bigger salary—so my employers used to remind me at frequent intervals—than any so-called country editor in the state. I was getting thirty dollars a week.[19]

The owners got their money's worth. Urey Woodson in a later tribute to Cobb described Cobb's talent as a "smoke-up" man, a person who could take extremely scanty or unpromising material and turn it into a full story:

> There are days when news just won't happen in Paducah and then you were at your best. On a dully foggy, misty day, or a sleety, snowy day, when nobody would venture out, not even a burglar, you were surely on the job, smoking up a half dozen corking first page local stories with scare heads.[20]

The foreman of the composing room, Will Cabell, told of Cobb's heroic efforts on August 19, 1901, when the riverboat *City of Golconda* sunk at Cottonwood Bar. A nervous eyewitness arrived in Paducah at 8 P.M., and shortly after that brief messages came in over the wire about the sinking. From such information as he could get, plus a lot of deduction and imagination, Cobb wrote nearly six columns for a special edition that was on the Paducah streets by midnight. It was, according to Cabell, "one of the finest examples of newspaper enterprise I ever saw."[21]

Cobb loved his first year or so back in Paducah. He loved the people, the town, and even the hard work. His old friends were glad to have Irvin, his funny stories, and his hearty laugh back with them. One acquaintance from those days tells this story:

> I remember one night about midnight I was walking past the newspaper office where he worked and heard him howling with laughter inside. I knew it was he because nobody in three counties had a mouth so big or could laugh so loud. I went in and

> he was almost rolling out of his chair. He had a big heap of letters and was putting stamps on them. Beside him was a big Newfoundland dog. He would tear off a stamp and the dog would stick out his tongue very solemnly and lick it. And then Cobb would laugh until the building shook. I never had so much fun as sitting there an hour listening to him laugh.[22]

But as the months passed and the work increased, the strain on Cobb's health became intense. He became irritable and jumpy—he even suffered from dizzy spells and once almost fainted in the office. His responsibilities were increased by the birth of his daughter in 1902, and he began to dream of being a city reporter again.

Laura Cobb had become pregnant before her first year in Paducah was over. She went to Savannah to spend the hot summer months of her pregnancy and to await the birth of her child. Elizabeth Cobb (she later changed the spelling of her name) was born in Savannah on October 8, 1902. Laura's recovery was slow, and then, after they had returned to Paducah, the baby was frequently sick. The doctors at several points thought that she would not live, and throughout her infancy she was thin, feverish, and almost constantly crying. Cobb walked her for hours at night after he returned from the newspaper, reading a book as he paced.

For about a year after their daughter's birth Laura was too weak and Cobb was too harassed to do much more than make it through the day. By 1904, however, things had settled down enough to make plans. Cobb had once confided to Laura his desire to work for a newspaper in New York City, and she had immediately taken that dream as her own. Without her encouragement he might never have taken the chance, because Cobb was always modest about his own abilities and cautious where money was concerned. For a while Cobb thought of trying Chicago, since he'd already had a big story published in the *Tribune,* but Laura held out for New York. She had fallen under the spell of its excitement and sophistication during one brief visit and was sure that she wanted to live there forever. Chicago would have been a poor substitute. She felt that Cobb was the best newspaperman in the world and told him so. When Cobb brought home the news that a Paducah native who had worked on newspapers in St. Louis and Chicago was now making sixty-five dollars a week in New York, Laura immediately said, "If that man can make sixty-five, Irvin, *you* can make a hundred." She wrote her father, who agreed with her that Cobb was the "smartest" man around and arranged a two hundred dollar loan and an offer to take care of Laura and the baby until Cobb was settled and earning money in New York.[23] By August she had convinced him, and she took off for Savannah as he left for New York.

The decision was an extremely difficult one to make. Cobb's mother took his wish to leave as a personal affront and his actual departure as a desertion. She placed the blame solely on Laura, whom she viewed as "a wicked woman trying to take her son away from her."[24] Relations between the two women became even more strained; in later years when Cobb went back to Paducah he usually went alone. Cobb had no job waiting for him in New York, and in many ways it was a foolhardy decision for a man with five females to support: quitting a well-paying job and a respected position in the community in hopes of finding something in a city two thousand miles away. But Laura had enough optimism and determination for both of them, and Cobb took the plunge. It was almost a year after he had put her on the train before he could afford to bring her to join him.

## Notes

[1]Neuman, *Cobb* (1924), p. 24.

[2]E. Cobb, *Wayward Parent,* pp. 28-30.

[3]E. Cobb, *Wayward Parent,* p. 30.

[4]Carol Sutton, "A Visit with Mrs. Irvin S. Cobb," *Louisville Courier-Journal* April 26, 1964, III, 1.

[5]Sutton, *Courier-Journal,* April 26 1964.

[6]E. Cobb, *Wayward Parent,* pp. 31-32.

[7]Sutton, *Courier-Journal,* April 26, 1964.

[8]E. Cobb, *Wayward Parent,* p. 28.

[9]Cobb, *Myself to Date,* pp. 89-90.

[10]E. Cobb, *Wayward Parent,* p. 40.

[11]Jillson, p. 6.

[12]Cobb, *Exit Laughing,* pp. 222-223; Louisville *Courier-Journal,* Oct 10, 1900, 1:2; Memphis *Commercial Appeal,* Oct. 16, 1900, 1:7.

[13]Cobb, *Exit Laughing,* pp. 223-225. This is one of several Cobb stories that probably grew in the retelling. James C. Klotter doubts it happened at all.

[14]Thomas L. Masson, *Our American Humorists* (Freeport, N.Y.: Books for Libraries Press, 1931), p. 98.

[15]E. Cobb, *Wayward Parent,* p. 51.

[16]Paducah *News Democrat,* Dec. 30, 1922.

[17]Boyce House, "I Give You Texas," Texas City *Sun,* March 24, 1944.

[18]Interviews with Cobb's grandchildren

[19]Cobb, *Myself to Date,* pp. 99-101.

[20]Paducah *News Democrat,* December 30, 1922.

[21]Neumann, *Cobb,* (1934), p. 65.

[22]Townsend, *Concerning Cobb,* p. 7D.

[23]Sutton, *Courier-Journal,* April 26 1964.

[24]E. Cobb, *Wayward Parent,* p. 56.

## Chapter Six

For the rest of his life the view of the Manhattan skyline from the Hudson River brought to Irvin Cobb the intense feelings—a combination of dread and anticipation—that he felt on the night of August 4, 1904, as he rode the ferry from Jersey City into New York for the first time.

> It was the greatest sight I had ever seen, the most inspiring, the most exhilarating—and the most daunting. It stirred me clear up to the roots of my back hair, and it scared me clean down to the nails of my toes. This was the oyster I had come to open and find the meat inside—and maybe, if I had luck, a pearl or two. All of a sudden I realized what a whale of an oyster it was! If my legs had been cut off at the ankle I reckon I shouldn't have bled a drop; but if I had cold feet in the most aggravated form I likewise had the courage of desperation that keeps a forlorn hope from being too forlorn. I had burned the woods behind me. I just had to make good—that was all.[1]

Cobb was intimidated by the size and strangeness of the city—he later said he knew exactly how an immigrant must feel as he views the city from the steerage deck—and he decided to wait until the next day to try to find the boarding house that had been recommended to him instead he went to the Hotel Marlborough, which he had heard was a favorite with Southerners. Already lonely and eager to hear familiar accents, he approached a man in the lobby wearing a white goatee and a slouch hat. Although the stranger proved to be friendly and talkative, he soon explained that he was from Michigan and the disappointed Cobb went to bed.[2] The next morning he moved to the boarding house, at 3348 West Fifty-seventh Street, and set out to find a job. He soon discovered what really big disappointments New York could deliver.

Cobb thought he had two really good possibilities. One was the Paducah friend who was making sixty-five dollars a week; the other was a letter praising Cobb's talents that Urey Woodson had written to Caleb von Hamm, Woodson's friend and in 1904 the managing editor of the New York *Evening World.*[3] In addition, he had a sheaf of recommendations, "To Whom It May Concern," from Woodson and others. Von Hamm acknowledged receipt of Woodson's letter but said that there were no vacancies at the *Evening World.* Cobb's interview with the successful Paducahan was even more disappointing: he had just been dismissed from his job and was looking for an opening himself. Cobb soon found out what he had not known, that August was the slowest month for New York newspapers, the time when they traditionally cut back their staffs. Cobb found himself in competition for the almost non-existent positions with men with impressive New York experience, and his Kentucky references and experiences were apparently worthless. He knew one other man in New York—a copy-reader on a tabloid. This man responded to his call with suspicion, became less icy but hardly friendly when he found out Cobb was not looking for a loan, and told him he was crazy to have left his Paducah job. He was too busy trying to keep his own job to help Cobb find one. When that interview was over, Cobb knew he was on his own. The only thing worse than trying to find a job under such circumstances would have been to write Laura that he was giving up, so he grimly set up a plan of attack.

Every morning he toured all the afternoon papers; after lunch he made the circuit of the morning papers. He never got past the waiting rooms; he never saw anyone more important than an office boy. Everywhere, every day, the response was the same: no vacancy.

When he was not pleading with office boys or writing falsely cheerful letters to Laura—containing a lot of funny stories about New York and very little about the job situation—Cobb investigated New York and studied the New York newspapers. Detailed knowledge of streets and neighborhoods is as important to a reporter as it is to a taxidriver, and Cobb went about his task quite systematically. He would pick a cross-town streetcar—he soon had ridden them all—and take it until he reached a district that looked interesting and unfamiliar. He would walk around, noting street names and ethnic identifications, and then would ask a policeman how to get back to Broadway or Sixth Avenue. By using this method Cobb became familiar with the Bowery, the East Side, Harlem, Chinatown, Greenwich Village, Little Italy, the Waterfront, Wall

Street, the Syrian Quarter, the Greek Quarter, connecting the mental images of each in his mind with a route from the central district.

Also Cobb bought and read newspapers. He studied their make-ups and their treatments of stories, both to differentiate among them and to isolate any general New York style. He was amazed by the flippant tone used to describe even those in positions of importance and by the apparent desire of New Yorkers to be shocked by what they read in the papers. He ranked the papers according to their general merits and to the ease with which he thought he could duplicate their style. None of this effort made any difference at this point; the office boys still grinned and said that nothing had changed.

After two weeks of this routine, Cobb's money and self-confidence had dwindled alarmingly. One noontime his poverty made him afraid to eat lunch and his discouragement made him uninterested in exploring the city, so he sat on a park bench in Madison Square, thinking how much more he looked and felt like the down-and-outers around him than he had two weeks before. At this point he had the idea that, he says, "lifted me off that bench as if I had been bee-stung." New Yorkers liked flippancy, didn't they? They liked to be shocked? He would send a letter to every managing editor in the city that would be so impudent they would be forced to notice him! Cobb went home to compose his letter.

Apparently there is no copy of Cobb's letter in existence today, but Cobb reconstructed it in *Stickfuls*. He began by calling himself "the best writer and the ablest editor that had ever come to New York to uplift its journalism to the highest level," claimed to be able to do any job on any paper better than the person then holding it, and expressed amazement that no one had yet grabbed up this prize. The last paragraph went like this:

> This is positively your last chance. I have grown weary of studying the wall-paper design in your anteroom. A modest appreciation of my own worth forbids my doing business with your head office boy any longer. Unless you grab me right away I will go elsewhere and leave your paper flat on its back right here in the middle of a hard summer, and your whole life hereafter will be one vast surging regret. The line forms on the left; applications considered in the order they are received; triflers and professionals flirts save stamps. Write, wire, or call at the above address.[4]

When the letter was drafted he went to a stationary shop and bought some expensive paper, heavy and gilt-edged. Then he hired a public stenographer in a hotel lobby to make thirteen separate copies of the letter, one for each managing editor in New York. She giggled at the difference between the tone of the letter and the appearance of the gawky young man in front of her, but did her work.[5] Cobb mailed the letters that afternoon and went to bed feeling that New York had not defeated him yet.

Cobb had decided while studying newspapers that the New York *Evening Sun* was the best written and edited paper in town. (He later discovered that morning papers were considered more prestigious by New York reporters.) The next morning, his better suit newly pressed (he only owned two), he set out for the offices of the *Sun*. As usual, the head office boy was there to take his card, but this time the managing editor followed him back to the anteroom, waving Cobb's letter.

"Are you the same man who wrote this damn fool letter?" When Cobb acknowledged it, he responded, "If you've got half as much ability as you have gall, consider yourself hired." "All right." Cobb said. "I'm hired."[6]

They went in to talk things over. Cobb told of his varied experiences as reporter and editor. The *Sun* editor was impressed; such a general knowledge of the newspaper business was difficult to get on a metropolitan paper, where employees were quickly categorized. So he was willing to take a chance on this outsider. But all newcomers at the *Sun* began at fifteen dollars a week, with a chance of regular raises if they proved themselves. Cobb's enthusiasm was deflated by this news—fifteen dollars a week minus family expenses would hardly support him in New York, much less Laura and the baby! But he liked the editor and his description of the kind of reporter he was looking for, and he agreed to start work the next morning.

When Cobb returned to the boarding house four letters awaited him—one promising to consider him for the next vacancy and three offering him jobs outright. Two of them were from morning papers which Cobb later realized would probably have paid more than the *Sun*. But he never regretted accepting the *Sun* job—the editor had made him feel welcome, and that to Cobb was very important. Elisabeth Cobb says that the most amazing thing about her father's letter was that *he* had written it—his nature had none of the impudence and gall the letter displayed. Even in desperation, she thinks, he could only have got away with it on paper; had he attempted such flippancy in person, his natural humility would have ruined his act. When he walked out of the *Sun* office, he had a job to prove himself with, and there was no need to sustain the sassy tone of the letter. He wired Laura the happy news, but did not reveal the amount of his salary until later.[7]

Cobb still had a lot to learn about the New York newspaper business—including how seldom a cub reporter is given the chance to prove himself. He must have had some uneasy memories of Cincinnati the next morning when he was assigned to edit telegraph dispatches. His co-worker, a bald, melancholy man of about Cobb's age, regarded him sourly as he explained the *Sun* format. While grabbing all the more interesting dispatches for himself, this journalistic Uriah Heep told Cobb that the *Sun* was the worst-run, lowest-paying shop in the business, that its only virtue was that it fired its workers less frequently than the other newspapers. Cobb later realized that such remarks were typical of the New York style—all reporters criticized their own papers among their co-workers and defended them as vociferiously in the presence of employees of other papers.

After two days of cutting and pasting telegraph dispatches, Cobb was given a chance to write up an advance story about a naval review. He spent a whole day on the story, giving it his glossiest stylistic polish, only to find that it had been cut severely before it appeared in the paper. This was another New York fact-of-life: only the work of top reporters went into the paper as they turned it in, and the copy readers were severe toward any cub reporter who tried fine writing.

When on his fourth day Cobb was sent out to investigate a possible strike threatening the public transportation system, he had a chance to learn some more about the New York reporting business. He was afraid to tell the acting city editor that he had no idea how to cover the story, so he pocketed the clippings he was given from the morning papers and set out. The clippings indicated that a meeting might take place at the office of the general manager of the particular system under threat, so Cobb went there. The secretary told him to wait, and he was soon joined by a group of five men, obviously reporters, who came in together. When the secretary handed out copies of a statement, one reporter suggested going to strike headquarters and others agreed. Cobb considered this strange behavior and went back to the newspaper to write up his story.

One matter was cleared up as soon as he got to the *Sun* office, where the city editor told Cobb he wasn't supposed to write anything. In New York, especially on the evening newspapers, what Cobb considered to be one reporter's job was divided between two men, the leg man, who ran the story down, calling in information as he found it, and the rewrite man, who stayed at the newspaper office and wrote up the stories he took over the telephone. This division of labor permitted the coverage of many more stories in the vast area of New York City than would have been possible if each leg man did his own writing.

When Cobb had turned in his notes on the strike situation, he went to the hotel where the labor leaders were meeting, to discover the same group of reporters he had seen earlier. Talking with them soon explained the lock-step movements that had surprised Cobb that morning. Leg men in New York did not work independently, but those covering the same story for different newspapers banded together for mutual assistance. Reporters who discovered one of their ranks was holding out on some useful item would ostracize him in the future, but a member of the group in good standing would not only get all the pooled information, but also could depend on the other reporters to supply him the whole story if for some excusable reason he failed to show up at all. This practice, unlike that in any other city, was disliked by the city editors, who felt it hurt their chances to score on the opposition, but the reporters, who knew that the man working alone was far more likely to be fired for missing a story than to be promoted for scooping one, stuck together out of a sense of self-preservation. So Cobb was given a post guarding the front door of August Belmont, the head of the threatened line. When a labor union official left, another reporter peeled off to follow him, to return later to tell Cobb and the other reporters what he had learned before he called it in to his own newspaper.

Cobb, who worked as a leg man for several months, soon adjusted to this assembly-line method of reporting. While he sometimes despaired of making an impression because he was denied scoops on one end and distinctive writing on the other, he was receiving a valuable education in New York journalism. His forays into various parts of the city escorted by a band of experienced reporters increased his knowledge of New York geography, and the form in which his stories finally made the *Sun* taught him what New Yorkers consider news. The city editor, Tommy Dieuaide, a soft-spoken, diminutive man, was impressed with Cobb's energy, and, discovering that he had done humorous writing in the past, suggested that he vary the routine of his legwork by submitting items to the *Sun's* Saturday humor page. Cobb later was responsible for most of the page in addition to his regular work.

But, although Cobb found kindness and encouragement at the *Sun,* he didn't find many friends. The atmosphere at the *Sun* was businesslike, and few employees seemed to have time for Cobb after hours. Cobb's early months in New York, while profitable, were extremely lonely. As his services became more valuable, he received raises, five dollars at a time, but the income he needed before Laura and the baby could join him seemed to get larger every time he calculated the expected expenses.

Later in *Cobb's Bill of Fare* he wrote about the loneliness of his first Christmas in New York by way of explaining "the finest music I ever heard." On Christmas Eve he sat in his tiny boarding house room, watching the shoppers through the curtain of falling snow and feeling sorry for himself. He half-listened as an Italian music grinder positioned himself in front of the boarding house and started cranking out a wheezing, jerky tune. Suddenly Cobb recognized the song as "My Old Kentucky Home." The musician played the song twice, Cobb says, "once on his own hook and once because I went downstairs and divided my money with him."[8]

Laura was equally lonely in Savannah. She enjoyed the comforts of her parents' house, but, as the original visit of a month or two stretched out, she became anxious to conquer New York herself. Cobb wrote her long letters in which he tried to hide his misery, but Laura knew he needed both her company and her encouragement, and she added up expenses as often as Cobb did and usually came up with a smaller sum. The baby—now called "Buff" because one of the Savannah servants had declared "Elizabuff" too long and pompous a name for a baby—had grown fat and healthy, and Laura was anxious for them to be a family again. Finally, in early Spring, Cobb wrote that he had been picked to edit the early morning "lobster" edition of the newspaper, with a raise that would bring his salary to thirty dollars a week.

By Cobb's calculations that was only three dollars less than their projected expenses if all of them lived in one room at the boarding house. Laura wrote that she would do three dollars of laundry a week herself and that she and the baby would be up on the next train. Laura's parents supplied her with gifts to make their new life easier—clothes for her and Buff and a basket of goodies which included several jars of Irvin's favorite—Mrs. Baker's pickled shrimp.[9]

Laura's train was due at the same Jersey City station at which Cobb himself had arrived, and Cobb was so excited that he got there two hours ahead of time, only to miss Laura when her train came in. Cobb was frequently the butt of jokes and curses because of his powers of total concentration: when Cobb was reading nothing could disturb him, not even, it turned out, the long delayed arrival of his wife and child. Because Cobb got to New Jersey so early, he sat inside the station and read a magazine. When Laura's train came in, she climbed down onto the platform struggling with Buff, bags, wraps and baskets. Her husband was nowhere in sight. After waiting on the platform until she was convinced Irvin was not coming, she called a porter and got all her paraphenalia to the ferry, then into a cab and to the boarding house all by herself. By the time Cobb finished his magazine, realized what must have happened, and headed home as fast as he could, Laura was unpacked, had the baby in bed, and was sitting by the window holding a jar of pickled shrimps, planning to throw it at Irvin when he showed up. When his cab finally arrived below the window, however, and he was so flustered that he practically fell out its door and then dropped all his money in the gutter trying to pay the driver, his behavior was so typical and touching that she hugged him instead. But after that she always tried to arrange for someone else to meet her at the station.[10]

Laura's life that first summer was not easy. To get out the lobster edition Cobb worked all night and slept in the daytime, which meant that Laura had to keep Buff out of their one room so that he would not be disturbed. Laura and Buff thus spent most of their days in a park near the boarding house that was only slightly less cramped and dusty than the parlor of their landlady. Laura had few friends and found the other boarding house guests uncongenial. But she was in New York and her pleasure in that fact kept her cheerful no matter how difficult things got. Cobb's spirits improved greatly with her around, and he later told his daughter that any time in their later prosperity that he got mad at Laura, the memory of how sweet and understanding she had been that first year in New York would lead him to forgive her.

The Cobbs lived in or near New York City for twenty-nine more years, and Laura never lost her enthusiasm for the city. Irvin Cobb was more affected by the bitterness of his early experiences there, and even after New York gave him money, fame, and friends he felt a lingering dislike of the place, which he always described as cold and heartless, in contrast to his romanticized notions of Kentucky hospitality. Laura, who did not keep her opposite views of Kentucky hospitality to herself, was buoyed in those early months by a faith in Irvin much greater than his faith in himself, and, while he worried about bringing up a child in a New York boarding house, she confidently ignored the dirt and the noise because she was certain that New York would have to appreciate her husband's talents sooner or later—after all, he was an editor already—and that they wouldn't be in the boarding house for long.

Cobb's position as editor of the lobster edition carried little of the prestige or power of other editorships, but it did show that his bosses at the *Sun* were recognizing his talents and his previous experience. His hours were terrible—he left home at 1:30 A.M. and returned when the paper hit the streets at 8 A.M. But he could see things in the paper that he had put there—there were no copy readers between him and publication. This feature of his new position provided him with the opportunity Laura had told him was sure to come.

Working with Cobb was a reporter, Max Fischel, whom he later described as the best leg man in the business. One early morning Fischel called in a story of a stabbing at a dance hall in the Tenderloin District. There was no rewrite man in the office at the time and so Cobb prepared to write it himself; besides, he was familiar with the dance hall because once on his rambles he had sat there for several hours watching the patrons, who had seemed to him the epitome of sordid despair. The murder, although brutal, was by no means unusual, and might have merited only a few paragraphs, except that Fischel, too, was struck by the dismal atmosphere, and his account triggered Cobb's memory of his earlier reactions. Cobb wrote the murder up as a feature story, weaving in his impressions of the dance hall with Fischel's account of the events leading up to the murder. Because there was no one to stop him, Cobb put the story on the front page, and when the city editor came to work and saw it, he liked it and kept it in that position for the subsequent editions. The story created a mild stir in journalistic circles, and Cobb received three offers from other newspapers. He turned them down but enjoyed the greater respect with which his work was treated at the *Sun* after the story appeared. After almost a year in New York, Cobb was looked on as a man with a future. Cobb later used this story to explain the problems of the leg man: Fischel got no credit at all. Cobb remembered him, however, and later when he had a position of some importance at the *Evening World* he convinced the editor to hire Fischel and they worked together on several stories.

# Notes

[1]Cobb, *Myself to Date,* pp. 107-08

[2]Townsend, *Concerning Cobb,* p. 112.

[3]Neuman, *Cobb* (1934), p. 73.

[4]Cobb, *Myself to Date,* p. 118.

[5]E. Cobb, *Wayward Parent*, p. 69.

[6]Cobb, *Myself to Date,* p. 119.

[7] E. Cobb, *Wayward Parent,* p. 70.

[8]Irvin S. Cobb, *Cobb's Bill of Fare* (New York: George H. Doran Co., 1913), pp. 72; 77.

[9]Sutton, *Courier-Journal,* April 26, 1964.

[10]E. Cobb, *Wayward Parent,* pp. 81-82.

# Chapter Seven

One night in early August, 1905, Cobb, happier than he had been since Laura and the baby had arrived in New York, awoke his wife to tell her some exciting news: the *Evening Sun* was going to send him as special correspondent to the Portsmouth Peace Conference, with a by-line for his stories. It was the big break he had been waiting for, and could she endure spending the rest of the summer alone in the detested New York boarding house? Laura compromised on a trip to Savannah, and so, after putting her and the baby on the train, Cobb packed his bags for New Hampshire.

That the *Evening Sun* sent such a novice, however promising, as Cobb was unusual; other newspapers sent much more renowned journalists including Samuel Blythe, the Washington correspondent of the New York *Evening World*, and Charles Hand of the London *Daily Mail*, both of whom were good friends of Cobb by the end of the Conference. The Conference, which President Theodore Roosevelt had arranged between Russia and Japan as an attempt to end their war and thus to preserve the open-door policy, promised to be a great press event, and the other reporters tended to be those with experience at interpreting diplomatic innuendo. Irvin Cobb's experience was mostly at the city desk, and he immediately sensed that he was out of his league. So he decided to do what he knew how to do best—to report on the colorful if unimportant events and scenes outside the meeting rooms: the cut of a Russian's coat, the brilliance of a Japanese robe, the provisions for feeding these exotic foreigners in a New Hampshire navy yard.

While Cobb was sending home two columns of vivid description a day, the other reporters found themselves stymied. The ambassadors and emissaries moved from their bedrooms to the meeting rooms without a word to the reporters. All announcements to the press were short and practically worthless. Even the subtle signs such as private meetings and raised eyebrows were very rare and thus over-worked. Editors despaired over the meager stories their expensive reporters were sending back. Sam Blythe said later, "All of us Washington correspondents rushed up there, but we could not find an earthly thing to write about. But that made no difference to the Paducah boy; he wrote it anyway. He scooped the life out of all of us."[1] The public, who wanted to read about the Portsmouth Peace Conference, found something to read only in the *Evening Sun.* It didn't matter that, as Bob Davis put it, "there wasn't a single fact in the entire series;"[2] Cobb presented the excitement and drama of the Conference, and that was enough. Cobb's editor quickly realized he had a bonanza, and the series of columns written throughout the entire month of the Conference were syndicated all over the United States, bylined "Irvin S. Cobb." The Portsmouth Peace Conference brought Theodore Roosevelt the Nobel Peace Prize; it spread Irvin Cobb's name across the country and Laura Cobb never had to live in a boarding house again.

Cobb returned to New York and the *Evening Sun* in triumph to find five or six offers from other newspapers awaiting him. He chose to move to Joseph Pulitzer's *Evening World,* perhaps out of appreciation for the recommendation Sam Blythe gave Editor Van Hamm after returning from Portsmouth, perhaps because their offer of $60 a week was the most impressive one made. Cobb stayed on the *Evening World* for six years, only leaving in 1911 to become a staff contributor of the *Saturday Evening Post.*

In the first decade of this century the *World* newspapers were recovering somewhat from the yellow journalism of the nineties; as Cobb says, "they were over the yellow fever but still had the yellow jaundice." The *Evening World* had always been slightly in the shadow of its morning counterpart, Pulitzer's pride, where Arthur Brisbane and Herbert Bayard Swope reigned, but it was a good solid newspaper even if it still preferred its news sensational. The dominant figure from a reporter's viewpoint was Charles Chapin, the city editor, a gray, sour devil of a man, contemptuous of the reporters who worked for him and of the public who bought his newspapers. Chapin had an instinct for blood and sentiment, and Cobb insisted that he thought in headlines; "Tiny Tot with Penny Clutched in Chubby Hand Dies Under Tram Before Mother's Eye," he would cry, beaming with pleasure at the possibilities of a story before him. Cobb felt that Chapin was able to suspend his human sympathies in the newsroom; most other reporters were less charitable, and assumed he had none.

Shortly after Cobb joined the *Evening World* he made one of his most important and long-lasting friendships—that with Robert Hobart Davis. Bob Davis had joined the *World* in 1903 under editor F.L.H. Noble and stayed on when Caleb Van Hamm took over. Davis had many talents, one of which was finding talent in others.

While working for Noble, he had sought out and encouraged O. Henry, becoming his friend and editor. When he met Cobb, he was also impressed with his abilities and remained his friend, confidant and literary advisor after he left the *World* to take an editorial position at *Munsey's Magazine*.[3]

Davis was a tall, homely man with wide-spaced eyes, prominent ears and a big smile. His midwestern accent and his relaxed ways made him many friends, and he and Cobb found much to like in each other. Davis has written an account of Cobb's early experiences at the *World* offices. Cobb moved into the Pulitzer Building rather inobtrusively—it was only one door down from the *Sun* offices. In spite of his hefty increase in salary and his recent success, Cobb was not given any important assignments right away, and he felt himself every much an outsider in the offices. But Cobb did not remain friendless for long. As Bob Davis explains:

> One afternoon in the *Evening World* office I. Cobb strolled over the copy desk and told three inoffensive little short stories. Everybody laughed.
>
> A high-priced re-write man asked Cobb to lunch the next day. The city editor began to loosen up, the copy desk let some of his best stuff get through and into the paper—which is a very great concession in any section of Park Row.
>
> The *entente cordiale* spread into the morning department and then into the Sunday room, and finally downstairs and sat on Don Seitz's desk.

Don Seitz was Joseph Pulitzer's representative at the *World,* so Cobb was becoming welcome indeed. Cobb relaxed in this atmosphere as he had not since coming to New York. The *World* offered him a home and an audience that he had not found at the *Sun*—maybe because he had been too timid to seek it. Davis noticed a new bouyancy and purpose in Cobb, and attributed it to the demand for his stories and his friendship. "He held a levee daily in the city room. The cubs and the bosses, the stars and the stalk horses, the best and the worst of the staff attended. It was a brief half hour of the day when every man was at par."[4] Even the fiendish Chapin could not ruin such an atmosphere.

Laura Cobb relaxed in the new prosperity also. The Cobbs moved from the boarding house on west Fifty-seventh Street to an apartment on West One Hundred and Forty-sixth Street. Laura was in charge of a real household for the first time since her marriage, and she delighted in selecting furniture and decorations. Soon the Cobbs had a maid to cook and care for Buff and thus were able to entertain new friends such as Harry and Helen Burke, a newspaperman and his wife who lived in the same building. Laura even accepted Cobb's suggestion that his younger sister Manie come up from Paducah to live with them. Although Laura would probably have preferred to put the Paducah Cobbs behind her, and although Manie's fierce demands on her brother's time and attentions always irritated Laura, still Manie was pleasant company when she wanted to be, and Laura was quick to acknowledge that Manie's chances for a happy future were better in New York than under her mother's and Reubie's watchful eyes in Paducah.[5] Manie later married Hewitt Howland, a literary advisor for Bobbs-Merrill who later became editor of *Century* magazine, thus finding the successful marriage her brother had hoped for her. Whether Howland was equally blessed is another matter.

Cobb's responsibilities on the *World* went far beyond telling stories. Chapin, whatever his personality faults, knew a good reporter when he saw one, and Cobb within a year of joining the *World* was being given top assignments. His greatest feat during his early years on the paper was his coverage, in 1907-08, of the trials of Henry Thaw for the murder of Stanford White. The story satisfied many of Chapin's demands for the perfect news story: in Cobb's words, it had "wealth, degeneracy, rich old wasters; delectable young chorus girls and adolescent artists' models; the behind-the-scenes of Theaterdom and the Underworld and the Great White Way; the abnormal pastimes and weird orgies of overly aesthetic artists and jaded debauchees."

The woman in the case was Evelyn Nesbitt, a beautiful model whose face was seen all over the county on calendars, advertisements, and magazine covers. She had been painted by James Montgomery Flagg and Charles Dana Gibson; indeed, she seemed the Gibson girl personified, with a slender body, a graceful neck, a head held high, light brown hair and large, expressive eyes. Evelyn was married to Henry Thaw, the extravagant, pleasure-loving son of a wealthy Pittsburgh family. Stanford White was an architect famous for the design of the Madison Square Garden of his day, for the extravagance of the parties he gave for a fast crowd, half Bohemian and half aristocratic, and for the number of ladies he was rumored to seduce in such a setting. Evelyn Nesbitt, who was a part of his social group, had been involved in an affair with White before her marriage and continued to rely on his advice afterwards, stirring her husband's jealousy.[6]

Thaw's revenge was dramatic. On a summer evening of 1906 a

smartly dressed crowd arrived on the roof garden of White's Madison Square Garden for the opening of a new show. The roof garden was a fashionable spot that year, and all seats were filled to see the comedian Harry Short and the Garden's chorus line. Instead, for their first night tickets, the crowd watched in horror as Henry Thaw shot Stanford White, who was sitting at a front table. Evelyn Nesbitt then rushed to embrace her husband, who was waving his gun and cried out to him, "Oh, Harry, why did you do it?" Thaw was immediately arrested; the trial was delayed until January.[7]

Chapin sent Cobb to cover the story of the trial, allowing Cobb to decide how many and what kind of assistants he wanted. Cobb decided that he preferred to do all the reporting himself, requesting only a messenger boy to run the copy to a telegraph operator in the basement, who would send the copy over a private wire to a *World* stenographer a mile away. Another boy stood behind Cobb, keeping him supplied with the sharpened pencils. Since the other newspapers had shifts of from four to five reporters covering the trials, Cobb's request seemed bizarre, but he felt his experience at the Goebel trials had prepared him to perform best in this way. Certainly Cobb's one-man show gave the *World* coverage a unity of viewpoint and a greater awareness of the total picture than that of any other newspaper. Chapin had nothing but praise for Cobb's production. In his autobiography Chapin claims that Cobb turned out twelve thousand words per working day with full coverage of the speeches and testimony, descriptions of the participants, background explanation, interpretation of new developments, and leads for future articles.[8]

The first trial was long, with batteries of lawyers on both sides. There were some days filled with legal quibbling when Cobb's output was far less than Chapin's estimate, but when Evelyn Nesbitt Thaw took the stand, wearing a demure schoolgirl dress with sailor collar, to tell plaintively of resisting White's offers until she fell a victim to drugged champagne, the coverage expanded rapidly. Evelyn was not loved by Thaw's family or by his lawyers. Cobb was convinced that she had been paid off by the family to behave herself and testify in Thaw's behalf, for there was little sense of family unity in the courtroom. Another feature of the first trial was Thaw's chief counsel, Delphin Delmas, a legendary San Francisco master of oratory, whose gifts, unfortunately for Thaw, had faded. Actually, even in its prime, his oily delivery would probably have not been successful with a New York jury. His strategy, besides his oratory, was to present a bevy of psychiatrists to demonstrate that Thaw was not responsible for his actions when he shot White. District Attorney William Travers Jerome was able to turn all Delmas' gestures and periods against him and to counter the defense psychiatrists with his own crew, who proclaimed that Thaw had been perfectly sane when he shot White. When the pyrotechnics between the lawyers grew wearisome, reporters hoped for new testimony on the strange life style and sexual highjinks of Stanford White, who was made to sound the star cuckolder of all time. (Such public figures as Richard Harding Davis and Charles Baldwin insisted that White did not deserve the labels.) The first trial produced a hung jury but some clear decisions: the next time around Chapin kept his reporter, but Henry Thaw got another lawyer.[9]

Henry Thaw's new chief counsel, Martin Littleton, proved more skillful then Delmas had been, and the second trial was less a sideshow than the first. Littleton dressed Evelyn in more appropriate clothes and convinced Thaw's family that a mental institution was better than a prison. He met Jerome objection for objection, and finally convinced the jury to send Thaw not to Sing Sing but to Matteawan State Hospital for the Criminally Insane.

Cobb's journalistic involvement with Henry Thaw was not over yet, however. The Thaw family petitioned for a release for their son and the case was heard in the summer of 1909. Cobb and the expected mob of other journalists convened to cover it. The decision rested with the New York State Supreme Court Justice Isaac N. Mills, a self-taught, clear-headed man whom Cobb admired for his desire to cut through the fogs the medical witnesses were throwing up and to get down to the bare facts of the case. On Saturday night, after a full week of testimony, Jerome suddenly rested his case for the state, foregoing a closing speech. Thaw's lawyers, rattled by this development, felt they could only do likewise. The justice then decided against the petitioners and Henry Thaw returned to the Matteawan State Hospital for the Criminally Insane.

In *Exit Laughing* thirty-five years later Irvin Cobb claimed that earlier that evening the presiding justice whom he does not identify by name, had sought him privately at his hotel during the dinner break, praised his reputation for honesty and close observation, and asked his opinion about Thaw's sanity. "Judge," Cobb reports himself as saying, "he's as crazy as a creek crane." The justice nodded, asked but did not demand confidentially, and three hours later declared Thaw insane.[10]

Cobb's reputation for honesty and accuracy had spread out only to the justice but also to all the *World* readership. He was already being called Charle Chapin's star reporter, and in early 1908 he had signed a three year contract for the impressive salary of $7,500 a year, with permission to sell anything he wrote that the *World* couldn't use.

## Notes

[1]Neuman, *Cobb,* (1934), p. 79.

[2]Robert H. Davis, *Irvin S. Cobb: Storyteller* (New York: George H. Doran, 1923), p. 11.

[3]Davis, *Over My Left Shoulder,* pp. 150-154.

[4]Davis, *American Magazine,* May 17, 1917, p. 14; clipping, Kentucky Library, Western Kentucky University.

[5]E. Cobb, *Wayward Parent,* p. 89; Cobb's grandchildren explain that their mother's picture of Manie was kinder than was accurate; unlike Reubie, Manie was still alive.

[6]Charles C. Baldwin, *Stanford White* (New York: Dodd, Mead, 1931); Reprinted as vol. 39 in *Da Capo Press Series in Architecture and Decorative Art,* ed. Add K. Placzek (New York: De Capo, 1971), p. 310.

[7]Baldwin, pp. 304, 309. "Judge Sends Thaw Back to Matteawan," New York *Times,* 13 Aug 1:1.

[8]Charles E. Chapin, *Charles E. Chapin's Story* (New York: Putnam, 1920), p. 190.

[9]Cobb, *Exit Laughing,* pp. 227-231; Baldwin, pp. 304-307.

[10]Cobb, *Exit Laughing,* pp. 246-248.

# Chapter Eight

During Cobb's six years on the *World* he turned out many different kinds of writing. Straight reporting like the Thaw trial was his staple at first, but he was so skilled at feature stories, especially those covering occasions in which the atmosphere was more important than the events, that his editors used him more and more to cover such spectacles as horse shows, baseball games, political rallies and prize fights. And it was not long until humorous articles by Irvin S. Cobb began to appear, especially in the joint edition called the *Sunday World.*

Newspaper humor at the turn of the century was developing in new directions and becoming an increasingly important part of the humor being published. Its antecedents in the nineties were the cynical, dry observations of Mark Twain, E. W. Howe and Ambrose Bierce. Norris W. Yates traces the development early in the twentieth century of three types of journalistic humor, which he characterizes by their typical personae as "the crackerbox philosopher," "the solid citizen," and "the little man." He points out that Irvin Cobb was unusual in that he successfully used all three types of humor at various points in his career.[1]

The stance of the "crackerbox philosopher," a recognizable American type which goes all the way back to Franklin's "Poor Richard," is a small-town unsophisticate whose wisdom lies in using common sense and barn-yard comparisons to deflate the pomposities of the more subtle and powerful. Bill Nye, Sut Lovingood, and Josh Billings were writing columns in this vein when Cobb began writing humor columns for the *World.* The "solid citizen," as Yates describes him, is a character of a more respectable class, less fancy-free than his crackerbox counterpart, but also more apt to be preoccupied with family matters—noisy children, whimsical wives—than with world issues. He is always correct in his behavior and polished in his manners, and frequently this care about standards gets him nowhere. The "Autocrat of the Breakfast

Table" was an early model. The "Little Man" is more hapless still; less assured of his insights than the crackerbox philosopher, less assured of his position than the solid citizen, he pictures himself at the mercy of a modern civilization which threatens to destroy him. Cobb found crackerbox philosopher and solid citizen types of humor already in existence and used them to suit his own ends; later, according to Yates, he, along with Robert Benchley and James Thurber, was one of the chief developers of the "Little Man" humor which gained such popularity in the teens and twenties.[2]

The popularity of the cracker box humor of the turn of the century can perhaps be attributed to the number of small town folks who found themselves living in big cities and not liking it very much. Certainly the newspapers were staffed with a disproportionate number of southerners and mid-westerners, always ready to praise the small town virtues in contrast with the city realities. George Ade's "Stories of the Streets and of the Town" in the Chicago *Record* included both crackerbarrel and solid citizen types. Abe Martin, the country spokesman for Kin Hubbard, must have struck some important response in the newspaper audience to make them willing to decipher the heavy dialect in which his aphorisms were recorded. Even Peter Finley Dunne's Mr. Dooley, an Irish Chicago bartender, has a neighborhood setting which gives his observations the clarity and simplicity of a small town performance. O. O. McIntyre, soon to be one of Cobb's best friends, wrote his column "New York Day by Day" as though it were a letter to his friends back home about the strange goings-on in New York; he can be classified with those who use a solid-citizen persona, although he would never have thought of himself as doing anything so literary. Even the more urbane Franklin P. Adams frequently wrote with an outsider's appreciation of the absurdities of New York. In such an atmosphere Irvin Cobb seemed a natural for a humor column. He was an outsider, he wrote well, and he was funny. By 1906 Cobb had a double column in the *World*, eight inches long, headed "New York Through Funny Glasses" with not only a by-line but a picture. Perhaps this was the first time Cobb decided to use the humor of his rather unusual looks publicly; at any rate Cobb stared balefully out of the page at the reader, his frowning lips protruding, his ears obvious, his new double chins on display. (Cobb, who had been tall and lanky all his life, suddenly ballooned into a fat man when he went to work at the *World*. He attributed the change to his newly acquired desk job; probably prosperity and a more settled home life helped also.) Bob Davis insisted a new reader was forced to examine the column to find out what such an apparently ill-humored person would think was funny.

"New York Through Funny Glasses" was moderately successful. It had no fictional framework, but consisted only of Cobb's vivid observations about the city from his Kentucky viewpoint. It ran for more than two years, when it was replaced by other Cobb columns. While most columnists tended to find a workable framework and to stick with it, Cobb liked to experiment. Some of his columns were planned as limited series, and he always had a new idea to follow up the old.

In 1908 the "Hotel Clerk" series began to appear in the *Sunday World* magazines section and ran for over five years. Each article covered about a third of a standard newspaper page, and each featured three to four illustrations. In many ways they are the best of the Irvin Cobb columns. They use the fictional setting of the Hotel St. Reckless. The hotel guests, the bell-boys, the house detective and others discuss items in the news, the theater, fads, and celebrities. The Hotel Clerk is the fountain of wisdom, a cynical but warm version of Mr. Dooley without an accent.[3]

Cobb's humorous columns by no means detracted from his authority as a writer of news stories; in fact, they gave him an opportunity to editorialize on the news. There was no problem at this stage in his career with becoming only a humor writer; on the contrary, his columns show his own views at the time more clearly than his other writing does. Those views seem surprisingly liberal and clear-headed for the jingoistic Roosevelt years. On August 9, 1908, the House Detective asks "What's Teddy going to Africa for?" The Hotel clerk replies, "For a dollar a word."

Cobb's sentiments were usually with the workers and the poor, but he drew the line at socialism. When a discussion of a public meeting of socialists causes the Hotel Clerk to say, tongue in cheek, "It's been a great month for the Downtrodden," the House Detective replies:

> Nobody ain't been around handin' me any asparagus tips or uncut emeralds. From where I sit it looks like the customary relations between Labor and Capital is still bein' preserved—Capital's keeping all the capital and Labor's doin' the bulk of the laborin'.

The Hotel Clerk distinguishes between the professional socialist, a foreigner, and the amateur, who "was born here but can't remember anything else of real importance that the U.S. has been able to pull off." He concludes that most socialists are not members of poor families, but poor relations of rich families. He describes an acquaintance who was an ardent socialist until he inherited his uncle's estate. Suddenly he forgot about share-the-wealth. Instead he dressed richly, enjoyed luxurious living and started criticizing Theodore Roosevelt. In fact, "he said he was going to hang around the car in the hope that he might get a chance to run over Upton Sinclair."

The crew at the Hotel St. Reckless also discuss the unequal treatment of the courts toward rich and poor, the strange new custom of women smoking in public ("If the American woman should decide to smoke in public, you might as well be a gentleman about it and pass a light") and the difficulties of keeping a show alive on Broadway. In 1910 Cobb initiated "Live Talks with Dead Ones," a series of about a hundred columns involving fictional and humorous interviews with figures from Cleopatra to George Washington. These, too, were of excellent quality and especially noteworthy for their clear-eyed look at what was and was not right about America. In "Live Talk number 83," the Statue of Liberty is being interviewed by the reporter, who as usual has all the straight and solid lines while the "Dead One" is far more penetrating. Discussing liberty and equality, the Statue points out some inequities.

> The poor murderer gets a swift speedy trial and seven thousand volts of electricity, all donated free by the state. The rich murderer gets the most expensive brand of insanity that his relatives can afford to buy for him....
>
> All men are born free and equal. That immortal statement, you will recall, was penned and adopted by gentlemen largely engaged in owning slaves. Yet nonetheless it is true that all men are born equal unless they happen to be Indians or negroes or Chinamen or Japanese or Hindoos or Mexicans, in which case it would have been much better for them if they had not been born at all. Likewise all men are born free and equal unless they happen to be born women, in which case they rank with the habitual criminals and the congenital idiots.

This passage points out some of the perenial subjects in Cobb's more serious columns—the inequities among rich and poor, the problems of racial prejudice, and the need for greater freedom for women. Cobb heartily supported the vote for women, greater education for women—and shorter skirts. His new prosperity had made the support of his mother, his two sisters, his wife and his daughter much easier, and he never complained about the burden (even though his wife would have welcomed some complaints about the Paducah dependents), but he always insisted that girls—including his daughter—should be brought up with the education, skills, and sense of independence that would allow them to support themselves. Fewer than half the columns dealt with serious subjects, however; many were pure nonsense.

Some other series of columns that appeared in the *World* during Cobb's years there were "Judge Hightower," which had the same impressive layout as "The Hotel Clerk" and "Live Talks" and featured a solid-citizen persona; "Gotham Geography: Just a Simple Guide to a Complex City," which was more satirical than geographical—lesson six, for example, was entitled "Politicaledonia, the Land of the Campaignia"; and a series that ran in 1910 and 1911 called "The Browe Brothers: Hiram and Loerum." The brothers' dialogues covered more than the cultural and intellectual cross-purposes their names suggest, with Hiram appearing as the idealistic and perhaps naive proponent of society and progress, while Loerum takes the cynical and less conventional viewpoints. Like his counterparts in the other columns, Loerum usually has the last word. Some of Cobb's columns were syndicated and appeared in newspapers throughout the country. If Americans first heard of Cobb through his Portsmouth Peace Conference stories, now they began to remember who he was.

In addition to these and other series, Cobb frequently wrote humorous articles for the *Evening* or *Sunday World*, each of which was presented with full treatment: by-line and illustrations. For example, in August of 1908, the *World* featured "New York to Have Only Seven Kinds of Plays this Season—Here They Are." (The types of plays included the musical, the western, the "George Cohan thing," and the Belasco show.) He also got full treatment for his interviews with sports figures and other celebrities, and readers came to expect a Cobb by-line to mean a humane, pithy, humorous treatment. Perhaps Cobb's most famous stories of this sort were his two installments on the New York Horse Show in 1910. He treated the aristocracy with his usual searching lack of awe and set the town laughing with his comparison of a particularly impressive matron's emerald earrings to the engine lights on the Lenox local.[4]

Cobb had a particular talent not only for making friends, but for keeping them. The newspaper connections he had made on the *Sun* and the *World* remained his friends as his importance and his income increased. One reason was his total lack of snobbery. Many of his reporter friends later praised him for always considering himself just a reporter. One of his colleagues on the *World*, Bill Johnston, in a humorous tribute in 1915, described Cobb this way:

> In all the years he wrote for the *Sunday World* he never was late in turning in his copy, reaching the pay window, going to luncheons, buying a drink, laughing at his own jokes, or demanding a raise in salary.[5]

Cobb's down-to-earth manner was in direct contrast to the behavior of other rising stars in the newspaper world, and his colleagues loved him for it and despised such snobs as Franklin P. Adams.

Damon Runyon's experiences with the two celebrated writers were typical. Runyon came to town around 1910 and got a job as a sports writer on the *World.* Runyon had heard of Cobb out in San Francisco and when he heard the rumor that Cobb was making $90 a week (Cobb was actually making twice that much), it only confirmed his conviction that Cobb was the best newspaper writer of his time. Bozeman Bulgar, the *World*'s chief baseball writer and a good friend of Cobb's, introduced Runyon to Cobb, who took a great interest in the young reporter. They met often in the press box at the Polo grounds and became close friends. While all the regulars at the Polo Grounds welcomed Cobb, they dreaded the appearances of Franklin P. Adams. Adams was a self-appointed guardian of correct grammar who enjoyed pointing out the errors of the sports writers in his column, causing Runyon to lie awake nights worrying that he would lose his job. Adams was apparently totally unaware of the difference between the warm welcome the sports writers extended to Cobb and the icy reception his condescensions received.[6]

O. O. McIntyre, another newspaperman who admired Cobb's primary loyalty to reporting, years later recalled somewhat romantically:

> He belonged to that illustrious period when clean-minded newspaperman drank their rye neat at the Martinique and Doc Perry's, got drunk like gentlemen and took over the lines of the cab driver for a spin up Broadway as a red sun bleared an eye over Manhattan.[7]

## Notes

[1]Norris W. Yates, *The American Humorist: Conscience of the Twentieth Century* (Ames: Iowa University Press, 1964), p. 129.

[2]Yates, passim; p. 133.

[3]Near complete runs of Cobb's *World* columns are in the possession of Thomas Cobb Brody, Greenwich, Conn.

[4]Sloan Gordon, "The Story of Irvin S. Cobb," *Pearson's Magazine* (March, 1915), p. 281.

[5]tribute in *Irvin S. Cobb: His Book* (New York: George H. Doran Co., 1915), n.p.n.

[6]Ed Weiner, *The Damon Runyon Story* (New York: Longmans, Green, and Co., 1948), pp. 98-100.

[7]Neuman, *Cobb* (1934), p. 13.

# Chapter Nine

By the time Cobb joined the *Evening World* in 1905 his circle of acquaintances included not only newspapermen but also many of the dramatists, actors and actresses who made their living on Broadway. Reporters and Broadway figures shared many of the same haunts and clubs in turn-of-the-century Manhattan, and a gregarious man like Cobb soon found himself and his funny stories welcomed into some very glamorous company.

Cobb's earliest theatrical connections were probably made at the Algonquin Hotel. Although the Algonquin is now best known for the Round Table, the group of precocious writers and editors who met there during the twenties, it had attracted literary and theatrical celebrities since Frank Case took it over before the turn of the century. Case, whom Cobb described as "a long-legged, smooth-faced Santa Claus on a diet," was loved on Broadway for his wit, for his good humor, but above all for his willingness to extend credit to his frequently broke patrons. In "Casey's Owl Wagon," his tribute to Case, Cobb describes his first acquaintance with this Broadway Saint. At midnight in late 1904 Cobb was broke, hungry and prowling the streets when he ran into Frank O'Malley, who suggested they borrow some money from Frank Case at the Algonquin. Cobb was skeptical that anyone would loan money to reporters, but O'Malley replied, "Listen, kid, he even loans money to actors." Cobb and Case became fast friends and remained so even after Cobb could pay his own way.[1]

The location of the Algonquin Hotel on 44th Street between Fifth and Sixth Avenues made it convenient to Broadway. The Hippodrome, where Fred Stone and DeWolfe Hopper headlined, was across the street, the Lambs' Club was a block away and the restaurants Sherry's and Delmonico's were both nearby. Among the Broadway regulars whom Cobb met there were John and Ethel Barrymore, Mary Pickford, and Douglas Fairbanks, Sr. (Douglas Jr. was a small boy running through the halls and playing hide-and-go-seek with the busboys.) All lived at the Algonquin at least part of the time, along with Fred Stone, DeWolfe and Hedda Hopper, and a number of stars of the day not now so well remembered. Other celebrities, including Flo Ziegfeld and members of the "Follies" cast, Lillian Russell, and David Belasco met there for lunch.[2]

Writers found the Algonquin congenial, too, not only as a place to meet friends but also as a place to work. Richard Harding Davis, Booth Tarkington, Harry Leon Wilson, and Gertrude Atherton all lived there at times during this period, and H.L. Mencken joined them after the *Smart Set* offices moved to 45th Street in 1915. Gertrude Stein stayed there when she came to New York.[3] Writers and actors became superstitious about the Algonquin: it produced success, they thought. It certainly attracted those soon to be successful and gave them comfort, encouragement, and the atmosphere of a club.[4] The mirrored dining room at the Algonquin was a favorite meeting place, and the glamorous Broadway patrons attracted businessmen and ladies meeting for lunch who wanted to ogle the celebrities. Newspaper columns reported on who was seen eating there and passed on the quips for the regulars. For example, when the foppish Davis registered as "Richard Harding Davis and man," O'Malley signed in below him as "Frank Ward O'Malley and two men." The newspaper accounts also increased the clientele. Frank Case may have befriended the actors and reporters out of kindness, but he proved to be a Santa Claus with an astute business sense.

Irvin Cobb was soon transformed from another penniless reporter to one of the regulars, and eventually to one of the celebrities to stare at. He found both the atmosphere and the company congenial at the Algonquin and remained a regular until he moved to Hollywood in 1934. He and his family lived at the Algonquin on several different occasions in the teens, during the winters of 1912, 1913, 1914 and 1918.[5] Of course Cobb went to other Broadway haunts also, such as Lindy's, Lahiff's, and Dinty Moore's and became acquainted with George Gershwin, George Cohan, Irving Berlin, Al Jolson and a young songwriter named Jimmy Walker, who later became mayor of New York.[6] During the summers when the Cobbs lived in one of their suburban homes the Broadway crowd frequently visited them and Clare Booth Luce recalls her wonder and excitement when she, a childhood friend of Buff Cobb, was introduced to Flo Ziegfeld and Fanny Brice at the Cobbs' home, Rebel Ridge.[7]

Through his friendships with theatrical people, Cobb was soon asked to join several of the men's theatrical clubs in Manhattan. The most renowned of these was the Lambs'. It had been founded in 1874 by three homesick British actors who longed for its counterpart in London, the club which was located in the former house of Charles and Mary Lamb. Charles and Mary Lamb had welcomed actors and writers to their home during their lifetimes and at their deaths left their house to be used to continue this hospitality. In their memory members usually referred to the London and the New York clubs as "the Lambs' " as in "Let's go around to the Lambs'," rather than as the "Lambs' Club." By 1910, when Irvin Cobb was a member, the Lambs', in its beautiful building on 44th Street at Fifth Avenue, was a Broadway tradition. It enjoyed a playful rivalry with the other theatrical clubs, the Players' and the Friars', but the Lambs' reigned supreme. In spite of the rivalry many members belonged to more than one club—Cobb was also a member of the Players' Club. The rivalry was most intense when two stage rivals headed two of the clubs, for example the year that DeWolfe Hopper was Shepherd of the Lambs' and George M. Cohan was Abbot of the Friars' Club.[8]1 Like the other clubs, the Lambs' produced an annual show written, produced, choreographed and acted by its talented members. In the Lambs' this show was called the "Gambol." Membership in the Lambs' was by invitation. Legitimate stage actors and creative writers made up most of the membership, but exceptions were made, and several reporters besides Cobb were considered literary enough to qualify. Devoted friends of members were also often asked to join, including lawyers, agents and Frank Case. Case complained a decade or so later when some radio actors were proposed for membership—the Lambs' should be kept for legitimate actors, he argued.[9]

At these clubs Cobb made even more friends. A member of both the Lambs' and the Players' Club was the artist James Montgomery Flagg, who used himself as the model for Uncle Sam in the famous World War I recruiting posters. Flagg was also the author of several plays. When Cobb first knew him, Flagg was a dashing young man who loved drinking and chasing women with his best friend Jack Barrymore. Flagg's luscious nudes, with Gibson girl figures and coy eyelashes, decorated the Lambs' dining room. (When the Lambs' admitted women a few decades later, the nudes were all decorously clothed.)[10] Ring Lardner was a member of the Lambs' also, an unusually anti-social one. Sometimes he sat alone at the piano, ignoring the bonhomie around him while he played an endless series of chords. At other times he attempted to trick the members with crude jokes, such as telling involved, purposely unfunny stories to a confederate who laughed uproarously.[11] Lardner had a distinct dislike for stories and story-tellers, Irvin Cobb among them, but he was in a small minority, for stories were a staple feature of the bars and dining rooms of the clubs, and Cobb's talents with a story soon made him in demand as a humorous speaker at club banquets. At the Players' Club Oliver Herford, Don Marquis and Rollin Kirby were among those that matched Cobb story for story.

One of the Cobb's frequent companions at the Lambs' was James O'Neill, then retired from the stage. O'Neill worried about his son Eugene, whose instability in the early teens would have worried any parent. One day the elder O'Neill gave Cobb four plays his son had written—early versions of *The Moon of the Caribbees, Bound East for Cardiff, The Emperor Jones* and *Anna Christie*—and asked Cobb's opinion about Eugene's chances as a playwright. In *Exit Laughing* Cobb reports that he felt the raw power of the plays and believed they might have some future as short stories for a few more daring magazines. "But as play material—well, I don't believe you'd ever find a manager to produce it or a critic who'd endorse it or a public that would go see it."[12] The productions of the Provincetown Players soon proved Cobb wrong, but his caution and literary conservatism continued.

Cobb also became a member of the Dutch Treat Club, an organization of artists and writers formed around 1906 which had no club building but met once a week for lunch at a restaurant. Around 1910 the meetings were held at Keen's English Chop House every Tuesday. Membership, by invitation only, was limited to one hundred men, but guests were sometimes included. The most important rule of the club was that everyone, including the most distinguished guests, was required to pay his own bill. Stories, wisecracks and humorous speeches were features of the weekly meetings. James Montgomery Flagg was a guiding light of the club, whose members also included the writers Rupert Hughes and Charles Norris, the critic George Jean Nathan, Frank Crowninshield of *Vanity Fair,* the columnist O.O. McIntyre, and Ray Long of *Cosmopolitan.*[13] Cobb may have first met Theodore Dreiser when he was the guest of William Lengel at the Dutch Treat Club.[14]

Despite his love of male company and good drink, Cobb was not a night owl. He was a hard working reporter during the day and except for his Tuesday lunches with the Dutch Treat Club, most of his social activities were restricted to the late afternoon and early evening. His letters mention family parties for dinner and cards as often as they do evenings at the all male clubs. Although Cobb enjoyed the moderately scandalous shows and the titillating conversations of the clubs (Ring Lardner once complained about sitting between Cobb and George Doran and being subjected to the off-color stories they told each other),[15] and although he considered the avid girl-chasers like Hopper and Flagg good friends, he preferred the company of other members who were devoted family men like himself. Unlike Hedda Hopper, whose dismay at DeWolfe's habit of staying at the Lambs' or other night spots until daybreak finally led to their divorce, Laura Cobb had no complaints about her husband's gregarious ways. She had friends and activities to fill her time, and she always knew that he would be home early. Their daughter says that Cobb always wanted to be in bed by ten-thirty if he could manage it.

It is not surprising that a man like Cobb, dramatic by nature and interested in experimenting with different literary forms, would in such theatrical company turn to playwriting. In *Exit Laughing* Cobb says he had started his first play at age fifteen while he was a reporter in Paducah. During the first decade of the century Cobb wrote several of different types and occasionally with different collaborators. These plays were not successful and Cobb himself in various later articles did an excellent job of explaining where he had gone wrong. He wrote no plays after the mid-twenties, but his early playwriting experience undoubtedly gave him skills used in his more successful writing of captions and plots for the movies.

In November, 1908, Cobb published in *Munsey's Magazine* an article entitled "The Strange Adventure of the Man Who Wrote a Play" about his attempts to rewrite the play he had started in Paducah, finally entitled *The Sure Return,* during the first winter he was in New York. He says his boarding house landlady probably thought he was a secret alcoholic, hiding away in his room upstairs, but he was wrestling with something stronger than gin—characters who wouldn't stay put:

> It started out to be a problem play of modern life, full of terse epigram and gripping satire, with touches of comedy deftly interspersed here and there, like the onion in a hamburger. After I had got to work on Act I, scene I, I discovered, to my surprise and at first to my chagrin, that my characters absolutely refused to stand for any problem business. I wish I might make the reader understand how I thrashed around with that obstinate crowd until my typewriter was as limp as a rag.... They had their own way and I wrote a comedy.[16]

Although Cobb sent *The Sure Return* to all the producers he could find, none accepted it, each finding a different set of flaws from the last. In this article Cobb claimed to be keeping it in anticipation of the day when a demand rises for a "play made up of flaws." Of three other early plays, *The Gallery God, The Yeggman* (written with Paul East), and *Daffy-Down-Dilly,* Cobb once wrote, "One was accidentally destroyed, one was lost, and one was loaned out and never returned."[17]

In spite of the fun Cobb makes of his early rejections, response to his dramatic work must not have been as negative as he implies, for some other early efforts did get produced. He wrote several vaudeville sketches, including Ed Wynn's first starring vehicle. He wrote the book and some of the lyrics for *Funabashi,* a comic opera with a *Madame Butterfly* setting which ran on Broadway for five weeks. Its failure at that point was probably not the fault of Cobb's script but of the strange conditions of the production. An earlier show, a straight stage play presenting a romance between a Japanese heroine and a naval ensign, had failed and the backer wanted a new show, a musical this time, which could use the same sets, props and costumes as the old show. The cast members were picked less for their singing and acting talents than for their dress sizes. Cobb wrote the book in five days and never received the promised five hundred dollars. Laura Cobb cried when the critics panned the show, but Cobb, who was also always hurt by bad reviews, was ready to try again. He had a hand in *Mr. Busybody,* 1908, also a failure. Shortly after that, Cobb's short stories became quite successful, and he entered into several collaborations, as writer or advisor, to reproduce some of them on the stage.

## Notes

[1]Irvin S. Cobb, "Casey's Owl Wagon," printed in Frank Case, *Tales of a Wayside Inn* (New York: Frederick A. Stokes Co., 1938), pp. 315-322.

[2]Margaret Case Harriman, *Blessed are the Debonair* (New York: Rinehart and Co., Inc., 1956), pp. 117-120; Case, *Wayside Inn,* pp. 41-47.

[3]Case, *Wayside Inn,* pp. 71; 77; 349.

[4]Margaret Case Harriman, *The Vicious Circle: The Story of the Algonquin Round Table* (New York: Rinehart and Co., Inc., 1951), p. 22.

[5]Case, *Wayside Inn,* p. 317.

[6]Gene Fowler, *The Life and Times of Jimmy Walker* (New York: Viking Press, 1949), p. 61.

[7]Stephen Shadegg, *Clare Booth Luce* (New York: Simon and Schuster, 1970), p.

[8]Hedda Hopper, *From Under My Hat* (Garden City: Doubleday and Co., 1952), p. 112.

[9]Harriman, *Blessed,* p. 120.

[10]Susan E. Meyer, *James Montgomery Flagg* (New York: Watson Guptill Publ., 1974), p. 30.

[11]Donald Elder, *Ring Lardner* (Garden City: Doubleday, 1956), p. 129.

[12]Cobb, *Exit Laughing,* p. 366.

[13]Meyer, p. 29; George H. Doran, *Chronicles of Barabbas,* 1884-1934 (New York: Harcourt, Brace and Co., 1935), p. 207.

[14]W. A. Swanberg, *Theodore Dreiser* (New York: Charles Scribner's Sons, 1965), p. 287.

[15]Elder, p. 129.

[16]Irvin S. Cobb, "The Strange Adventures of the Man Who Wrote a Play," *Munsey's Magazine* (November 1908), p. 276.

[17]Townsend, *Concerning Cobb,* p. 13.

# Chapter Ten

By 1907, the year of *Funabashi* and the first Thaw trial, the Cobbs had begun to look for a suburban home. City living never suited Cobb, and Laura began to dream of trees and flowers and room for Buff, who turned six that year, to play. After they could afford it they had regularly taken cottages for the summer; in the summer of 1907 and several summers thereafter, the Cobbs and the Samuel Blythes rented adjacent cottages at Poorhouse Point on Lake Champlain in Vermont. But they wanted to own a house and to live there year round.

In the fall of 1907 they purchased a "plain little box of a house" in the Yonkers suburb of Park Hill. It was cheap, it had good plumbing and on one side of its yard was a rocky boulder which Buff imagined to be a house, a ship, or a fortress. On the other side was a sunny strip on which Laura planted her first flower garden. Laura's gardens—meticulously planned and beautifully cared for—became a family institution; the fact that the Cobbs always moved when she got the garden the way she wanted it became a family joke.

Elisabeth Cobb's earliest vivid memories of her father date from the five years they lived in the house in Yonkers. During those years Cobb's newspaper career flourished—the "Hotel Clerk" and "Live Talks" series were both written during this time—and his cautious experimentation with short stories brought him the immediate recognition that led to the offer of a staff position at the *Saturday Evening Post* which he accepted in 1911. But Cobb did not relax in his success and prosperity; he worked very hard, and he found the demands of a weekly column exhausting. The strain seemed to lie not so much in preparing the next Sunday's column, for humor came very easy to him in those days, but in the possibility his vivid imagination presented to him of a day in the future—in a week or a month or a decade—when the funny topics would all be exhausted. In his prosperous days as in the belt-tightening periods, the greatest threat to Cobb's contentment was his fears about the future. So when a Yonkers neighbor asked Elisabeth if her father was Cobb the humorist, she had to ask what the word meant. In response to the definition, a person who entertains people and makes them laugh, she shook her head. "That can't be my Daddy. He's never very entertaining around the house with me and my Moie." (Buff's mispronunciation of "Ma" became a standard nickname for Laura among those who did not adopt Cobb's "Lolly.")

Cobb adored his daughter, however, even if he could not always stay cheerful for her sake, and he spent all the time available in her company. The Cobbs frequently took Buff with them to social events, even those at which no other children were present, and Cobb glowed whenever anyone praised her beauty or her precocity. Buff in turn worshipped her father and treasured vivid memories of their times together:

> It was a hot summer afternoon and probably he was taking his vacation, for else how was it I was lying by his side in a darkened room in the daytime? He was never home in the daytime, except on Sundays, and this has no Sunday "feel." No—it was an unusual occasion and I remember it as such. He read me the first story from *The Jungle Book*. He read wonderfully, leaving me gasping with the thrill of that trip to the Seconee Wolfpack's cave in the hills. Lordy! Lordy! This moment I can hear Shere Khan roaring from the pain of his burned foot and for his lost prey, Mowgli the Frog. Yes and long for that broad kind back to cuddle against and take comfort from, as I suffer a most luscious sort of fear!
>
> When he stopped reading I assaulted him. It was intolerable that all, *all*, that book be not read to me now, at once, straight through and without stopping! He swung me in the air, laughing, while I spit with fury. "I know, kid...I know!" he said.
>
> That is a fine memory.

Several other of Elisabeth Cobb's favorite childhood memories concern times when her father read aloud to her. He was a dramatic and entertaining reader who loved to tease his daughter by interpolating his own dialogue and descriptions into the stories. Romantic favorites such as *Ramona* were subjected to a complete transformation which delighted adult household guests and frustrated his daughter.[1]

Cobb's work on the *Evening World* in those years was by no means limited to his humor columns; in fact, his role as a humorist was only a small part of his value to the *World*. His superiors at the newspaper continued to rely on him to cover the big stories. They also found his skill at dealing with people useful on at least one occasion.

In 1908 the *World* newspapers began an ambitious investigation into the purchase of the property in Panama on which the canal was to be built. They turned up some extremely questionable financial manipulations involving prominent citizens, among them a relative of President Roosevelt. Joseph Pulitzer, who was frail, practically blind and usually unable to leave his house, had years earlier delegated the work of directing his newspaper empire to three administrators, Don Seitz, Florence White and Bradford Merrill, but the illusion was maintained that he was still in charge. Thus the accused manipulators demanded that a warrant for the arrest for libel be issued for Joseph Pulitzer himself. These demands were made to William T. Jerome, the District Attorney of New York County, who had recently been the victim of a *World* attack for what the editors saw as too gentle treatment of George W. Perkins, a socialite accused of financial misleadings. There was great fear at the Pulitzer Building that Jerome would take what the editors suddenly realized must be a tempting opportunity—to send policemen to drag old, sick Joseph Pulitzer off to jail as they had suggested Perkins should have been treated. Jerome delayed from day to day the indication of how he would meet the demands placed by Roosevelt's relative and his cronies, and the atmosphere at the *World* offices grew more and more tense. As Cobb later found out, the Pulitzer organization in an attempt to determine what Jerome would do hired detectives to shadow Jerome and his staff and to question the clerical workers in the Criminal Courts Building. For four weeks Jerome did nothing and the detectives got nowhere, so Seitz, White and Merrill called Irvin Cobb in to take over the assignment.

Cobb was chosen because of his stature on the paper, because he was acquainted with Jerome and because he had a reputation for getting information that other reporters missed. Cobb's path had crossed Jerome's many times—Jerome had been the prosecutor at the Thaw trials and at several other trials Cobb had covered and they had met at social occasions hosted by mutual friends. Although they had not talked since the publication of the Perkins editorials and the Panama purchase exposures, Cobb's faith in Jerome's integrity led him to doubt that Jerome would be vindictive toward Pulitzer. The paranoia at the *World* offices was pervasive, however, and Cobb was as tense as his bosses as he listened to them outline his task. They gave him three questions about Jerome's intentions that they wished answered and according to Cobb's account of the interview, empowered him as follows:

> Take as much time as you please on this proposition—you will make your report to us here and to no one else.

> If you desire the aid of anyone to assist you, from the top to the bottom of this organization, you have only to mention his name and he will gladly work with you or under you until further notice.... Your expense on this work is unlimited. No one in the cashier's department or elsewhere will question any item of any size which you care to charge up.

Cobb enjoyed telling the story of his successful completion of this mission as an after-dinner speech and the punch line was always the expense statement he turned in to the cashier: five cents for carfare to the Criminal Courts Building and five cents back. He went to Jerome's office, sent in his card and, as they were talking over beer at a neighborhood tavern, discovered that Jerome was glad to supply the answers to the questions. He admitted that he had no intention of prosecuting Pulitzer and that his four weeks' silence had been a deliberate attempt to make the Pulitzer organization sweat. His delay was not in retaliation for the earlier attack in the Perkins matter, however, but merely a reaction to the hordes of detectives that had been plaguing him and his staff. Had the Pulitzer organization sent a man four weeks earlier to ask him what they wanted to know, he insisted, the whole situation could have been avoided.

Cobb returned with the answers less than an hour after he had been given the task. The triumvirate, much relieved at the news, immediately put a call through to Pulitzer's home and Cobb relayed the message to Pulitzer's secretary. Pulitzer had scarcely left his house in the years that Cobb had worked on the *World*, and Cobb never saw him in person, but he claimed he could hear his voice in the background as the secretary gave him the good news. The secretary then relayed to Cobb a question from Pulitzer as to how he had obtained this information. Cobb explained that he had gone straight to Jerome and asked him. After this statement was passed to Pultizer, Cobb could hear his voice distinctly, "Well I wish I might be God-damned!" Cobb insisted that this story illustrated his "only method of approach" in running down stories—going straight for the facts with no subtleties or deceptions.[2]

Cobb's bosses apparently learned nothing about the benefits of openness from his success; they pledged him to secrecy about his role in the affair and made him no specific reward for his services. But on numerous occasions in the weeks that followed an announcement was posted that, on accout of some insignificant article he had written, Cobb was to receive a fifty dollar bonus. The situation, which caused some of his puzzled colleagues to call him "Teacher's Pet" made Cobb extremely uncomfortable.

There was duplicity involved in other areas of the *World's* payment system. Employees who made less than one hundred dollars a week were paid each Saturday in cash from one cashier's window, while those who made more than that amount, usually those in editorial or administrative positions, were paid by check at another window. Cobb had already passed the one hundred dollar mark by the time of the Jerome affair, but it was thought that paying him at the appropriate window would have a bad effect on the morale of the other reporters. So his various assignments were each treated as a separate job and on pay day he picked up as many as four different envelopes at the cash window. By the time he left the *World* in 1911 his salary was $99 a week from the *Evening World* and $51 from the *Sunday World* for his duties as a reporter, plus extra amounts (in a separate envelope) for his columns and humorous features. A fourth envelope might contain special bonuses. Many of his articles and features were picked up by the McClure syndicate and marketed to newspapers across the country; payment for his syndicate work frequently brought his monthly income to a thousand dollars. His success was well enough known for him to be called the highest-paid reporter in the country—but he and his colleagues never remarked on the irony of the situation as they stood in the hundred dollar line together.

Also during this period Cobb made his first major venture into writing advertising brochures. In 1909, the first year that Model-T Fords were produced, Cobb met Gaston Plantiff, Henry Ford's publicity man and chief advisor. Plantiff volunteered that both he and Ford admired Cobb's "Hotel Clerk" series and wished that it were possible to inject some light-hearted humor into automobile advertising. By the time the evening was over Cobb had agreed to write the text of five short pamphlets promoting Ford cars for the sum of five hundred dollars. Cobb, who had been hoping to take an extended summer vacation to try his hand at writing free lance fiction, was delighted at the chance for extra money and produced the five manuscripts, entitled "Talks with the Fat Chauffeur," in three days. Plantiff and the company were so pleased with the copy that they made Cobb a special offer: if he chose, he could take some or all of the five hundred dollars in Ford stock, which Plantiff assured him would be extremely valuable in a few years. Cobb thanked him but requested the cash; automobile companies seemed an extremely risky venture in 1909 and besides he wanted the vacation. Cobb sometimes amused himself in later years by calculating how many hundreds of thousands of dollars that block of stocks would have been worth in only a few years, but he never really regretted having turned it down. His six weeks of writing fiction paid good dividends also.

Like Cobb's early desire to be a dramatist, his yearning to write serious fiction is in contradiction to his "I-am-just-a-reporter" badge, although many of his reporter friends were also experimenting with fiction. The type of fiction that had the most appeal to Cobb at this period was as different as possible from the wry humor of his columns. Cobb's earliest short stories are carefully crafted works which display both gothic horror and psychological realism in differing proportions. Cobb was fascinated by the use of atmosphere and mental anguish to create the kind of effects seen in the works of Edgar Allan Poe. Like Ambrose Bierce, Cobb experimented with producing such Poe effects in more realistic and more obviously American settings. Like O. Henry, whom Cobb knew in New York, Cobb preferred a tight structure whose tidy ending often featured a "twist," a reversal of the reader's original expectations.

In spite of his long interest in such fiction, Cobb had only attempted one such story before the summer of 1909, an early version of the gothic tale "Fishhead" which he had written in Louisville. Serious doubts about his own abilities had kept him from attempting more. But he had shared this dream with Laura, as he had his earlier dream of going to New York, and once again she took it as her own and encouraged and bullied him to achieve it.

Others besides Laura felt that Cobb had the ability to write fiction. Samuel Blythe, who in 1907 had quit the *World* to be a political writer for the *Saturday Evening Post,* assured Cobb that George Horace Lorimer, the editor of the *Post* and a close friend of Blythe, would be interested in publishing anything Cobb could produce. Finally Laura and Blythe presented the summer vacation plan: both families would take summer cabins at Chazy Lake in the Adirondacks and for six weeks while their families played and swam the men could write and give each other mutual encouragement. Cobb wanted to revise the "Fishhead" story and had another tale he wanted to get down, so he agreed. With the windfall of the "Fat Chauffeur" check, he set out to become a fiction writer.

Cobb's stories of terror and retribution—for a later collection he authorized the term "grim tales" for the category, and it seems as good as any—may have little connection with the Hotel Clerk, but they were frequently based on crimes or personalities Cobb had encountered as a city room reporter. The story that Cobb had in mind when he went to the Adirondacks was suggested to him by the defendant at a trial he had covered, Charles W. Morse. Morse was a financial genius whose Wall Street manipulations were frequently illegal. Cobb was fascinated not so much by Morse's crimes as by his personality. He intimidated his own lawyer and defied the judge and seemed a man of almost inhuman nerve and stratagem. Cobb recreated his personality in a tale which traced the gradual mental breakdown of Hobart Trimm, a wily banker convicted of embezzlement, who manages to elude his guards because in a train wreck a corpse is mistakenly identified as Trimm. It seems a perfect opportunity to escape, then to collect his stolen millions through the aid of his lawyers and live a life of luxury under an assumed name. Trimm is finally and horribly defeated, however, by the handcuffs he wears, and the pain and despair of his attempts to remove them is graphically portrayed. At the end of the story as he gives himself up, he is more a monster than a man. Cobb tells the story in the third person with careful attention to detailed descriptions of scenes and actions, but the depiction of the mental state of Hobart Trimm is the story's focus. The following passage describes events after Trimm escapes a dog by kicking it, only to have its yowls arouse a farmer:

> Back and forth along the lower edge of his yard the farmer hunted, with the whimpering, cowed terrier to guide him, poking in dark corners with the muzzle of his shotgun for the unseen intruder whose coming had aroused the household. In a brushpile just over the fence to the east Mr. Trimm lay on his face upon the wet earth, with the rain beating down on him, sobbing with choking gulps that wrenched him cruelly, biting at the bonds on his wrists untnil the sound of breaking teeth gritted in the air. Finally, in the hopeless, helpless frenzy of his agony he beat his arms up and down until the bracelets struck squarely on a flat stone and the force of the blow sent the cuffs home to the last notch so that they pressed harder and faster than ever upon the tortured wrist bones.
>
> When he had wasted ten or fifteen minutes in a vain search the farmer went shivering back indoors to dry out his wet shirt. But the groveling figure in the brushpile lay for a long time where it was, only stirring a little while the rain dripped steadily down on everything.[3]

Cobb claims to have made a bet with his wife before he wrote this story, which was entitled "The Escape of Mr. Trimm," that it would not have an intentionally funny line in it. He certainly won the bet.

George Horace Lorimer was enthusiastic about "Mr. Trimm" when Cobb submitted it to him and immediately sent a check for five hundred dollars and a request for more stories.[4] "The Escape of Mr.

Trimm" appeared in the *Saturday Evening Post* in the November 27, 1909, issue. Popular response was enthusiastic. It remains one of the most anthologized of Cobb's works.

If the terrifying psychological realism of "Mr. Trimm" proved to be just what the public wanted, however, the story Cobb revised in the summer of 1909, "Fishhead," was judged too grim for popular taste. This tale describes the murder of a misshapen half-breed on Reelfoot Lake in Tennessee and the revenge on his murderers accomplished by the giant catfish of the lake. It is a gothic fantasy whose effect of horror is produced by Cobb's diction and style. Cobb sent "Fishhead" to numerous editors, but it was not published until Bob Davis decided to include it in his *Cavalier* in 1913. Even Davis felt the need to preface it with a warning that readers might find it offensive. Cobb kept the letters of rejection that it attracted. Lorimer at the *Post* had said, "It pains me to send back one of the best written stories I have seen in years." The editor at *Everybody's Magazine* said, "I don't know when a short story has impressed me more strongly or more unpleasantly." The editor of *Redbook* also praised the story but explained, "readers aren't educated up to raw beef yet." At least twelve magazines rejected it as too experimental, too shocking and too sophisticated for their readers.[5]

After his first appearance in the *Saturday Evening Post* Cobb did not immediately abandon the newspaper business for magazine work. He continued at the *World* for almost two more years, preparing himself to make the plunge. Elisabeth Cobb remembers her father during this period pacing back and forth, twisting buttons off his vest in a characteristic nervous gesture. George Doran, his publisher and friend, explained his anxiety at leaving a regular paycheck as that of a solicitous husband and father, citing ample instances of his courage at other times, especially during his war experiences, to demonstrate that Cobb was no coward:

> His physical courage was that of a superman. His self-confidence in the pursuit of his vocation was phenomenal, his courage—some call it nerve—superb.... Yet when confronted by a change of living which was to affect the fortunes of his family he was as timid as a fawn. But if he was timid, wife Laura was not. A delicate little person, she had the soul and the courage of the most adventurous campaigner. She brought her troops to order; she was prepared for a new campaign.[6]

While Laura encouraged, Cobb wrote. After several false starts, he completed "The Exit of Anse Dugmore" to his satisfaction and sold it to Lorimer. The story was probably suggested by the situation of Jim Howard, the eastern Kentuckian whose feuding past was so damaging to his case in the Goebel trials, Anse Dugmore is a mountaineer, imprisoned for a feud murder, whose life comes to a horrible end after a benevolent governor pardons him and sends him back home, where his sense of honor requires more killings from him. "The Exit of Anse Dugmore" appeared in *The Saturday Evening Post* on December 17, 1911. Cobb accepted the title of staff contributor to the *Post* in January of 1912 and finally quit his *World* job that September. One of the first stories published in the *Post* after he had made the break was "Words and Music," a story more concerned with compassion than with criminal psychology. Its protagonist was a homey Paducah lawyer, Judge Priest, whom Cobb certainly did not envision as a continuing subject of his fiction at the time. But the *Post* readers loved Judge Priest and asked for more. Cobb was to write over fifty short stories about the shy but skillful lawyer who gently imposed justice on his unruly townspeople. But in 1912 when he quit the *World* Cobb had only published three short stories and he was terrified that he could never publish another one. His daughter writes:

> He told me that when the first week rolled by and payday came, though not for him, he went near crazy. He could concentrate on nothing; he just stayed near a telephone, so that if the pressure grew unbearable he might call the *World* at any moment and ask them to take him back. And twiddled two sets of buttons off his vest.

Actually his nervousness does not seem to have affected his output. From the beginning of his full time work for the *Post,* a piece by him appears in almost every issue of the magazine. His work for the *Post* was by no means limited to short stories, but included humorous essays as well.

Cobb's admiration of G. H. Lorimer grew. He describes Lorimer as a "benevolent satrap" who indicated his satisfaction with a writer by his off-hand manner of giving important assignments and his generous payments and bonuses. Cobb called him a natural actor, not because there were any false notes in his speech and gestures, but because he was so adept at using his expression and intonation to reveal more than was said by his words alone. They had a Kentucky childhood in common; in fact, Lorimer's father, a Baptist minister, had moved from Paducah to Louisville only three months before his son's birth.[7] The relationship between Cobb and Lorimer was never as close as that between Cobb and his later publisher George H. Doran, but the two men respected each other and worked together successfully.

## Notes

[1]E. Cobb, *Wayward Parent,* pp. 101-106.

[2]Cobb, *Exit Laughing,* p. 156.

[3]Irvin S. Cobb, *The Escape of Mr. Trimm: His Plight and Other Plights* (New York: George H. Doran Co., 1913), pp. 49-50.

[4]Doran, p. 235.

[5]Letter, Irvin S. Cobb to Robert H. Davis, June 1, 1913; Davis Collection, New York Public Library.

[6]Doran, pp. 245-246.

[7]Townsend, *Concerning Cobb,* p. 14B.

# Chapter Eleven

One day in 1909 Buff came running into the Park Hill house to tell her parents that some lovely people were moving into the house behind them; she knew they were nice because they had such "swell garbage." The neighbors turned out to be George Henry Doran and his wife and daughter, moving to New York from Toronto. Doran, who had begun as an office boy but risen rapidly in publishing businesses in Toronto and Chicago, had organized his own publishing house in Toronto in 1907. The George H. Doran Company published native authors, but its early success was based on an arrangement with the British firm of Hodder and Stoughton for the rights to print and release the works of their authors in the United States and Canada. In 1909 Doran moved both the company and his household to New York. After Buff had introduced the two families, Doran and Cobb became close friends. Over the years Doran introduced Cobb to an international literary society he might otherwise never have encountered and published over forty of Cobb's books.

Doran's first best seller was Arnold Bennett's *Old Wives' Tale.* It was included in a parcel of books from Hodder and Stoughton that Doran took home to entertain his wife while she was recuperating from a brief illness. She singled out Bennett's novel and insisted that her husband publish it. The book, which had gone largely unnoticed in England, was an immediate success in the United States, which in turn created an interest among the British, so George Doran and Arnold Bennett each created the first major success of the other. The Dorans visited Bennett in Paris that Christmas of 1909 and the two men got along so well that the families spent the next fourteen Christmases together.

Doran and Bennett were an interesting pair. Doran was exuberant, handsome and self-confident. Bennett was awkward, unattractive and ashamed of his lower-class origins and of his tendency to stammer. Bernard Shaw once said that Bennett looked like "a fourth-rate clerk from the potteries and out of work at that." To some Bennett's shyness and frequent silences seemed disdain, but his good friends such as Doran found his company most enjoyable. Doran followed up the success of *The Old Wives' Tale* by bringing out Bennett's earlier novels, one every few months over the next three years. Doran begged Bennett to take a tour of the United States to see the country as Doran's guest, to receive the adulation of his American following and, incidentally, to create publicity that would drive sales figures even higher. A six-week tour was finally set for the late summer of 1911.

Doran was an attentive host who left hardly a moment of Bennett's visit unscheduled. When his ship approached the harbor Doran jumped on a tender and went out to meet him. From that point they were not separated for more than a few hours during the entire six week period. Doran even slept in a room of the suite he had rented for Bennett at the Waldorf-Astoria. Some members of Bennett's party found the attention undesirable; one wrote home:

> His publisher clings to him jealously and so B. hasn't really seen the best Americans, as Doran (the publisher) is a good sort but about what a publisher might be in London—or even a little less important. However B. is having a good time and that's the main thing.[1]

It was just such British snobbery that made Cobb suspicious of Bennett and later of all Doran's British authors. In all cases his response to them was cordial whatever his misgivings and with several he did establish warm friendships. Cobb never shared Doran's enthusiasm for Bennett's company, however, even though the publisher included Cobb in many of the activities on Bennett's schedule.

Cobb first met Bennett as one of the "great names in American journalism"—the others were Richard Harding Davis, Dorothy Dix and Franklin P. Adams—whom Doran had arranged to interview Bennett when he first left the ship. Cobb's article based on that interview was published in *American Magazine* that November. In it he described Bennett as "a smallish, slightly wearied-looking man, with a small impediment in his speech,... and in his head the brightest, quickest brown eyes you ever saw—an eye that is interested in everything that has happened, is happening or is going to happen."

Later, Cobb attended many of the social events planned for Bennett. He served as Master of Ceremonies at a special dinner given by the Dutch Treat Club. According to a newspaper account, the speeches and stories continued until daybreak and Bennett was "the only one [who] didn't say something." Not only Cobb but also

Laura and Buff were frequently included in the party as Doran showed Bennett the town, and *Your United States,* the book Bennett wrote about his tour, contains a tribute to Buff, who is described only as the young daughter of "one of the foremost humorists in the United States." Of Buff he says,

> this captivating creature, whose society I enjoyed at frequent intervals throughout my stay in America, was a mirror in which I saw the whole American race of children—their independence, their self-confidence, their adorable charm and their neat sauciness.[2]

Bennett's tour was compared by Doran to the earlier tour of Charles Dickens, but the books they wrote about the United States were quite different. Unlike Dickens' caustic attack on American scenery, manners and sanitary conditions, Bennett's book, which was of course published by The George H. Doran Company, displays a tame but agreeable enthusiasm for the United States. There is no way to know if he really found Buff Cobb's sauciness so delightful.

Bennett and Doran did not stay in New York, but also travelled to Washington, D.C., Chicago, Indianapolis, Boston and Philadelphia. In each city there were crowds waiting to meet Bennett and dignitaries or literary figures anxious to entertain him. Booth Tarkington, who had known Bennet in Paris, gave a reception for him in Indianapolis. Cobb travelled to Philadelphia to join G. H. Lorimer and Samuel Blythe in giving a luncheon for Bennett there. Bennett's behavior on this occasion reinforced Cobb's private dislike of Bennett. Lorimer had put meticulous care into his plans for the luncheon at the Bellevue Stratford, especally the menu. Lorimer decided to serve typically American dishes. The first course was terrapin stew, Philadelphia style, and Lorimer had sent all the way to the Chesapeake Bay to get the most appropriate kind of terrapin. This explanation did not impress Bennett, who said, "a sort of turtle, eh?" pushing back his plate. "I shan't touch it." According to Cobb's account of the luncheon, a chill fell over the company at this insult which had not dissipated when the oblivious Bennett left, rudely early, to go to another engagement. Bennett was certainly oblivous: he later recalled the luncheon in this way: "I heard more picturesque and pyrotechnic wit at one luncheon in Philadelphia than at any two repasts outside it." He recalled the conversation as consisting of "racy tales and slang. Politics and murder. . . ."[3]

Unlike Will Rogers, Cobb never claimed to like all the men he met. Some of his acquaintances assigned this virtue to him, however, because he usually hid his dislike of other person behind a mask of witty geniality. His relationship with Arnold Bennett is an interesting example of this behavior. Bennett admired Cobb's humor and assumed they were friends: the Bennetts entertained the Cobbs when they came to Paris in 1913. Cobb nursed his grudge and only exposed it to a few confidants. It is his treatment of Bennett in *Exit Laughing,* written when Bennett had been dead for ten years, that is most interesting, however. He talks specifically of his acquaintance with Bennett at one point, praising him as a novelist and regretting that the English caste system had saddled him with an inferiority complex. Fifty pages later he tells the terrapin stew story without identifying the author who, Cobb says "made the mistake of believing that calculated rudeness was an outward evidence of genius."[4] He is identified as Bennett by Cobb's daughter.[5] Cobb's code of politeness kept him from publicly denouncing others for their rudeness, but the men he sought as friends held the same standards of courtesy as he.

An interesting example of an observer who was unaware of Cobb's capacity for judgmental attitudes is seen in this description by E. V. Lucas, another British writer:

> Beneath Mr. Cobb's fun is a mass of ripe experience and sagacity. However playful he may be on the surface, one is aware of an almost Johnsonian universality underneath.... Don Marquis, while equally serious (and all the best humorists are serious at heart), has a more grotesque fancy and is more of a reformer, or, at any rate, a rebel. His dissatisfaction with hyprocisy provided a scorn that Mr. Cobb is too elemental to entertain.[6]

Although George Doran never again attempted to give one of his British authors as grand a tour as that he masterminded for Arnold Bennett, others also came to the United States to garner publicity and material for new books and Doran made sure that all of them met Irvin Cobb. Frank Swinnerton, E. V. Lucas and Cosmo Hamilton all praised Cobb in their descriptions of their American travels; one of the best descriptions of Cobb's ability to entertain is this tribute by Hamilton.

> I cannot remember in whose house it was that I first met Irvin Cobb, but his lightning flashes of humor and his sudden infectuous laugh was unforgettable. From the beginning to the end of that evening he made the laughter echo from the walls, went from one gorgeous story to another, built up an Eiffel Tower of right and Cobbish words and fired off his various points with a sharpshooter's aim.[7]

H. G. Wells came through, to impress Cobb with his geniality and his lack of snobbery; Somerset Maugham and G. K. Chesterton, who also seemed unusually modest to Cobb for Englishmen and the equally charming P. G. Wodehouse.

When Cobb was not helping Doran entertain visiting Englishmen, he frequently met Doran's American authors at his house. Frank Norris's brother Charles, who wrote rather daring novels based on scientific and political theories and Charles' wife Kathleen Norris, whose romantic novels enjoyed far greater sales, were both Doran authors who became good friends of Cobb. Mary Roberts Rinehart, whose son was later to marry Doran's daughter and join the Doran firm before founding his own, and her husband Dr. Stanley Rinehart became frequent companions of the Cobbs. They had many friends in common: Bob Davis first accepted Mrs. Rinehart's stories for *Munsey's Magazine* and encouraged her to write a book length work. The editor who came from Bobbs-Merrill to help her with that book, *The Circular Staircase,* was Hewitt Howland, who later married Manie Cobb.[8]

Even before Doran published his first Cobb books in late 1912 Cobb's stories in the *Saturday Evening Post* were attracting attention. His most enthusiastic fan besides Laura was Bob Davis; a mutual friend once said that if there were a vacancy on the twelve apostles Davis would have nominated Cobb for the position.[9] In October of 1912 one of Davis's friends on the New York *Sun* asked him who he thought was "the foremost writer on the horizon" and laughed at the answer, "Cobb." Davis's long article "Who's Cobb and Why?" defending his choice was published in the *Sun* on October 19, 1912. The praise he gives Cobb is fulsome:

> One is impressed not only with the beauty and simplicity of his prose, but with the tremendous power of his tragic conceptions and his art in dealing with terror. There appears to be no phase of human emotion beyond his pen.... Thus in Irvin Cobb we find Mark Twain, Bret Harte and Edgar Allan Poe at their best. Reckon with these potentialities in the future. Speculate, if you will, upon the sort of a novel that is bound, some day to come from his pen. There seem to be no pinnacles along the horizon of the literary future that are beyond him....
>
> There are critics and reviewers who do not entirely agree with me concerning Cobb. But they will.[10]

By 1923, when Doran published a volume entitled *Irvin S. Cobb: Storyteller* containing the original Davis article and two others, Davis felt that his extravagant remarks had been vindicated. In 1912, however, both Davis and Cobb took a lot of good-natured ribbing about Davis' predictions. Since he had made a serious attempt at fiction only three years earlier, however, Cobb must have found even the denials of his pre-eminence in American letters exciting.

The first Cobb book that Doran published was *Cobb's Anatomy,* a collection of four humorous essays, "Tummies," "Hair," "Hands and Feet," and "Teeth," that appeared in *The Saturday Evening Post* in the summer of 1912. The book came out that fall shortly after Davis' *Sun* article. In these essays Cobb first cast himself as the comic fat man, vulnerable to the insults and callousness of the thin world:

> It is all right for a thin man to be grouchy; people will say the poor fellow has dyspepsia and should be humored along. But a fat man with a grouch is inexcusable in any company—there is so much of him to be grouchy. He constitutes a wave of discontent and a period of general depression. He is not expected to be romantic and sentimental either. It is all right for a giraffe to be sentimental, but not a hippopotamus.[11]

*Anatomy* is simple description; Cobb would later develop this comic fat man into the bumbling persona of his semi-autobiographical essays.

Far more important to Cobb, however, than the publication of *Anatomy* was the volume Doran brought out in November, 1912: *Back Home: Being the Narrative of Judge Priest and His People.* It collected the ten Judge Priest stories that had been published in *The Saturday Evening Post* in 1911 and 1912. To these was added a "Preface" in which Cobb sets forth his serious purpose for the Judge Priest tales: to correct the Northern view of Southerners as either "venerable and fiery colonels with frayed wrist bands and limp collars" or "snuff-dipping, ginsing-digging clay-eaters." Instead, Cobb insists, Southerners are typical Americans, "having the same aspirations, the same blood in their veins, the same impulses and being prone under almost any conceivable condition to do the same thing in almost the same way" as citizens of the Northern states. He explains in the "Preface" that many of the events in his stories are based on fact and that many of his characters are modelled on actual Kentuckians.[12]

Most of the stories are set in the Paducah of the eighties; although Cobb never specifically names the town, he represents Paducah geography quite faithfully, only occasionally altering the name of a street or the location of a public building. Cobb pictures the town as ruled by a natural aristocracy—Judge Priest and his cronies Dr. Lake, Sgt. Jimmy Bagby, and Herman Felsburg—who are middle-class, small town property owners, not descendants of old plantation families. Frequently their good judgment and moral superiority are enough to maintain their political and social ascendency; at other times, however, Judge Priest uses force or polite blackmail to make sure that justice triumphs and innocence is protected. If to a modern reader Judge Priest and his cronies seem too noble and unprejudiced—and their accomplishments too miraculous—to be taken as an accurate portrayal of the Paducah civic leadership of 1885, there is nothing sentimental about Cobb's representation of the Paducah citizenry. They are an unruly lot, composed not only of shopkeepers and laborers but also of grafters, prostitutes, gamblers and crooks. Judge Priest has to quell lynch mobs and local con-men as well as Eastern racketeers and riverboat evangelists. He protects the victims of local prejudice—a group that includes not only blacks seeking protection from whites but also a black turned out by his own race (and then accepted into the all-white Gideon K. Irons Camp by the votes of Judge Priest and his friends after the black man tells a story of loyalty to a white master during the Civil War), a young prostitute who before her death requested a church funeral, Italian railroad workers falsely accused of stealing and an innocent man accused of murder who makes the mistake of hiring a Yankee lawyer. The short story format both points up the benevolent dictatorship that Judge Priest maintains and suggests its necessity—the citizens learn nothing from one story to the next and any natural sense of justice or decency that is buried within them must be forced out each time by the heavy-handed persuasion of Judge Priest.

One story in this early collection which demonstrates both Judge Priest's methods and the serious problems he deals with is "The Mob from Massac." It is based on an actual incident in Bowling Green, Kentucky; in moving it to Paducah, Cobb changed the origin of the lynch mob to Massac, a tiny settlement on Massac Creek, which runs into the Ohio near Paducah.[13] A white girl in Massac is raped by an unidentified black man; bloodhounds lead the sheriff's men to a pitiful Negro hiding in a tree. He is dragged back to town and locked in jail under the care of the cowardly, prejudiced deputy jailer Dink Bynam, while all of the other officials go to a town picnic and political rally. When the lynch mob from Massac arrives only Negroes are in the streets:

> Down through the drowsing town edge they stepped, giving alarm

only to the chickens that scratched languidly where scrub-oaks cast a skimpy shade across the road; but as they reached the town line they passed a clutter of negro cabins clustering about a little doggery. A negro woman stepped to a door and saw them. Distractedly, fluttering like a hen, she ran into the bare, grassless yard, setting up a hysterical outcry. A negro man came quickly from the cabin, clapped his hand over her mouth and dragged her back inside, slamming the door to behind him with a kick of his bare foot. Unseen hands shut the other cabin doors and the woman's half-smothered cries came dimly through the clapboarded wall; but a slim black darky darted southward from the doggery, worming his way under a broken, snaggled fence and keeping the straggling line of houses and stables between him and the marchers. This fleeing figure was Jeff, Judge Priest's negro bodyservant, who had a most amazing faculty for always being wherever things happened.[14]

Judge Priest reaches the jail just as Dink Bynam is about to release the prisoner into their charge. The judge intimidates Bynam, but stopping the mob proves more difficult. He explains to them the purposes of legal procedures, but they become impatient. He tries an appeal to their friendship:

"Boys," said the judge, "most of you are friends of mine—and I want to tell you something. You mustn' do the thing you're purposin' to do—you mustn't do it!"

A snorted outburst, as of incredulity, came from the sweating clump of countrymen confronting him.

"The hell we mustn't!" drawled one of them derisively, and a snicker started.

The snicker grew to a laugh—a laugh with a thread of grim menace in it and a tinge of mounting man-hysteria. Even to these men, whose eyes were used to resting on ungainly and awkward old men, the figure of Judge Priest, standing in their way alone, had a grotesque emphasis. The judge's broad stomach stuck far out in front and was balanced by the rearward bulge of his umbrella. His white chin-beard was streaked with tobacco stains. The legs of his white linen trousers were caught up on his shins and bagged dropsically at the knees. The righthand pocket of his black alpaca coat was sagged away down by some heavy unseen weight.[15]

When Judge Priest's efforts to stop them with words fail and the mob is about to push him aside, he resorts to force:

"One minute!" The judge's shrill blare of command held them against their wills. He was lowering his umbrella.

"One minute and one word more!"

Shuffling their impatient feet they watched him backing with a sort of ungainly alertness over from right to left, dragging the battered brass ferrule of his umbrella after him, so that it made a line from one curb of the narrow street to the other. Doing this his eyes never left their startled faces. At the far side he halted and stepped over so that they faced this line from one side and he from the other. The line lay between them,

> furrowed in the deep dust.
>
> "Men," he said and his lifelong affectation of deliberately ungrammatical speech was all gone from him, "I have said to you all I can say. I will now kill the first man who puts his foot across that line!"
>
> There was nothing Homeric, nothing heroic about it. Even the line he had made in the dust waggled and was skewed and crooked like the trail of a blind worm. His old figure was still as grotesquely plump and misshapen as ever—the broken rib of his umbrella slanted askew like the crippled wing of a fat bat; but the pudgy hand that brought the big blue gun out of the right pocket of the alpaca coat and swung it out and up, muzzle lifted, was steady and sure. His thumb drew the hammer back and the double click broke on the amazed dumb silence that had fallen like two clangs upon an anvil. The wrinkles in his face all set into fixed, hard lines.[16]

The threat works and the mob goes home. Cobb goes on to give the story a typical tidy ending: the actual rapist is found and shot while resisting arrest (but survives just long enough to make a full confession), the innocent man is freed and Judge Priest is reelected by the largest margin ever.

In *Exit Laughing* Cobb discusses the chief models for Judge Priest. Foremost was Judge William S. Bishop, a Paducah judge of Cobb's childhood. From Judge Bishop Cobb took Judge Priest's appearance, his gentle manner, his absentmindedness and his keen intelligence. Judge Bishop was such a unique personality that he was a favorite topic of conversation in Paducah and stories about him are numerous, divided equally among those that demonstrate his absentmindedness and those that indicate his grasp of the law. Alben Barkley, later Vice President of the United States, knew Bishop when he was reading law in Paducah in the late nineties and give him this tribute:

> Judge Bishop was one of the squarest, most brilliant jurists I have ever known and he fully deserved his reputation of being able to look "straight as a gun barrel" at the law, the facts and the justice of every case that came before him.[17]

Another Paducahan who contributed some features to Judge Priest was Judge Hal Corbett, a contemporary of Cobb who later became a resident of New York. Corbett actually inspired the first Judge Priest story. In the winter of 1911 while his family was away for several weeks Cobb stayed at the Algonquin, where he suffered from a severe attack of tonsilitis. Corbett visited him there and to entertain him told of defending a man for murder in Ripley, Tennessee, by using Judge Bishop as a character witness. Judge Bishop's tales of the Civil War, backed up with a harmonica playing outside the courtroom window, moved the jury to acquit the defendant.[18] Cobb turned Corbett's story into "Words and Music" and added some of Corbett's traits to his main character. Judge Priest's deliberately folksy talk is a Corbett characteristic, as is his ability to make himself a celebrity among Easterners. In "Stratagem and Spoils" Judge Priest goes to New York to save some Paducahans who have lost their money to a fast-talking swindler. Judge Priest succeeds by being such a character that the New York reporters are willing to follow him around—even to the swindler's office—in search of a story. This story exaggerates the impact of Judge Hal Corbett on the New York press, but not by too much. Cobb saw Judge Priest as a "gallon" of Judge Bishop, a "pint" of Judge Corbett and a "gill" of his own father—his gentleness, his pride and his love of children.[19]

Many of the other characters had their Paducah prototypes, most of them dead by the time Cobb began writing the stories. Paducahans delighted in identifying the sources of characters and plots and those still living, such as Connie Lee, the black chiropodist with a flair for clothes who was the model for Judge Priest's servant Jeff Poindexter, became local celebrities. Herman Wallerstein, the original of Herman Felsburg, died before the stories were printed, but his son Herbert Wallerstein, who took over the family clothing store, capitalized on his friendship with Cobb.

*Back Home* received cautiously favorable reviews and good sales. Cobb's growing celebrity and his involvement in the prosperity of The G. H. Doran Company are indicated in the first mention of him made by his later antagonist H. L. Mencken. In a 1913 letter to his protege Theodore Dreiser, Mencken advises:

> Take the Doran offer by all means. I hear only good of Doran, despite his publication of bad books by Irvin Cobb, Will Levington Comfort, *et. al.* He is more secure financially than the Harpers and he has an incomparable finer taste in books. I think you will find him a comfortable publisher.[20]

## Notes

[1]Reginald Pound, *Arnold Bennett: A Biography* (London: William Hernemann, Ltd., 1952), p. 227.

[2]Arnold Bennett, *Your United States* (New York: George H. Doran Co., 1912), p. 148.

[3]Pound, p. 234.

[4]Cobb, *Exit Laughing,* pp. 353-394.

[5]E. Cobb, *Wayward Parent,* p. 119.

[6]Townsend, *Concerning Cobb,* p. 2.

[7]Cosmo Hamilton, *People Worth Talking About* (London: Robert M. McBride & Co., 1933), p. 220.

[8]Mary Roberts Rinehart, *Mary Roberts Rinehart* (Chicago: E.M. Hale & Co., 1931), pp. 91; 96.

[9]Gordon, *Pearsons* (March 1915), p. 284.

[10]Davis, *Cobb: Storyteller,* pp. 10; 13-14.

[11]Irvin S. Cobb, *Cobb's Anatomy* (New York: George H. Doran Co., 1912), p. 11.

[12]Irvin S. Cobb, *Back Home: Being the Narrative of Judge Priest and His People,* (New York: George H. Doran Co., 1912), pp. vii-ix.

[13]Townsend, *Concerning Cobb,* p. 50.

[14]Cobb, *Back Home,* p. 263.

[15]Cobb, *Back Home,* p. 267.

[16]Cobb, *Back Home*, p. 271.

[17]Allen W. Barkley, *That Reminds Me* (Garden City: Doubleday & Co., 1954), p. 65.

[18]Katharine Logsdon, *Irvin S. Cobb and the Judge Priest Stories* (unpubl. thesis, Western Kentucky University, 1936), p. 16.

[19]Cobb, *Exit Laughing,* p. 340.

[20]Guy J. Forgue, ed, *The Letters of H. L. Mencken* (New York: Alfred A. Knopf, 1961), p. 36.

## Chapter Twelve

1913 was an extremely busy year for Cobb. He made two long trips that year, one to the Western United States and one to Europe, he continued to appear in at least two or three issues of *The Saturday Evening Post* each month, he published two more books, and he completed several other projects. Cobb's newspaper experience made his position as staff contributor to the *Post* seem easy by comparison; the *Post* was anxious to publish as much as he wanted to write, but there were no deadlines and no daily columns to fill. Under such conditions Cobb had no difficulty keeping a backlog of stories and essays in Lorimer's office. His inclination to write both humor and fiction in continuing series made completing a month or two's contributions in advance particularly easy for him; items from different series would alternate in different issues of the *Post,* or sometimes two different items, such as a Judge Priest story and an *Anatomy* essay, would appear in the same issue. Lorimer, while making suggestions and offering assignments, apparently gave Cobb free rein to write what he pleased and to abandon projects that proved disappointing. For example, between December, 1912 and May, 1913, five stories with Manhattan settings and the running title "The Island of Adventure" appeared in the *Post.* Cobb later explained to a friend why the series had been discontinued: "Personally, I didn't like 'em; that's why I stopped 'em when I did."[1]

Cobb's judgment of his own work was also important in determining which of his *Post* contributions were collected into volumes published by Doran. During 1912 and 1913 the *Post* ran ten humorous essays on the pattern of his *Anatomy* pieces that ranged in topics from "Duds" to "Law." Cobb and Doran selected four of them, "Vittles," "Music," "Art," and "Sport," for publication in a volume called *Cobb's Bill of Fare* that Doran brought out later in 1913. Perhaps in gratitude for the *Sun* article, Cobb dedicated the book to Bob Davis, although as was common in their friendship he made a joke out of the gesture. Davis and Cobb both liked to invent insulting names for each other or to imitate the errors of those who confused them with other celebrities. Davis thus frequently pretended that his friend was the newspaperman Frank Cobb or the baseball player Ty Cobb, or spelled his first name "Irving."[2] So the dedication to *Cobb's Bill of Fare* reads: "To R. H. Davis (not Richard Harding—The Other One)."

At some time during the winter of 1912-13 Cobb also made his first attempt at drama in five years. The sportswriter Bozeman Bulgar, a good-natured, warm-hearted Alabama native who had been a good friend of Cobb for years, felt that the Judge Priest stories had dramatic possibilities and convinced Cobb to collaborate on a modest one-act play, *Sergeant Jimmy Bagby*. The play, which was produced in early 1913, was a reasonable success; it ran on the Keith vaudeville circuit for a year and a half.[3]

Cobb's humorous travel writing was Lorimer's idea. Cobb's essays were frequently compared to those of Mark Twain; Lorimer thought it would be amusing for Cobb to do an updated version of Twain's *Roughing It* as a series in the *Post*. Cobb was delighted with the prospect of a two month western trip at the *Post's* expense, so in February of 1913 he settled Laura and Buff in a New York city apartment (the Park Hill house was becoming less appealing, especially in the winter)[4] and set off for Chicago and the luxury train that would carry him to the Grand Canyon and California.

The five installments that Cobb wrote about his western trip appeared in the *Post* in June, July and August of 1913 under the series title of "Roughing It Deluxe." Cobb's *Post* work had been illustrated by various staff writers; these essays were the first to be accompanied by the witty drawings of John T. McCutcheon. Doran brought the series out in book form under the same title and with the same illustrations in 1914. In these essays Cobb expanded his use of himself as a subject for humor (as seen in the *Anatomy* essays) to a narrative form. The personality of the narrator is not emphasized as heavily here as it is in later works, however, because the main sources of humor are the behavior of the other tourists, the luxury of their accomodations, and the strange habits of the natives:

> Starting out from Chicago on the Santa Fe, we had a full trainload. We came from everywhere: from peaceful New England towns full of elm trees and old line Republicans; from the Middle States; and from the land of chewing tobacco, prominent Adam's Apples and hot biscuits—down where the r is silent, as in No'the Ca'line. . . we were going West to see the country and rough it—rough it on overland trains better equipped and more luxurious than any to be found in the East; rough it at ten-dollar-a-day hotels; rough it by touring car over the most magnificient automobile roads to be found on this continent. We were a daring lot and

> resolute; each and every one of us was brave and blithe to endure the privations that such an expedition must inevitably entail.... If there wasn't any of the hothouse lamb, with imported green peas, left, we'd worry along on a little bit of the fresh shad roe, and a few conservatory cucumbers on the side.[5]

Still, there are some appearances of the resolutely cheerful, but cautious and self-effacing, narrator of his later humorous works, as in this discussion of the mule that he rode down the trail into the Grand Canyon:

> When she came to a particularly scary spot, which was every minute or so, she would stop dead still. I concurred in that part of it heartily. But then she would face outward and crane her neck over the fathomless void of that bottomless pit and for a space of moments would gaze steadily downward, with a despondent droop of her fiddle-shaped head and a suicidal gleam in her mournful eyes. It worried me no little and if I had known, at the time, that she had a German name it would have worried me even more, I guess. But either the time was not ripe for the rash act or else she abhorred the thought of being found dead in the company of a mere tourist, so she did not leap off into space, but restrained herself; and I was very grateful to her for it. It made a bond of sympathy between us.[6]

In few of the drawings McCutcheon followed the illustrator of the *Anatomy* and *Bill of Fare* essays in introducing a recognizable Cobb caricature; fat, with prominent eyes, unruly hair and a bemused but hopeful expression. The tradition was maintained, and over the years such artists as Tony Sarg, Herbert Johnson and F. Strobel took their turn at drawing the comic Cobb persona.

The trip included Cobb's first visit to California; he mostly limited his jokes on that state to the tendency of the residents of Los Angeles to praise the climate even during a drizzle and of the residents of San Francisco to honor all native sons except fleas. In Los Angeles Cobb visited Charley Van Loan, a former *World* reporter who was then a *Post* writer located on the West Coast. *Back Home* was attracting nationwide attention at the time, so Van Loan decided to play a trick on his friend. Before Cobb's arrival he went to six bookstores in Los Angeles and bribed the proprietors to go along with the joke. Early in Cobb's visit Van Loan suggested they purchase several copies of *Back Home* so that Cobb could autograph them for California friends. They toured the bookstores only to be told by the forewarned salesmen that they had never heard of either Cobb or *Back Home*.[7] Cobb took the joke much better than Van Loan himself would have; in *Exit Laughing* Cobb remembered, "There was a ton of sweetness in Van's huge frame, but. . . like the average practical joker, [he] couldn't stand being joked himself." On March 13 they sent a joint post card to "Old Bob Davis": "Greetings from the Van Loan—Cobb Atlantic and Pacific Marching and Chowder Club First annual reunion."[8]

Cobb left California at the end of March for Paducah to visit his mother and Reubie. There was no problem in finding copies of *Back Home* there and, even though Paducah was recovering from another spring flood, the citizens gave Cobb a royal welcome. He also stopped at Louisville, his first visit there since his days on the Louisville *Evening Post.* Louisville also treated him as a celebrity, running newspaper stories on his career and his western trip.[9] He reached New York in mid-April and the family soon moved back to the Park Hill house.

Much of the trusting ingenuousness of his literary persona was part of Cobb's own character, although he tried to hide it behind a facade of blustering pragmatism. One of his wife's favorite stories involved an unprofitable investment Cobb made shortly after his return to New York. During Cobb's absence Laura had been pestered by a man claiming to be an old friend of her father who wanted to sell her a Georgia pecan grove. Laura expressed no interest but was not able to discourage the man. Their daughter recreates Cobb's reaction to this problem in this way:

> "Now Laura! You haven't bought a pecan grove?... There's a woman for you! Leave her for six weeks—and she bankrupts you."
>
> "Certainly I haven't bought a pecan grove. I've only been driven half crazy getting away from the old man."
>
> "Let him come up," said Irvin grandly. "I will tend to him. And afterward we will hear no more of this nonsense."

In the Cobb family records is a letter written to Irvin Cobb on April 18, 1913, by Fred Geiger, acknowledging payment for five acres of land and one hundred pecan trees in Sumter County, Georgia. In exchange for the original investment and the property taxes, the Cobbs received a bag of pecans every Christmas.[10]

Shortly after Cobb's return—but probably written before he left—a three part series "Breaking Into New York" appeared in the *Post.* It traced Cobb's newspaper career from his first job in Paducah to his Portsmouth Peace Conference assignment on the *Sun.* Unlike all Cobb's other long *Post* contributions, these were unsigned; perhaps Cobb and Lorimer felt that anonymity would allow Cobb to be more candid. There were enough biographical details in the series, however, to identify it as Cobb's to anyone familiar with his career. In 1923 the three essays, retitled "Stickfuls," were incorporated in the volume *Myself to Date*, with Cobb identified as author.

During the summer the Cobbs decided that the Park Hill house was no longer a desirable year-round residence. Laura had enjoyed her winter in the city and was anxious to maintain an apartment there on a permanent basis; in addition, the Cobbs wanted to buy some property in the country for relaxation and flower growing in the summers. As Cobb explained in an essay published in the *Post* that September, finding an abandoned farm was all the rage, so he and his family decided to become "abandoned farmers" too. Abandoned farms were not plentiful, however, and their unsuccessful research was interrupted by a European trip and then by the World War. It is not clear when the Cobbs sold the Park Hill House, but they did not live there after the summer of 1913.

The 1913 European trip was a sequel to Cobb's western trip. Lorimer was so pleased with the "Roughing It Deluxe" essays that he sent Cobb and Laura on a three month tour of Europe so that Cobb could do an updated version of Mark Twain's *Innocents Abroad.* They sailed on September 23 on the *Lusitania* for London, where they stayed about three weeks before moving on to France, Germany and Italy. They sailed back from Naples on the *City of Berlin* in December.[11] The series describing the trip, which was entitled "An American Vandal," ran in the *Post* in eleven installments from March through July of 1914. Doran published the essays under the title *Europe Revised* later that year. This series was also illustrated by John McCutcheon and once again the drawings of the narrator presented not merely the perplexed but cheerful expression suggested by the tone of the book, but also a caricature of the features of Cobb himself.

Like *Innocents Abroad, Europe Revised* is doggedly low-brow and pragmatic in its approach to the cultural treasures of Europe. Cobb adopted this tone for its humorous value and in imitation of Mark Twain, but he probably had to exaggerate his own feelings only a little:

> It was after we had gone from France to Germany and to Austria and to Italy, that I learned the great lesson about art—which is that whenever and wherever you meet a picture that seems to you reasonably lifelike it is nine times in ten of no consequence whatsoever; and, unless you are willing to be regarded as a mere ignoramus, you should straightway leave it and go and find some ancient picture of a group of overdressed clothing dummies masquerading as angels or martyrs and stand before

that one and carry on regardless.

When in doubt, look up a picture of Saint Sebastian. You never experience any difficulty in finding him—he is always represented as wearing very few clothes, being shot full of arrows to such an extent that clothes would not fit him anyway. Or else seek out Saint Laurence, who is invariably featured in connection with a gridiron; or Saint Bartholomew, who, you remember, achieved canonization through a process of flaying and is therefore shown with his skin folded neatly and carried over his arm like a spring overcoat.

Following this routine you make no mistakes. Everybody is bound to accept you as one possessing a deep knowledge of art and not mere surface art either, but the innermost meanings and conceptions of art.[12]

Cobb is also similar to Twain in his insistance on comparing European scenery to less hallowed American counterparts:

On the whole Venice did not impress me as it has impressed certain other travelers. You see, I was born and raised in one of those Ohio Valley towns where the river gets emotional and temperamental every year or two.... The Grand Canal did not stir me as it has stirred some—so far back as '84 I could remember when Jefferson Street at home looked just like that.[13]

But, like *Roughing It Deluxe, Europe Revised* is hardly a close copy of its Twain inspiration. Cobb was not on a guided tour, as Twain had been,and his trip did not include the Holy Land. Because Cobb stayed longer in the European countries and because he had friends—Arnold Bennett and other Doran authors, the newspaperman Charles Hand—to entertain him, he had the leisure and the opportunity to study the Europeans more closely than Twain did. He shares Twain's interest in differentiating between American and European character traits, but he also tries to depict other national differences. Cobb devotes more space to the personalities and habits of the Europeans than to the tourist sights and his tone is frequently more thoughtful and authoritative than that of either *Roughing It Deluxe* or the two Twain books. Unlike Twain, Cobb made his European tour as an established writer with a national audience and he must have felt some responsibility to educate his readers as well as entertain them, as is seen in this explanation of English reserve:

An English cannot understand an American's instinctive desire to know about things; we do not understand his lack of curiosity in that direction. Both of us forget what I think must be the underlying reasons—that we are a race which, until comparatively recently, lived wide distances apart in sparsely settled lands and were dependent on the passing stranger for news of the rest of the world, whereas he belongs to

> a people who all these centuries have been packed together in their little island like oats in a bin. London itself is so crowded that the noses of most of the lower classes turn up—there is not room for them to point straight ahead without causing a great and bitter confusion of noses; but where it points upward or outward or downward the owner of the nose pretty generally refrains from ramming it into other folks' business. If he and all his fellows did not do this; if they had not learned to keep their voices down and to muffle unnecessary noises; if they had not built tight covers of reserve about themselves, as the oyster builds up a shell to protect his tender tissues from irritation—they would long ago have become a race of nervous wrecks instead of being what they are, the most stolid beings alive.[14]

*Europe Revised* also contains many examples of the vivid description that was to make Cobb's war reports so moving, as in this recreation of an automobile trip along the Bay of Naples:

> Then for a distance we would run right along the face of the cliff. Directly beneath us we could see little stone huts of fishermen clinging to the rocks just above highwater mark, like so many gray limpets; and then, looking up, we would catch a glimpse of the vineyards, tucked into man-made terraces along the upper cliffs, like bundled herbs on the pantry shelves of a thrifty housewife; and still higher up there would be orange groves and lemon groves and dusty-gray olive groves. Each succeeding picture was Byzantine in its coloring. Always the sea was molten blue enamel and the far-away villages seemed crafty inlays of mosaic work; and the sun was a disk of hammered Grecian gold.[15]

If *Europe Revised* contains less of the "Cobb-as-inept-yokel" persona than the other books, however, it was a misrepresentation of his behavior in Europe according to his wife, who later liked to laugh at the gaucheries they innocently displayed in their attempts to cope with foreign languages, wily guides, superior waiters, and European telephones. She also professed amazement to discover on reading the finished account that, as far as one could tell, Cobb had travelled alone![21] Perhaps he was depending here on his Twain model, or perhaps he was not yet sure how to treat Laura as a literary character. At any rate, she came into her own as a subject for Cobb's humor in the later "Abandoned Farmer" essays.

As autobiography, then, the *Europe Revised* essays slightly alter the facts—or at least leave some out. The questions that always arise about the accuracy of someone's account of himself become even more pointed when entertainment, not information, is the purpose of that account. Cobb loved telling and retelling his stories and they frequently grew better as the years passed, but if Cobb occasionally reworded the conversations or the characters in his anecdotes, there were no contemporary charges that he totally fabricated a significant event in his autobiographical books. Only a couple of his stories have ever been challenged by witnesses and those only on minor details. One of Cobb's favorite stories about his European trip, not told in *Europe Revised* but repeated in many after dinner speeches and written down later, involves the time in Paris that Lady Randolph Churchill's male secretary called Cobb's hotel room by mistake. The secretary was returning a call and Cobb had difficulty making him understand that he had the wrong number. Cobb's version of the rest of the conversation goes like this:

> "What! You don't want Lady Upchurch [Cobb's disguised version of her name]?
>
> "Well," I said, "if you're going to make an issue of it I may take the proposition under consideration. When did Her Ladyship start doing this sort of thing?"
>
> "Oh, God bless my soul! What a frightful Yankee bounder! Oh, God bless my soul!"[16]

Elisabeth Cobb tried to check on the accuracy of this story by asking her mother, who agreed that Cobb did talk to someone by mistake at the Hotel Lotti in Paris that September—but she was not sure just how the conversation went. Even if Cobb polished up the dialogue, however, apparently the incident did take place; or at least Cobb was confident enough about his version to tell it to Lady Churchill herself on a later trip to London. She laughed heartily.[17]

Another feature of the European trip that Cobb left out of *Europe Revised* was his meeting with Rudyard Kipling. An article based on that interview appeared in the New York *Evening Post* on December 11, 1913. In February of 1914 the periodical *Book News Monthly* published a special issue on Cobb and Kipling, with portraits of and articles about both authors, to commemorate their meeting. Excerpts from the *Post* article, "Kipling at Home," were reprinted there.

Cobb had written Kipling to request an interview without any real hope of a reply. Kipling handwrote a cordial note, however, inviting the Cobbs to luncheon.[18] In the *Evening Post* article Cobb describes strolling in the Kipling garden on their arrival, to hear a shout and see Kipling running toward them. Kipling welcomed them warmly and kept them for most of the afternoon so that he and Cobb could discuss the state of literature in England and America. Both agreed in their mistrust of the "ultramoderns." Cobb was delighted and impressed with his host:

> What's he like? Well, to me he appeared, at first flush, a combination of Theodore Roosevelt, William Travers Jerome, and Bob Davis. He has a big jaw and he wears shiny glasses and shows his teeth like T. R. and he's a short man and blocky, with a big strong hand...
>
> It didn't take me two minutes in that walk...up to the house to find out that in spite of his great work and his experience he feels a tremendous ethusiasm about everything that is worthwhile. He's not a bit blase, but he isn't Englishy English...but is cosmopolitan in the real meaning of the word.[19]

After their return from Europe the Cobbs spent the rest of the winter in the Algonquin Hotel. The *Post* was still running a Cobb humorous essay series, "Shakespeare's Seven Ages and Mine," begun while they were abroad. These essays, which use the seven stages of life enumerated by Jacques in *As You Like It* as a basis for comic analysis of human types, were reprinted in *Prose and Cons* in 1926. About the time of their return Doran published *The Escape of Mr. Trimm,* a volume of *Post* stories including several of the grim tales, a few stories with New York settings and one Judge Priest story. The reviews it received that January and February were the best a Cobb book had ever produced; *The New York Times Book Review* praised the book's dramatic force, admirable psychology, "the very clever way in which the climaxes are reached," and its "human quality."[20]

Cobb spent the rest of that winter preparing the *Europe Revised* essays and writing a new supply of short stories for the *Post.* That spring the Cobbs moved to an apartment on West 110th Street that they kept through 1917. In June, 1914, they rented a lake cottage at North Hatley in Quebec, expecting to stay the whole summer. Their vacation was interrupted, however, by the telegram from Lorimer that sent Cobb on his first trip to Europe as a war correspondent.

## Notes

[1]Townsend, *Concerning Cobb,* p. 60.

[2]Cobb-Davis correspondence, Davis Collection, New York Public Library.

[3]Townsend, *Concerning Cobb,* p. 64.

[4]E. Cobb, *Wayward Parent,* p. 126. She has confused the chronology of the Western and European trips.

[5]Irvin S. Cobb, *Roughing It Deluxe* (New York: George H. Doran Co., 1914), p. 17.

[6]Cobb, *Roughing,* pp. 44-45.

[7]Unidentified newspaper clipping, Crabbe Library, Eastern Kentucky from Universeity.

[8]Davis Collection, New York Public Library.

[9]Louisville *Post*, April 9, 1913; clipping in Louisville Free Public Library.

[10]E. Cobb, *Wayward Parent,* p. 128.

[11]Letter, Irvin S. Cobb to John Wilson Townsend, February, 1922, Crabbe Library, Eastern Kentucky University.

[12]Irvin S. Cobb, *Europe Revised* (New York: George H. Doran Co., 1914), pp. 390; 393.

[13]Cobb, *Europe Revised,* pp. 125; 126.

[14]Cobb, *Europe Revised,* pp. 319; 320.

[15]Cobb, *Europe Revised,* p. 409.

[16]Cobb, *Myself to Date,* pp. 323-325.

[17]E. Cobb, *Wayward Parent,* pp. 115-117.

[18]The letter is in the Brody collection.

[19]Irvin S. Cobb, "Kipling at Home," *Book News Monthly* (February, 1914), pp. 276-277.

[20]*New York Times Book Review* (January 1, 1914), IX, 776.

# Chapter Thirteen

The short telegram that Cobb received from Lorimer contained a reference to one of Cobb's jokes and the only essential information:

> Seems like this here war has done busted right in our face. Your ship sails Thursday.

It was a typical Lorimer assignment: no polite inquiry, no explanation of duties, no discussion of terms. The Cobbs packed up immediately and left for New York. Also typically, Lorimer's provisions for Cobb were generous: he had ready for him a letter from Secretary of State William Jennings Bryan commending him to all American diplomats in Europe, an automatic revolver, a letter of credit, a good supply of travelers' checks and a satchel weighing about forty pounds which contained six thousand dollars worth of gold sovereigns. Cobb was to represent *The Saturday Evening Post* and the Philadelphia *Public Ledger*, going wherever possible in the war zone and writing about what he saw. Cobb sailed on the St. Paul on August 7, 1914, with three other reporters: Will Irwin, famous for his article on San Francisco at the time of the earthquake and representing *Collier's* magazine, Arnot Dosch of *World's Work* and John McCutcheon, the illustrator of Cobb's books who was also a reporter for the Chicago *Tribune.* Two days earlier five other reporters had sailed on the *Lusitania,* including Richard Harding Davis, Cobb's only rival at the time for the title of most famous reporter in the United States, representing the New York *Tribune,* and Gerald Morgan of the *Metropolitan Magazine.*[1]

These eight men hoped to find the warring nations willing to accredit and to provide accomodations for reporters from a neutral country (Woodrow Wilson reemphasized the unbiassed neutrality of the United States in an appeal made on August 19), but there were no assurances and no accepted international policy. They discovered after their arrival that the governments of all three countries—England, France and Germany—were unwilling to cooperate and anxious to keep the news of what was actually happening from their own countrymen and from the rest of the world. Both the French and the British felt that the presence of war correspondents had hurt them by providing information to the enemy in previous wars: the French in the Franco-Prussian war and the British in the Boer War. They were anxious to avoid such a danger in this conflict and thus were willing only to issue optimistic, misleading and basically useless bulletins to the press. The German position was similar; they did not want the French and British to be aware of the power and extent of their attacking armies or of the movements of their troops. In spite of President Wilson's declaration of neutrality, they mistrusted the American reporters and suspected them of being spies for the British. So the reporters found themselves on their own, with a war to cover and no credentials that would prevent their being harassed, arrested, or shot as spies.

The attempts on both sides to fight a war in secret—and the state of communications technology in 1914—affected the type of journalism the men produced. Stories could go back to the United States by cable from England, which was controlled by English censorship, by wireless from various locations, the main source of German propaganda and information, or by ship. Before the American reporters landed the only information about the war available in the United States (and in the European countries as well) was in the short bulletins released by the various governments. So Americans were anxious to know not only about daily developments but also about the full scope of the war: the relative power and preparation of the countries, their aims in the war, the amount of distress and destruction in the war theater. The stories sent back by the reporters, especially those representing magazines, were not curt announcements of developments but long feature articles which tried to reproduce for the American readers the atmosphere and scenes of the war. The communication difficulties, the uneasy status of the reporters and the more leisurely nature of the articles led to unusual publication delays; although Cobb left New York on August 7, his first story on the war did not appear in the *Post* until October 10. The official United States neutrality made the task more difficult, but the reporters, Cobb especially, tried to pass no moral judgments on the armies of either side. All the warring countries were issuing propaganda about atrocities committed by their enemies; Cobb decided the only way to deal with the situation was to report as fact only what he saw with his own eyes.[2]

The Cobb party arrived in Liverpool, but finding no help or

information in England, went across the channel to Belgium. On August 18 they met Davis and Morgan, who had preceded them, in Brussels for dinner at the Palace Hotel. In the luxurious dining hall of the hotel it was hard to believe that Belgium was being invaded, but the streets were full of dazed refugees from the north. The next morning Cobb, McCutcheon, Dosch and Irwin hired a taxicab, told the driver to head north and set out to find the war. When they got close enough to hear the guns and see the smoke on the horizon, the taxi refused to go farther, but agreed to wait. The reporters started out on foot, leaving their overcoats in the car. They never saw them or the taxi again.

As the reporters walked toward the site of the smoke and gunfire, moving against a horde of refugees, they realized it was the city of Louvain under siege. (It was destined to be totally destroyed in the next week.) They stopped by the Church of Saint Jacques for bread and cheese and, while they were eating, the Germans arrived. Cobb described the event in this way in his second *Post* article:

> When we came to where the street leading to the Square of Saint Jacques joined the street that led in turn to the Brussels road, all the people there were crouching in their doorways as quiet as so many mice, all looking in the direction in which we hoped to go, all pointing with their hands. No one spoke, but the scuffle of wooden-shod feet on the flags made a sliding, slithering sound, which someway carried a message of warning more forcible than any shouted word or sudden shriek.
>
> We looked where their fingers aimed and, as we looked, a hundred feet away through a cloud of dust a company of German foot soldiers swung across an open grassplot, where a little triangular park was and straightened out down the road to Brussels, singing snatches of a German marching song as they went.
>
> And behind them came trim officers on handsome, highheaded horses and more infantry; then a bicycle squad; then cavalry and then a light battery, bumping along over the rutted stones, with white dust blowing back from under its wheels in scrolls and pennons.
>
> Then a troop of Uhlans came, with nodding lances, following close behind the guns; and at sight of them a few men and women, clustered at the door of the little wine shope calling itself the Belgian Lion, began to hiss and mutter, for among these people, as we knew already, the Uhlans had a hard name....
>
> Just then, from perhaps half a mile on ahead, a sharp clatter of rifle fire sounded—pop! pop! pop!—and then a rattling volley. We saw the Uhlans snatch out their carbines and gallop forward past the battery into the dust curtain. And as it swallowed them up we, who had come in a taxicab looking for the war, knew that we had found it; and knew, too, that our chances of ever seeing that taxicab again were most exceeding small.
>
> We had one hope—that this might merely be a reconnaissance in force and that when it turned back or turned aside we might yet slip

> through and make the Brussels afoot. But it was no reconnaissance—it was Germany up and moving. We stayed in Louvain three days and for three days we watched the streaming past of the biggest army we had ever seen and the biggest army beleaguered Belgium had ever seen and one of the biggest, most perfect armies the world has ever seen. We watched the gray-clad columns pass until the mind grew numb at the prospect of computing their number. To think of trying to count them was like trying to count the leaves on a tree or the pebbles on a patch.
>
> They came and came and kept on coming, and their iron-shod feet flailed the earth to powder and there was no end to them.[3]

The reporters had taken rooms at a small hotel in Louvain after a German adjutant had told them courteously but firmly that he doubted that they would survive if they tried to make Brussels without a safe conduct, which he refused to give. Finally on Saturday, August 22, the Germans had left and the party found a Belgian willing to take them back to Brussels.

On August 19 Harry Hansen of the Chicago *Daily News* and Roger Lewis of the Associated Press had arrived in Brussels and met Davis and Morgan. The next day they watched as the German army that had passed Cobb in Louvain marched in to occupy Brussels. Davis got out a dispatch to the New York *Herald Tribune* describing the spectacle; it was the first notice to the outside world of the size of the German army. Cobb and his three companions managed to enter occupied Brussels on August 22, to go back to their hotel, and to find the other reporters, whose party now included James O'Donnell Bennett of the Chicago *Tribune,* but their movements were restricted and their lives endangered. They could scarcely move from the hotel without being stopped by German soldiers who accused them of being British spies. Davis visited Major General Thaddeus von Jarotsky, the military governor, and managed to get a document entitling him "through all German lines to pass, in Brussels and its suburbs." He took the other reporters to von Jarotsky, who agreed to stamp similar documents for them if they would type up their own copies. When they went back to do this, Cobb suggested taking a gamble—omitting the phrase "in Brussels and its suburbs" from the documents—in the hopes that von Jarotsky would affix the stamp of the Imperial Government to them without noticing, giving the reporters credentials useful anywhere the German army happened to be. The other six men agreed, von Jarotsky didn't notice and the seven newly documented reporters—without Davis and Morgan—set off to find the war. The stratagem was a dangerous one; any high-level official would know that no neutral reporters were being permitted to travel freely past the

German lines, but the reporters hoped to find out something before they were caught.

The seven set out from Brussels in two hired horse carriages on August 23. At Nivelles the coachmen insisted on turning back and Irwin and Dosch went with them. On the morning of August 24, the other five reporters set out on foot. They arrived at Binche at nightfall with feet so sore and bleeding that they stayed there another day. So far they had seen German and Belgian soldiers but no signs of major destruction. On Wednesday morning, August 26, they acquired a dogcart, an ancient horse which they christened "Gray Gables" because of what Cobb called her "architecture," and two bicycles. Cobb, Bennett and Lewis rode in the dog car McCutcheon and Hansen took the bicycles. They set out in the direction of Mauberge, where they had reports of a battle. In the village of Merbes-Ste-Marie and Merbes-le-Chateau they came on the first signs of the war's destruction: some vandalized shops, a burned-out-mill, a dead civilian, some signs of gunfire. At the site of La Buissiere across the river, however, they found only a smoking ruin, policed by German soldiers and still inhabited by a few frightened natives and some wounded French prisoners. The French had fortified themselves there, digging entrenchments and providing supplies and the Germans had run over them like a machine.

The shelling of Louvain had been shocking, but its effect on the five men was nothing compared to that of the ruins of La Buissiere. It was Cobb's first view of war up close; he had tried to enlist for the Spanish American War but had been rejected because of his flat feet. Cobb had already lost most of the romantic notions about war that he had inherited from Uncle Jo Shrewsbury; after his inspection of La Buissiere Cobb equated war with mindless and needless destruction. He could admire bravery, he could understand self-defense, but from that day Irvin Cobb hated war, and his record of the war was more than anything else a record of destruction. When Cobb's *Post* articles were collected into a Doran book in 1915, they were given the stirring title of *Paths of Glory,* but Cobb used the phrase in a fashion more pessimistic than even the original Gray quotation. In the book, talking about German soldiers marching to a later battle—which they lost—he says:

> Viewed against the sunset yellow, the figures of the dragoons stood up black and clean as conventionalized and regular as though they had all been stenciled on that background.... It was as though they marched into a fiery furnace, treading the crimson paths of glory—which are not glorious and probably never were, but which lead most unerringly to the grave.[4]

The reporters stayed at La Buissiere only an hour before pushing on to the villages of Neuville and Montignies St. Christopher, where they found more destruction. In the latter village, which Cobb made the subject of his first *Post* article, the only living creatures they saw were an old woman and three cats. Outside the village some Red Cross workers dug graves for the corpses of French soldiers. Continuing along the path of the German advance, the party of reporters found themselves over the boundary of France and at the site of a major German encampment.

Cobb has written two versions of his encounter with and subsequent detainment by the German Army at Beaumont. The events are the same, but the *Post* version written in 1914 is terse and emphasizes the fear of the reporters and the danger of their situation. About eight years later Cobb wrote about it again in an essay entitled "The Funniest Thing that Ever Happened to Me." Here he elaborates on the ridiculous appearance they made as they rode up to the assembled ranks of the Seventh German Army in their dog cart and bicycles:

> It properly should have been a bit out of a Viennese opera. For all the world it was like a well-devised theatrical setting, like a scene from a production that had been mounted without regard to the expense. A jig-sawed sky line, where the serrated roofs of tall ancient houses cut across one's breadth of vision, made the chief detail of the back-drop. Just here, in the right wings, was set the town house of the Prince de Caraman Chimay, a picturesque old pile.
>
> At the lower left entrance was the medieval church and from its crumbling belfry the Prussian double-eagle showed, black against a white background, for proof that the church like all else in these parts, had been conquered and captured.... We swung out into the clear, the two bicycles leading on like outriders and the rest of our troop perched in the creaking ruin of the dog-cart....
>
> So far, we did not realize that we were cast to provide the low comic relief. How were we to realize it? Nobody else who was present knew it yet. We just had the feeling that we were out of place. Besides, we were not dressed for company.
>
> Take my own case: The night before, while we slept on the bare tiled floor of an abandoned schoolhouse, I rolled over on my straw hat and broke it so badly that the crown sloughed away. But I still clung to the brim, as a man will cling to the last remnants of his one-time respectability; and my mane, which was uncombed, stood up through the opening, in what my companions had described to me as being a very striking effect.
>
> Also, that morning, to save myself from the occasional showers, I had purchased from a wayside butcher his long canvas blouse, which I wore—and so coated over was this garment with suet and tallow and hog grease and other souvenirs of his calling, that had it caught fire I am sure it would have burned for at least half a day with a clear blue flame.
>
> Two days earlier than this I had walked the shoes off my feet and

with the shoes, some tender portions of the feet themselves. So, for this, the occasion of my advent into fashionable military society, I had on a pair of homemade carpet slippers which I had acquired by barter from an elderly Belgian lady. These slippers were gray in color, mottled with white and of a curious swollen shape, so that they looked rather like a pair of Maltese cats which had died of dropsy and then had been badly embalmed.

I might add that I probably, was the best-dressed person in my crowd; anyhow, I was the one with the most fanciful touches to his wardrobe. All of us still were wearing the light summer suits in which we had left Brussels five days before, ostensibly for a carriage ride to Waterloo; and all that time we had been constantly on the go, through everlasting clouds of thick white dust, sleeping at night in our wrinkled clothing; and for at least thirty-six hours none of us had washed his face and hands, or slicked his hair down, or roached it up, or anything. Do you blame us for feeling that we did not match in with the prevalent surroundings?

Nevertheless, there being nowhere else for us to go, we headed straight into the heart of that sunburst of military grandeur; and when we arrived there we stopped and Gray Gables, following her usual custom, put her long fiddle-shaped head down on the cobbles and took a nap and we dismounted and, five abrest, in all our grimed and gritty and frowsy untidiness, we advanced upon the Headquarters Staff of the Seventh German Army....

When we had approached quite near to it, a colonel stepped forward from the front line. With popping eyes he regarded us. In excellent English, but in the shocked tones of a tremendous astonishment, he asked the question: "Who are you?"

And then, when I, as unofficial spokesman for our delegation, spoke up and answered—at the same time jauntily lifting the brim of my straw hat—"A party of American war correspondents," the laugh that went up was the heartiest laugh, I think, which the German Army enjoyed during the early part of the war.

After the interruptive echoes had died down and after all the fat generals had stopped choking and beating one another on the back and after all those mere common soldiers quit leaning up against the handiest walls or up against their handiest comrades and were straight on their legs again, the colonel resumed.

"But we have no correspondents with the German Army," he stated; and then looked hard at us, as though to add, "What have you to say to that?"

It would never do to let the conversation sag here. An apt retort was needed to lift the situation and prevent an embarrassing stage wait. Somebody must do something and do it right away, to put all of us on an easier footing.

"Well, Colonel," I said in a sprightly manner, "if you'll be good enough to count, you'll see that you now have five."[5]

In the *Post* account Cobb attributes the retort to "one of us;" Harry Hansen claimed that it was actually his.[6] Whoever made it, however, probably did not do so in a "sprightly" fashion; the reporters were physically and emotionally exhausted and there was nothing funny about finding themselves at the mercy of the German army. They were not released for three weeks.

The Germans at first agreed to send the Americans back to Brussels but then changed their minds. After a day of semi-starvation and of uneasy company with the German soldiers, the five reporters found themselves on a train heading back to German territory. They were escorted to the train by a courteous German sergeant who assured them that, although the train was filled with prisoners, they were not prisoners but guests of the German army. He then requested that they shake hands all around as "a token of mutual confidence." Cobb felt relieved for a moment, but then:

> As he left us, however, he was heard, speaking in German, to say *sotto voce* to one of the guards:
>
> "If one of those journalists tries to slip away don't take any chances—shoot him at once!"
>
> It is so easy to keep one's honor intact when you have moral support in the shape of an earnest-minded German soldier, with a gun, stepping along six feet behind you. My honor was never safer.[7]

The train ride took two days. The five American reporters plus three other captured journalists, one American, one Frenchman and one Belgian, were crammed into a compartment meant for six. The other compartments in their car held German officers and wounded German soldiers. Behind them in the train was a long line of boxcars containing French prisoners, many of them wounded. No food was provided for the Americans; in "The Funniest Thing that Ever Happened to Me" Cobb describes his delight at sticking his hand out the window and getting a sausage intended for a German veteran. He ends that essay, "So we ate that sausage and lived happily ever after."

It did not seem a happy ending at the time. On August 30 the Americans were put off the train at Aix-la-Chapelle, a town over the German border. Here they finally got food, a chance to take a bath and even clean clothes, but there was no way to communicate their whereabouts to the outside world and no notion of when they would be released. No member of Cobb's party had been able to file a story or send a message of any kind since they had left Brussels.

The group of reporters they had left in Brussels had been a little more successful. Although Davis had some bad experiences with the Germans also—they threatened him with execution once and only released him at the last minute—he, Morgan and Irwin managed to leave Brussels on a train toward the Channel on August 27. From the train windows they watched the final destruction of Louvain. Irwin returned to the United States soon after and immediately published a description of the shelling of that city. Davis, who stayed in London, managed to get a story out which appeared in the New York *Tribune* on September 4, 1914. Under the headline, "Eight American Writers Arrested," it told of the various adventures of the reporters in Europe. Davis of course had not seen or heard of the members of Cobb's party since they had left Brussels and could offer no assurances that they were still alive.[7] Many rumors of atrocities committed by the German soldiers against the French and Belgians were circulating, so the families and friends of the missing reporters were understandably worried.

Cobb and the other reporters were allowed to contact the American consul at Aix-la-Chapelle, who helped them convince the Germans that they were not British spies, but the Germans still refused to let them leave Aix-la-Chapelle. They tried every means available to request permission to travel as neutral correspondents with the army. They were politely put off. They decided that the only thing to do was to write a letter to the Kaiser. A civilian whom they approached for help with the appropriate phrasing tried in shocked tones to talk them out of it; the emperor was unapproachable and etiquette did not allow such familiarities. The reporters wrote one anyway, explaining to the Kaiser that it would be useful to the German cause if the American people were informed of the German military situation. Their German friend overcame his amazement and polished their language, but predicted the letter would never make it through the first military censor. For three days they heard nothing; then a resplendent staff colonel arrived with parchment documents, decorated with seals and ribbons and signed by the Kaiser himself, allowing them to go and do practically as they pleased in Germany and behind the German lines.

The military establishment was apparently impressed with the reporters' argument about the need for good publicity in the United States; by special arrangement the first message the Americans were allowed to send out dealt not with their safety or with their new official status but with the atrocity rumors. The New York *Times* printed the text of their telegram in full on September 7:

> In spirit we unite in rendering the German atrocities groundless, as far as we are able to. After spending two weeks with and accompanying the troops upward of 100 miles we are unable to report a single instance unprovoked.
>
> We are also unable to confirm rumors of mistreatment of prisoners or of non-combatants with the German columns. This is true of Louvain, Brussels, Luneville and Nanbes, while in Prussia hands.
>
> We visited Chateau Soldre, Sambre and Beaumont without substantiating a single wanton brutality. Numerous investigated rumors proved groundless. Everywhere we have seen Germans paying purchases and respecting property rights as well as according civilians

> every consideration.
>
> After the battle of Beass [possibly Barse, a suburb of Namur] we found Belgian women and children moving comfortably about.
>
> The day after the Germans captured the town in of Merbes Chateau [possibly St Marie] we found one citizen killed, but were unable to confirm lack of provocation. Refugees with stories of atrocities were unable to supply direct evidence.
>
> Belgians in the Sanibre Valley discounted reports of cruelties in the surrounding countries.
>
> The discipline of the German soldiers is excellent as we observed.
>
> To the truth of these statements we pledge our professional and personal word.
>
> Roger Lewis, Associated Press
> Irvin S. Cobb, *Saturday Evening Post* and *Philadelphia Public Ledger*
> Harry Hansen, *Chicago Daily News*
> James O'Donnell Bennett and John T. McCutcheon, the *Chicago Tribune*

This telegram had an electrifying effect, although no one was sure what to make of it. Most Americans suspected—and feared—that the Germans had tortured the reporters to make them sign it. Both Cobb and McCutcheon were well known and a threat to them became for many Americans the first awareness that the United States might be affected by the war. Ironically—for the telegram, although set up by the Germans, reflected the reporters' actual experience and sentiments—the telegram probably hurt the German cause in the United States rather than improved it.[8]

Sending the telegram, however, did improve the lot of the five reporters considerably. The Germans not only allowed them to pass unmolested but took them on tours of their military operations. Cobb went up in a German observation balloon, toured the trenches near Rheims under fire while the cathedral burned over his head and viewed the technological marvels of telephone exchanges, portable field hospitals and an impressive array of military hardware. But Cobb's reports dwell on the destruction and the human suffering. A German officer explained the unfortunate smell at Cerny to him this way:

> The French and English, but mainly the English, held the ground first. We drove them back and they lost very heavily. In places their trenches were actually full of dead and dying men when we took those trenches....
>
> At once they rallied and forced us back and now it was our turn to lose heavily. That was nearly three weeks ago and since then the ground over which we fought has been debatable ground, lying between our lines and the enemy's lines—a stretch four miles long and half a mile wide that is literally carpeted with bodies of dead men. They weren't all dead at first. For two days and nights our men in the earthworks heard the cries of those who still lived and the sound of them almost drove them

> mad. There was no reaching the wounded, though, either from our lines or from the Allies' lines. Those who tried to reach them were themselves killed. Now there are only dead out there—thousands of dead, I think. And they have been there twenty days....
>
> "But in the name of God, man," I said, "why don't they call a truce—both sides—and put that horror underground?"
>
> He shrugged his shoulders.
>
> "War is different now," he said. "Truces are out of fashion."
>
> I stood there and I smelled that smell. And I thought of all those flies and those blood-stiffened stretchers and those little inch-long figures which I myself, looking through that telescope, had seen lying on the green hill, and those automobiles loaded with mangled men and War de Luxe betrayed itself to me. Beneath its bogus glamour I saw war for what it is—the next morning of drunken glory.[9]

Even more horrible to Cobb than the smell of the dead on the battlefields was the suffering of the wounded. The Germans permitted his party to go to Mauberge where trains carrying wounded German soldiers and wounded French prisoners stopped for medical aid and soup on the way to the interior of Germany. A single train would contain hundreds of men; sometimes the trains were only ten minutes apart, but never more than an hour apart. Exhausted doctors, nurses, and Red Cross workers rushed to do something for the men on board while the trains paused in the station. Cobb writes of his attempts to help:

> In the halted freight cars and cattle cars were dead men, dying men, men rolling in the festering stained straw from the pangs of untended and mortifying hurts.... The only two nurses still able to stand on their feet tottered back and forth, sometimes holding to solid objects for support.... Because intervals befell when there was no one else to do it,... my companion and I bodily lifted men out from where they wallowed in their own filth and half-dragged, half-led them indoors and there we stripped off clotted first-aid dressings and mended infected wounds and even performed minor operations under the eyes of the surgeon in charge, a frail middle-aged Saxon who had given out along with nearly all the members of his staff.... He was too weak to get up but able to direct our awkward ministrations. I aided at setting a cracked shinbone...and from the shattered hand of a young Hessian private two of us sheared away three fingers so far gone from gangrene they looked like rotten bananas; and the soldier...made little whimpering sounds, little mewing sounds, like a complaining sick kitten.[10]

In his lifting of the wounded soldiers Cobb suffered an umbilical hernia which was to cause him difficulties later.

The atrocity telegram had been sent through German military communications; the American consul at Aix-la-Chapelle made it possible for Cobb to send articles to Lorimer through diplomatic channels. After a few weeks of inspecting German military

*Saturday Evening Post* correspondent Irvin S. Cobb.
Photo reprinted by permission of Louisville Courier Journal and Times

operations the reporters wanted to move on to England and then to head back for the United States. Prudence suggested that they not tell their German hosts of their plans to stop in an enemy country, so they announced their departure for Vaals in the Netherlands, a port from which one could reach either London or New York. With great courtesy the Germans wished them good-bye; one major even requested that they take a letter back to the United States. Imagining a love note, Cobb agreed, only to find himself entrusted with a fat packet addressed to a German attache named von Papen which almost certainly contained top secret material. Cobb kept his word and delivered it, even though during his stay in London the presence of the German packet in his hotel room seemed more dangerous than a time bomb. On October 14 the New York *Times* carried the story that Cobb had arrived in Vaals, Holland, safely out of German territory. On Oct. 17 it carried an article in which Cobb explained that the atrocity telegram was sincere; that he and his party had seen no German actions that were not accepted wartime behavior.

While in London Cobb was offered the opportunity to talk with Lord Kitchener, the head of the British War Office. It was the only interview Kitchener granted a reporter during the entire war. Much of the official British paranoia about journalists originated with Kitchener; he hated reporters and felt that the British cause would be best served if no mention of the war were made in newspapers beyond the terse, occasionally misleading bulletins issued by the War Office. There was an unwritten stipulation that Kitchener himself was never to be quoted in the press, but no one thought to inform Cobb. Kitchener probably invited Cobb because he wanted to find out what Cobb knew about the German Army; perhaps it never occurred to him that Cobb might write about their meeting.

At any rate Kitchener was extremely candid, much more so than Cobb, who was still trying to obey Wilson's strictures about neutrality. Kitchener said the war would probably last three years—and most experts were predicting it would be over in a few months. He expressed disdain for trench warfare and insisted the war would be won in other ways. He remarked at great length on the stupid, cruel and uncivilized nature of the German people in general and certain German officers in particular. Cobb was stunned to have such volatile material thrown at him and not at all sure what to do with it. He had earlier been invited to lunch at the home of Lord Northcliffe, the British newspaper magnate, and Northcliffe had helped arrange the meeting with Kitchener. Afterwards Cobb asked him if it would be proper to write about the conversation and Northcliffe assured him that it would. Cobb did omit some of the malicious remarks Kitchener had made about the Germans because he feared German retaliation against the British soldiers if they were printed. Otherwise he wrote up the conversation as he remembered it. It was published in the *Post* on December 5—several weeks after Cobb's return to New York—and excerpts were immediately reprinted in the British newspapers.

Kitchener was incensed. He immediately had a bulletin released that the remarks attributed to him were fabrications and that, although he had once met Cobb briefly, there had been no such interview. The denial made the story even more newsworthy and newspapers all over the world printed extracts from Cobb's article, the Kitchener accusation and editorials defending the position of one or the other. Lord Northcliffe not only wrote Cobb a letter deploring Kitchener's reaction but used a public defense of Cobb to make a plea for freedom of information on many aspects of the war.[11] Kitchener only lived a few more months; after his death British newspapers were gradually given more information about the war.

## Notes

[1]Emmet Crozier, *American Reporters on the Western Front, 1914-1918* (New York: Oxford U. Press, 1959), pp. 17-18.

[2]Irvin S. Cobb, *Paths of Glory* (New York: G.H. Doran Company, 1915), p. 31.

[3]Paths of Glory, pp. 49-51.

[4]Paths of Glory, p. 261.

[5]Irvin S. Cobb, *Here Comes the Bride* (New York: G.H. Doran Company, 1925), pp. 104-109.

[6]Philip Knightley, *The First Casualty: From the Crimean War to Vietnam: The War Correspondent as Hero, Propagandist and Myth Maker* (New York: Harcourt, Brace, Jovanowich, 1975), p. 127.

[7]Crozier, pp. 50-53.

[8]Crozier, p. 42.

[9]Paths of Glory, pp. 292-293.

[10]Irvin S. Cobb, *Exit Laughing,* pp. 303-304.

[11]The letter is in the Brody Collection.

## Chapter Fourteen

Cobb's ship landed in New York on November 1, 1914, and he was immediately besieged by reporters who once more asked about the German atrocity rumors. Cobb was uncomfortable about the pro-German role into which he had suddenly been cast; as he explained in the article "Europe's Rag Doll" which appeared in *The Saturday Evening Post* on January 9, to him the destruction of Belgium was in itself an atrocity and strict military discipline did not insure that wars could be fought without human suffering. He took as the emblem of Belgium a torn, besplattered rag doll that he saw trodden under German boots on the muddy streets of a Belgian village. Malicious cruelty was not the threat, but the cold efficiency of modern warfare that could destroy more thoroughly than wanton hatred ever could. Spreading this message became Irvin Cobb's personal mission.

Cobb was given ample opportunity. Four articles on his war experiences appeared in the *Post* in December, three more in January, alternating with short stories. Doran was so anxious to get *Paths of Glory* into print that he did not wait to include the last two *Post* articles. The book came out in early February; a slightly edited version entitled *The Red Glutton* was published at the same time in London.[1] Neither contained the details of the Kitchener interview. The two books were well received by both the critics and the public. The *Journal and Tribune* reacted this way:

> There is scarcely an American who does not know of the part Irvin Cobb played in the early days of the war in following the German Army. . . the book cannot fail to increase his nationwide popularity. . . Cobb proves incontrovertibly that war is the most dreadful calamity that can befall a nation, without one word of preaching of the benefits of peace. . . . [He is] a man of genius. . . .[2]

The Manchester *Guardian* wrote of *The Red Glutton* on March 28:

> ...he will bring home to every reader the deadly realities of war and we English whose lot is to stay at home ought to thank him for helping us to visualize what our brave champions are enduring at the front.[3]

Cobb's war experiences strengthened his earlier attitudes about the capabilities of women. The New York *Tribune* on January 2, 1915, published a four column article entitled "Cobb a Suffragist." In it he stated that the women he had seen engaged in essential, exhausting work in Europe (perhaps he was thinking specifically of the nurses at the stations and field hospitals) had convinced him that women deserved the vote and an equal place in society.

> We have found that women are of use in the world aside from their being mothers and we have learned that the average woman is just as intelligent as the average man, possibly a little more intelligent.... If through their taking part in the government, women adjust wages so that they receive equal pay with men for equal work, this one thing alone would compensate amply any mistakes that might be made.

Print was not the only medium available to Cobb for spreading his views about the war. Soon after his return organizations began petitioning him to appear before them as guest and chief speaker. This was a new avenue for Cobb; he had frequently served as master of ceremonies or after-dinner speaker at banquets given by his various clubs, but on those occasions his remarks were expected to be light entertainment. In May of 1914 he had made his first serious speech, on advertising, before the National Newspaper Conference. Now he was asked to do something quite different: to explain the war and its effects to those who did not share his first-hand experience.

His appearances on the New York banquet scene that November and December of 1914 were extremely successful. So many guests wanted to hear his first speech, at a banquet given in his honor by the Twilight Club on November 23, that standing room tickets were issued when the banquet tickets were exhausted. "Cobb Tells Twilight Club of War Horrors" read the headline in the New York *Times* the next day. He continued to be honored and to make speeches about the plight of non-combatants and about the destruction of Belgium. Always the listeners were moved by his speeches, which contained some touches of humor but which were completely serious in their purpose. The most impressive banquet was the last one, give on December 13 by the Greenroom Club, a theatrical organization similar to the Lambs' and the Friars'. Because of the impact he made on his audience that night he was approached by two well-known Broadway managers and producers, the brothers Edgar and Archie Selwyn, to make a lecture tour telling of his war experiences. Cobb claims that he met the offer by insisting,

> "But I don't know anything about lecturing!"
> "And we," he retorted, "don't know a thing in the world about handling a lecturer, so it's as fair for one as it is for the other."

In spite of his protests, Cobb soon found himself signed up for a ten week tour in early 1915 that would cover much of the eastern United States.[4]

Although his relaxed manner and ready wit seldom betrayed it, Cobb was always nervous about speaking in public, even at a banquet attended mainly by his friends. The prospect of speaking not from a head table but from a podium to an audience that might include several thousand was frightening. He was quite insecure about his speech-making ability and even considered taking elocution lessons, although the Selwyns very sensibly insisted they were unnecessary. Cobb's story telling abilities needed no training, and essentially what he wanted to do was to tell a story, not to make a fiery speech. He did not use notes but talked directly to his audiences and they responded with warmth and enthusiasm.

But the opening speech of the lecture tour, made before a record crowd in New York City, was an agonizing experience. Cobb later wrote a humorous essay about his lecture tour entitled "Unaccustomed As I Am." He describes his debut this way:

> ...when the curtain rolled up before an assemblage of hardy adventurers who had gathered in out of the night, I was crouched back behind the protecting shadows of the proscenium arch. And I was perfectly calm and collected, except that I had already swallowed nine miles of Adam's apples and was still swallowing them at the rate of thirty or forty a minute.... But somehow I lived through it.[5]

Laura, who was in the audience, was almost as nervous as Cobb. Their daughter writes:

> I will never forget the little horrified cry that my mother gave from her box...the first night that he spoke, when a woman sitting very close to the platform suddenly keeled over in a faint. Laura was sorry for the woman; she was also in mortal terror that this interruption might throw Dad off so badly that he would be unable to collect this thoughts or his audience, knowing as she did just how fragile and uncertain was his poise. When he filled a glass of water from the pitcher provided for him

> on the rostum and signaled an usher to come up to him and get it and then waited, seemingly quite at his ease, without speaking until he saw that the woman had regained consciousness and was all right and then went ahead exactly as though nothing had happened to put him off his stride (only now of course his hearers were deeply in sympathy with him perhaps not knowing quite why, but liking him tremendously), I heard Laura let the air out of her lungs with a gasp, like someone who has been a long time under water.[6]

After the New York opening the tour went north into the New England states, then down into the Middle Atlantic and Southern states, then into the Midwest. The crowds were enormous; Cobb claims the tour made more money than any road show of the period except the Ziegfeld Follies. Americans perhaps would have been eager to hear any eyewitness of the war, but Cobb's national reputation and the praise his lectures were getting increased the size of his audiences even more. One of his largest receptions was at the McCauley Theater in Louisville, where he appeared on February 17. The account of his speech in the *Courier-Journal* was typical:

> His graphic story of the horrors of modern warfare, softened though it was by his irrepressible humor, made a profound impression on his audience and at times, when he described the misery of the unfortunate Belgians, some of his hearers were moved to tears.[7]

But Cobb's appearances were not all in city theaters; in fact, he claims to have lectured in "halls, skating rinks, opera houses, academies, armories, concert places, converted gymnasiums, auditoriums, coliseums—we played nearly everything except vacant lots and circus tents." They sold out in every town and thousands of disappointed ticket seekers were turned away.

The tour ended in Paducah, where Cobb arrived on April 12 to give his final lecture, to attend a banquet in his honor and to visit his mother and sister for a few days.[8] To Paducah Cobb was a combination of hero, mascot and guardian angel. Not only was he a famous native son who had made Paducah famous too, but on each return he remembered names and exchanged stories and seemed genuinely glad to be "back home" again. No Paducahan ever felt uneasy about stopping Cobb on the street, inviting him to supper, or asking him for a favor, and wherever he went in his hometown he was surrounded by an adoring crowd.

When Cobb left Europe in late October he planned to stay in the United States only a few months before returning. When the lecture tour was arranged, his return was postponed until May of 1915, but during the tour he frequently referred to his coming departure for the war front. After Cobb's stage fright subsided somewhat the lecture tour was a great pleasure to him; in fact from that point on in his life audiences became increasingly important to him. Elisabeth Cobb explains, "They brought him to life, or to it gave an accentuation and clarity that was lost for him without their aid. They excited him as nothing else did."[9] So it is possible that on the tour Cobb really believed that he was physically capable of more European adventures. But when Cobb left Paducah for New York in mid-April he was totally exhausted. Three months of living on bad food and close escapes in Europe followed by three months of one night stands on the lecture trail could break any man, and Cobb was an overweight, normally sedentary thirty-eight-year-old suffering from an unattended hernia. It is not clear just when the decision was made to postpone his return indefinitely; one complication was the banquet being planned by his friends in New York as a farewell gesture. The newspaper accounts of this dinner, which took place on April 25, refer to Cobb's imminent return to the battlefront, but it is almost certain that Cobb had privately changed his plans by that time. He entered the hospital for a hernia operation on May 1.[10]

The April 25 dinner was no ordinary honor. Instigated by some of Cobb's reporter friends, it was planned as the "biggest banquet ever given a writing man." Frank I. Cobb, who presided as toastmaster, explained that it was being given "to honor a reporter who measured up to the full responsibilities and opportunities of the occupation."[11] The committee who planned the dinner reads like a list of New York journalism and entertainment celebrities of the time. Herbert Bayard Swope was chairman and Frank Ward O'Malley, secretary. The committee of one hundred and thirteen included George M. Cohan, Grantland Rice, Frank Case, George H. Doran, Bob Davis, Charles Chapin, Tommy Dieuaide, George S. Kaufman, G. L. Lorimer, Edgar and Archie Selwyn, John McCutcheon, Franklin P. Adams, Douglas Fairbanks, Sr., Irving Berlin, James Montgomery Flagg and Roi Cooper Megrue.[12] The banquet was held at the Waldorf-Astoria and six hundred and sixty nine guests attended. According to established custom, the dinner guests were all male, but ladies were invited to sit in the balconies to listen to the speeches and other entertainment that followed the meal. In Cobb's family party were his wife, his sister Manie and his daughter, Laura's sister, Dorothy Dix, Margaret Ilington (an actress who was married to Major Eddie Bowes) and Mrs. George Doran. Among the other ladies present were Mrs. Frank Case, Mrs. Douglas Fairbanks, Mary Pickford and Hedda Hopper.[13]

The menu, labelled "Cobb's Bill of Fare," contained items both exotic and homey: crabmeat cocktail, creole gumbo, roasted filet, squab, corn bread and biscuits. The salad course was hearts of lettuce, Paducah, and the dessert, Savannah au rhum. The entertainment was even more unrestrained than the menu.

It began with a staged disturbance at the rear of the hall, from which a bill poster emerged to put up a notice announcing, "Town Hall Tonight! Irvin Cobb is Throwing the Bull!" Then the "Europe Revised Orchestra" that had played during the meal was replaced by an ensemble of Negro musicians, some of them from Paducah, that played and sang "My Old Kentucky Home."

Some of the early speakers on the program, such as George McAnemy, representing the current governor of New York, Martyn H. Glynn, a past governor, and Job Hedges, a political writer, delivered earnest assessments of Cobb's greatness, but most of the eight speakers strove to be humorous. Judge Hal Corbett told Kentucky stories and DeWolfe Hopper was encouraged to recite "Casey at the Bat," a perennial banquet performance. Franklin P. Adams read a message from Ring Lardner which included the following:

> You ast me I should write some thing about Irvin R. Cobb. Well frank I don't know nothing a bout him except he likes tuxedo tobacco and only met him oncet and that was under the grand stand up to the polo grds dureing the 1911 world serious and all of we base ball reporters humorist and evry body was down under the grand stand geting a sand witch and Bozeman Bulgar or 1 of them other bums says Mr. lardner shake hands with Mr. Cobb and I started to reach out my hand but I seen a fride egg sand witch in his hand. . . so I pertendit like my hand was hurt.[14]

Following the speeches was an unprecedented event; the lights were dimmed for the showing of a motion picture made for the occasion: *From Paducah to Prosperity or the Life of Irvin S. Cobb.* Several of Cobb's theatrical acquaintances were involved in the infant motion picture industry. In the early summer of 1914 Cobb had been filmed in conversation with the actress Norma Phillips, and the scene appeared in a Vitagraph short.[15] He had published a facetious article about the experience, entitled "How to Act in the Movies," in July of 1914. For the banquet the Vitagraph Company honored Cobb with a comic version of his biography written by Paul West and featuring a cast of over two hundred.[16]

Following the motion picture James Montgomery Flagg took the floor to present Cobb with a portrait in oils that he had painted. Finally Cobb stood up to receive the portrait and to thank his benefactors. He began by saying:

> I am proud of the fact that I have got so many friends, that so many of them are here tonight and that so many of them have every appearance of owning their own dress suits.

Each guest at the banquet was given a volume published by Doran entitled *Irvin Cobb: His Book*, which contained tributes and drawings by many of Cobb's friends. Two of the most interesting contributions are those by Arnold Bennett and Sinclair Lewis. Bennett cabled his tribute from London:

> Monumental on a boot cleaning stand, he is equally interested in cigars and in assassinations and he likes to wear his thinnest clothes in winter. His stories are always reliable, even when they deal with the British War Office. After annexing Broadway he took Belgium and his book thereon is history. He sees straight and writes straight and I am his friend and his fan.[17]

Unlike Arnold Bennett's, Sinclair Lewis' name was probably familiar to only a few of the recipients of *Irvin Cobb: His Book* in 1915. Lewis had published only one novel then, the unsuccessful *Our Mr. Wrenn*. He was acquainted with Cobb because in the summer of 1914 G.H. Doran had hired Lewis as editorial assistant and advertising manager. In that capacity Lewis wrote promotional material for Doran authors. Lewis also knew Cobb personally, although their relationship was not too close in April, 1915, because Lewis was so much in awe of the older man's success.[18] The extravagance of Lewis's praise must be viewed in terms of his role as Doran's press agent, but it probably also reflects Lewis's own attitudes at the time because, unlike all the other contributors to the souvenir book, Lewis discusses Cobb's fiction, not his humorous writing or war reporting. Had Lewis merely been puffing the latest Doran publication, he would have talked about *Paths of Glory*. Lewis' tribute includes the following statements:

> Cobb has made Paducah and all the other Paducahs—in Kentucky and Minnesota and California and Vermont—from which the rest of us came, live for us, in fiction which gets us as no foreign tale ever can. He makes one smell the soil—a thing that has been said of him so often that it is a platitude.
> [When "The Escape of Mr. Trimm" was published in the *Post*,] in that story, the dramatic structure of it, the words like sparks from a third rail in a snowstorm, the intensity with which the author saw himself as the chief character of the tale, there was evidenced a new American genius, Lord knows we needed him... where were the writers who could go out on

> the street, really see the folks going by and present them truthfully and interestingly in fiction? With one lone story, Cobb had elected himself as one member of that missing and much needed class of geniuses.... [a list of his titles] is enough to bring thrills to every reader of fiction.

It is interesting to see Lewis in 1915 praising Cobb for some of the same qualities that were praised in Lewis' *Main Street,* published in 1920. There is also an interesting passage in which Lewis uses rather xenophobic language to praise Cobb's national appeal:

> "Words and Music" might be used as a test for the Americanism of anybody. It's a seditious, Confederate Southern story, but anybody, Yank or Southerner, who doesn't thrill to it, doesn't feel all the old traditions of the real country when he reads it, is a fake-American, a person of hyphenation.

This rather heavy-handed judgment of Cobb's detractors (one thinks immediately of Lewis' later friend H. L. Mencken) is in jarring contrast to Lewis' final assessment of Cobb's behavior toward others:

> [Cobb] is one of the few big newspaper men in whose record there is not a single black spot, one single case of meanness of pettiness or failure in spirit.[19]

Shortly after the banquet Lewis managed to sell some of his short stories to *The Saturday Evening Post* and to publish another novel. On the strength of that success he quit Doran on December 3, 1915, and left for an extended trip to Florida. Just after Christmas he stopped off in Savannah to visit Cobb, who was staying with his in-laws. Now that they were on a more equal footing as *Post* writers the diffident Lewis was more at ease in Cobb's company. They kept in touch through Doran, who forgave Lewis his flight and became one of the chief promoters of *Main Street.*[20]

## Notes

[1]Irvin S. Cobb, *The Red Glutton* (London: Hodder and Stoughton), 1915.
[2]Feb. 21, 1915; clipping, Brody collection.
[3]March 27, 1915; clipping, Brody collection.
[4]Cobb, *Prose and Cons,* p. 263.
[5]1Cobb, *Prose and Cons,* p. 268.
[6]E. Cobb, *Wayward Parent,* p. 155.
[7]February 18, 1915; clipping in Louisville Free Public Library.
[8]Paducah *Evening Sun,* April 16, 1915.

[9]E. Cobb, *Wayward Parent,* p. 156.

[10]Letter, Irvin S. Cobb to John Wilson Townsend, May 27, 1915, Crabbe Library, Eastern Kentucky University.

[11]Neuman, *Cobb* (1934), p. 232.

[12]The committee is listed on the dinner program preserved at the Paducah Public Library.

[13]Louisville *Post,* April 28, 1915; clipping at Louisville Free Public Library.

[14]dinner program, Paducah Public Library.

[15]Townsend, *Concerning Cobb,* p. 106.

[16]New York *Times* (July 5, 1915), VII, 5, 3.

[17]*Irvin Cobb: His Book,* n.p.n. Paducah Public Library.

[18]Mark Schorer, *Sinclair Lewis: An American Life* (New York: McGraw-Hill Book Co., Inc., 1961), p. 216.

[19]*Irvin Cobb: His Book.*

[20]Schorer, pp. 229-230.

## Chapter Fifteen

Cobb's lifetime best-seller was *Speaking of Operations,* a wry account of his hernia operation in May of 1915. It appeared in *The Saturday Evening Post* that November and was brought out as a slender volume by Doran almost immediately. The first year it sold over a hundred thousand copies; it remained in print for years and was popular as a gift book for those entering the hospital. By the time of Cobb's death over a million copies in various editions and collections had been sold and the book had been translated into eight languages and Braille.[1]

The appeal of *Speaking of Operations* was the humorous treatment of what had been for Cobb a very serious matter. As in his war reporting, Cobb was able to look back on a dangerous and very painful experience and see the ridiculous aspects of his situation. In many ways the operation was more difficult for Cobb than his war adventures had been; in Europe Cobb found himself capable of enduring more than he had thought, but the operation that he had expected to recover from in a few days' time prostrated him for almost two months. Four days after the operation his condition was still listed as serious and he was denied visitors and books; twelve days later he wrote a friend, Harry Miner, "Your letter was one of the bright spots in a dark and dismal week."[2] By late June Cobb had recovered sufficiently to go to Atlantic City to recuperate some more. By accident or design Dr. Stanley Rinehart was also in Atlantic City, recovering from an appendectomy. The men of course swapped stories about the indignities suffered during their hospital stays and Mary Roberts Rinehart insisted that *Speaking of Operations* was the transcription of Cobb's part in these conversations.[3]

At the end of the summer, when Cobb's strength had returned and he could once again, in his words, "pass a display of adhesive tape in a drug store window without flinching," he was ready to put those experiences on paper.[4] Norris Yates in his *The American Humorist: Conscience of the Twentieth Century* sees the book as an early landmark in the humor of this century: the first full-blown example of what he calls the humor of the "Little Man." Only one earlier essay, written by Stephen Leacock in 1910, had attempted to find humor in modern medicine; Cobb pioneered the comic portrait of the patient as victim, trying desperately—and unsuccessfully—to retain his sense of importance and well-being while being treated as a case:[5]

> About eight o'clock I strolled in [the hospital where the operation would take place] very jauntily. In my mind I had the whole program mapped out. I would stay at the hospital for, say, two days following the operation—or, at most, three. Then I must be up and away. I had a good deal of work to do and a number of people to see on important business, and I could not really afford to waste more than a week-end on the staff of St. Germicide's. After Monday they must look to their own devices for social entertainment. That was my idea. Now when I look back on it I laugh but it is a hollow laugh and there is no real merriment in it.
>
> Indeed, almost from the moment of my entrance little things began to come up that were calculated to have a depressing effect on one's spirits. Downstairs a serious-looking lady met me and entered in a book a number of salient facts regarding my personality which the previous investigators had somehow overlooked. There is a lot of bookkeeping about an operation. This detail attended to, a young man, dressed in white garments and wearing an expression that stamped him as one who had suffered a recent deep bereavement, came and relieved me of my hand bag and escorted me upstairs.
>
> As we passed through the upper corridors I had my first introduction to the hospital smell, which is a smell compounded of iodoform, either, gruel and something boiling. All hospitals have it, I understand. In time you get used to it, but you never really care for it.
>
> The young man led me into a small room tastefully decorated with four walls, a floor, a ceiling, a window sill and a window, a door and a doorsill and a bed and a chair. He told me to go to bed. I did not want to go to bed—it was not my regular bedtime—but he made a point of it and I judged it was according to regulations; so I undressed and put on my night clothes and crawled in. He left me, taking my other clothes and my shoes with him, but I was not allowed to get lonely.
>
> A little later a ward surgeon appeared to put a few inquiries of a pointed and personal nature. He particularly desired to know what my trouble was. I explained to him that I couldn't tell him—he would have to see Doctor X or Doctor Z; they probably knew, but were keeping it a secret between themselves.
>
> The answer apparently satisfied him, because immediately after that he made me sign a paper in which I assumed all responsibility for what was to take place the next morning.
>
> This did not seem exactly fair. As I pointed out to him, it was the surgeon's affair, not mine; and if the surgeon made a mistake the joke would be on him and not on me, because in that case I would not be here anyhow. But I signed, as requested, on the dotted line and he departed.
>
> After that, at intervals, the chief house surgeon dropped in, without knocking and the head nurse came and an interne or so and a ward nurse and the special nurse who was to have direct charge of me. It dawned on

me that I was not having any more privacy in that hospital than a goldfish.[6]

The persona that appears here, like its forerunners in *Cobb's Anatomy* and *Cobb's Bill of Fare*, is a new and important voice in American humor, a character who is "not just an object of sympathetic laughter, but a norm of common sense and a defender of human dignity as represented by his own, however ridiculous." Soon Cobb was joined as a producer of this new type of humor by Robert Benchley and A. A. Milne; Charlie Chaplin's Little Tramp, James Thurber's Walter Mitty, and even the comic strip characters Casper Milquetoast and Dagwood Bumstead are later examples of this besieged and bemused Little Man.[7]

If the impetus for this type of humor was the growth of technology in the early twentieth century which gave the Little Man his feeling of having lost control over his own life and person, it became popular because readers could identify with the Little Man's struggles. The universality of his situation is described in this analysis by Thomas Masson, the editor of the humor magazine *Life:*

*Speaking of Operations* is funny because, in reality—although it may seem quite the opposite—it is impersonal. I remember when it first came out in *The Saturday Evening Post.* A number of people spoke to me about it. "Have you seen that thing of Irvin Cobb's? It's immense." And so on. You see, they were all taking it to themselves. They thought it had happened to them. And that, I take it, is one of the tests of real humor.[8]

If most of the summer of 1915 was lost to Cobb, he made up for it the rest of that year; in fact, he was incredibly busy until his return to the war front in December of 1917. One of his major interests during this time was drama. Cobb chose Atlantic City for his rest cure because a play, Bayard Veiller's *Back Home,* was trying out there before opening in Boston and New York.

Although several bibliographies list Cobb as a collaborator with Veiller on this play, probably the largest part of Cobb's contribution was the original stories on which the play was based. (For one thing, it is difficult to imagine when in the months preceding the play's production Cobb could have found time to do much playwriting.) The most important source of the play's action is Cobb's first Judge Priest tale, "Words and Music," and the trial scene from that story is reproduced quite faithfully in Act III. Some features of other stories are included also, the most important of which is probably Judge Priest's bodyservant, Jeff Poindexter, who does not appear in "Words and Music" but who became increasingly more important as the series continued. In *Back Home* John W. Cope played Judge Priest and Willis P. Sweatman played Jeff.[9]

The play opened in Boston in October of 1915 to what a friend of Cobb's described as an "enthusiastic" reception; the reaction was colder when the play opened in New York that November. A review in a New York newspaper panned the show and then continued, "Cobb's speech on the opening night was a huge hit, however, and there is a possibility that it will be sent on tour instead of the play."[10] This remark was presumably ironic, but the Selwyns, who were producers of the show, did approach Cobb with the suggestion that he act in the play. Cobb wrote his Kentucky friend John Wilson Townsend four years later that he "declined a chance to play the part of Judge Priest in *Back Home* at a salary which very few actors in the world were then receiving.... But I'm no actor and I know it."[11] *Back Home* was not the only play produced in 1915 in which Cobb had a hand; *Guilty as Charged,* a one-act play which Cobb and Harry Burke had written together a year or so earlier, was also presented that year.

Cobb's most ambitious—and ultimately most discouraging—attempt at drama came in 1916. Roi Cooper Megrue, a magazine writer who had already written the successful plays *Under Cover* and *It Pays to Advertise,* suggested that they collaborate on a drama that would deal with prison abuses and incorporate some of the ideas for prison reform that Thomas Mott Osbourne, the Warden of Sing Sing, was advocating. The play went through many rewrites; by the time it opened in New York in October of 1916 it was called *Under Sentence* and traced the career of a Wall Street financier, convicted of illegal money manipulations, who as a convict at Sing Sing set out to turn that prison into a paying business.[18] The play was given an impressive buildup, with wide newspaper and magazine coverage. *Hearst Magazine* featured a spread with pictures of the cast, including the young unknown, Edward G. Robinson, who played a convict named Fagan.[12] But in spite of numerous last minute revisions of the faulty third act, the play failed in New York and later in Chicago. Cobb and Megrue later realized that their crusader spirit had ruined the play's financial chances; the moralizing about prison reform in the third act was too heavy for the rip-roaring melodrama of the first two acts.

*Under Sentence* was Cobb's last stage drama, but his involvement with the movie business was growing. Many of the early motion picture entrepreneurs originally had Broadway or

Vaudeville connections and Cobb was acquainted with many of them at the time when movies were a means of making patrons leave vaudeville shows between acts. Cobb may have met Jesse Lasky, Cecil B. DeMille and Lasky's brother-in-law Samuel Goldfish at the Lambs' Club; at any rate it was in that club in late 1913 that the trio formed Jesse Lasky Productions and made arrangements for their first movie, *The Squaw Man*. Most motion pictures at that time were being made in New Jersey, but natural light in New Jersey in the wintertime was unreliable at best and the outside shots with real Western scenery dreamed of by the partners were impossible there. So the production crew, headed by De Mille, headed West. After a brief stop in Arizona, they ended up in Los Angeles, where they rented a barn at the corner of Hollywood and Vine as a makeshift studio.[13] On his lecture tour in 1915 Cobb visited Cecil B. DeMille's barn, where at that time *The Arab* was being filmed. A bit part, "American tourist," had not yet been cast and DeMille convinced Cobb to take the part as a joke between them and the audience.[14] Apparently DeMille felt that Cobb, who received no mention in the credits, would be recognized by a substantial portion of the film's viewers.

Cobb's first venture at writing for the movies came in early December, 1915, when he was the first author to participate in a plot-writing gimmick at Universal Studios. The notion was to make a serial with each installment written by a different "famous author." Cobb, as the writer of the first installment, was allowed to set up the situation and establish the melodramatic tone. It was the first attempt of a studio to emphasize the role of the scenario writer and the first time authors of established reputations agreed to work for the movies. Cobb was excited by the prospects of this new medium and in a syndicated news article he urged other writers to enter the movie field, which he described as "a wide-mouthed mill which is devouring an astonishing amount of dramatic material from all corners of the world every day in the week."[15]

In November of 1916 the first feature length film written entirely by Cobb was filmed at the Vitagraph Studios in New Jersey. Entitled *The Dollar and the Law*, the film began with shots of the actual printing of money and then traced its potential for good and evil through several fictional situations. Cobb frequently dropped in on the New Jersey studios, especially when he was involved in a project underway. In a novel Cobb wrote in 1922, *J. Poindexter, Colored,* he takes Judge Priest's servant to New York. Jeff's visit to the New Jersey studios gives Cobb the chance to describe the colorful, bustling world of movie-making. He describes the interesting mixture of technicians and actors, all lorded over by the director wearing the puttees and riding breeches so necessary to Cecil B. DeMille when he had made films in the cactus and rattlesnake-ridden desert, but hardly appropriate in New Jersey.

By early 1917 Samuel Goldfish had broken with Lasky and entered into a partnership with Cobb's friends and occasional agents and producers, Archie and Edgar Selwyn. They combined their names to create the name Goldwyn Pictures Corporation, a coinage that Goldfish took as his own last name a year or so later, much to the Selwyns' disgust. The Goldwyn company signed up a beautiful stage actress, Maxine Elliott, and hired Cobb and Roi Cooper Megrue to write a scenario for her that would be worthy of the first-class production they planned. The sets were designed by a well-known portrait painter and the most expensive director available was hired. The movie was a failure, however, both artistically and financially, for reasons beyond the control of the authors. First, Arthur Hopkins, one of the Goldwyn partners and the producer of *The Fighting Odds*, decided to make the movie without subtitles. His notion that the audience could follow the story without any explanation did not prove to be the case, and after a preview showing for a group of bewildered theater owners, some crude and frequently inappropriate subtitles, apparently not the work of Cobb and Megrue, were hastily inserted. Also, Maxine Elliott's acting, so compelling on the stage, proved unsuitable and even comic on film. These problems might not have been so devastating, however, had not the film been released in April of 1917, just as the United States entered the war.[16]

Cobb's writing output in other areas was also large in this period between his two trips to the warfront. He covered several important events—Billy Sunday's New York evangelistic campaign, the 1916 political conventions, the 1917 World Series—for various New York newspapers and their syndicates. Billy Sunday's attempt to convert New York in 1917 brought out Cobb's most flamboyant style:

> This man, Billy Sunday, for action, is the Charlie Chaplin of the pulpit. He is the Untired Business Man of theology. He is the boundin' bloomin', Fuzzy-Wuzzy who'll break the Manhattan crust. He is the Carrie Nation of his sex. . . .[17]

Billy Sunday's campaign created quite a stir, but it succeeded more as drama than as a call to repentance. As Cobb recalled later,

> You remember, the Rev. Sunday once came to New York with the intention of driving the devil off the island. At this time the betting was about even. Some had their money on Sunday to win, they were the ones who knew Sunday. Others had their money down on the devil, these being the persons who knew about New York.[18]

The Republican Convention, in Chicago, and the Democratic Convention, in St. Louis, were only a week apart in early June of 1916. Cobb's articles were the free-wheeling feature stories expected of him, with more attention to the pageantry and human insights than to the politics. He made no secret of his preference for President Woodrow Wilson, the Democratic nominee, over Justice Charles Evans Hughes, the Republican nominee. Even at a dinner at the New York Press Club—where partisan remarks were supposedly out of bounds—Cobb managed to indicate his aversion to the bearded Hughes by describing the better candidate as a "kind of a smooth-faced man."

Cobb had never before become involved in national politics in spite of his ingrained Democratic loyalty, but Wilson's determination to keep the United States out of the European war echoed his own convictions and Cobb helped him all he could. The men met, briefly, for the first time at the St. Louis convention and Cobb received a stiff note of thanks on White House stationery that June 23 for his "attitude" in St. Louis.[19] Cobb's offer to adapt his speech on the horrors of war as a campaign speech for Wilson was gratefully accepted, and Cobb spent three weeks in October making one-night stands at political rallies in New England and upstate New York at his own expense. This effort brought a much warmer note of thanks, this time signed "The smooth-faced man."

Cobb was called upon to make other speeches during these years, not all of them on the subject of the war. On May 17, 1916, he convulsed a convention of old soldiers at the Confederate Reunion in Birmingham. In January of 1917 before the American Irish Historical Society he delivered a fanciful speech, "The Lost Tribes of the Irish in the South," in which he insisted that all sorts of unlikely Southern customs and traditions were Irish.[20]

Cobb's *Saturday Evening Post* work was as extensive as ever during this period. From the time of his recovery in August of 1915 through December of 1917 he published at least two stories or articles in the *Post* every month and sometimes three. He also published occasionally in other magazines and wrote introductions for *Walt Mason: His Book* and Richard Harding Davis' *Ranson's Folly*.[21]

Doran continued to bring out collections of Cobb's magazine work. *Old Judge Priest,* which includes nine Paducah stories, and *Local Color,* whose frequently grim stories have mostly New York settings, came out in 1916, as did *Fibble, D. D.*, a volume containing three frothy sketches about an incredibly naive clergyman, the Reverend Roscoe Titmarsh Fibble. In 1917 Doran brought out *Speaking of Prussians,* a further consideration of Cobb's first trip to the war and *Those Times and These,* a mixed collection of short stories, five about Judge Priest and five with other settings and more recent times. Cobb almost always included a dedication in his books, honoring a friend or a member of his family. In *Those Times and These* the dedication reads:

> To the memory of Mandy Martin, whose soul was as white as her skin was black and who for forty-two years, until her death, was a loyal friend and servant of my people.

In May of 1917 *American Magazine* published a retrospective article by Cobb, "Looking Both Ways from Forty," in which he talks about his personal reactions to turning forty and his attitudes toward the changes in the country in his lifetime. The status of Cobb's reputation at the time is perhaps indicated by the caption of a full page portrait of Cobb in the same issue:

> "This Man is a National Institution"
>
> One of America's chief assets is Irvin S. Cobb. More people read him than any other contemporary writer—to be both amused and informed. He may not be the funniest writer in America, but if he isn't, who is? He may not be the greatest catch-as-catch-can reporter, but who could keep the title from him?
>
> He skimmed the cream off the European War in the first three months and has made nearly everything that has been written since seem dull and trite; and he lectures on the war as vividly and picturesquely as he writes. Cobb is only in his fortieth year, so we can look forward to enjoying him for years to come.[22]

## Notes

[1]Betty B. Burkhalter, *A Rhetorical Study of Irvin S. Cobb* (unpubl. thesis, Murray State University, 1967), p. 3; Neuman, *Cobb* (1934), p. 30.

[2]Irvin S. Cobb to Harry Miner, May 13, 1915, New York Public Library.

[3]Rinehart, p. 204.

[4]Irvin S. Cobb, "Speaking of Operations," in *Cobb Cavalcade* (New York: World Publishing Co., 1945), p. 17.

[5]Yates, p. 131.

[6]Cobb, *Cavalcade,* pp. 26-27.

[7]Yates, p. 132.

[8]Masson, p. 93.

[9]Logsdon, p. 21.

[10]unidentified newspaper clipping, Brody collection.

[11]Irvin S. Cobb to John Wilson Townsend, Jan. 7, 1922, Crabbe Library, Eastern Kentucky University.

[12]*Hearst Magazine,* January, 1917.

[13]Arthur Marx, *Goldwyn: A Biography of the Man Behind the Myth* (New York: Ballantine Books, 1976), pp. 42; 50-55.

[14]Cecil B. DeMille, *The Autobiography of Cecil B. DeMille* (Englewood Cliffs, N.J.: Prentice Hall, 1959), p. 136.

[15]Louisville *Post,* December 23, 1915; clipping. Louisville Free Public Library.

[16]Marx, pp. 92-100.

[17]Louisville *Post,* April 14, 1917; clipping, Louisville Free Public Library.

[18]Irvin S. Cobb, *Here Comes the Bride—And So Forth* (New York: George H. Doran Co., 1925), p. 274.

[19]The letter is in the Brody Collection.

[20]The MS of this speech is in The Kentucky Library, Western Kentucky University.

[21]Walt Mason, *Walt Mason: His Book* (New York: Barse and Hopkins, 1917); Richard Harding Davis, *Ransom's Folly* (New York: Charles Scribner's Sons, 1917).

[22]p. 18.

# Chapter Sixteen

In the September 13, 1913, issue of the *Saturday Evening Post* Cobb published a humorous essay "Life Among the Abandoned Farmers," in which he describes the futile attempts of himself and his wife to find an inexpensive, attractive "abandoned farm." Even though becoming "abandoned farmers" was all the rage, he says, finding the appropriate property selling for the reputed "song" turned out to be far more difficult than they had thought. The search for a country estate rather fancifully described in that article continued and in 1916 the Cobbs purchased sixty acres in the northern part of Westchester County near the town of Ossining, New York. Only one third of the land was cleared and that included many fine old trees standing singly or in small groves. The remaining forty acres was virgin forest, including the crest of a small mountain. The property had once been an impressive estate containing a frame residence, a farmer's cottage, a cow barn, a coach house, an ice house and numerous other outbuildings. All of these except the barn had fallen into such an advanced state of decay that they added little to the value of the property. But the chief attraction for the Cobbs was the natural features of the land, as Cobb explains:

> There were dells, glades, steep bluffs and rolling stretches of fallow land; there were seven springs on the place; there was a cloven rift in the hill with a fine little valley at the bottom of it and the first time I clambered up its slope from the bottom I flushed a big cock grouse that went booming through the underbrush with a noise like a burst of baby thunder. That settled it for me. All my life I have been trying to kill a grouse on the wing and here was a target right on the premises. Next day we signed the papers and paid over the binder money. We were landowners.[1]

The estate, which the Cobbs christened Rebel Ridge, had other attractions too: several of their friends also owned country homes in the area. Edgar Selwyn and his wife Margaret Mayo, George Creel,

Major Eddie Bowes and his wife Margaret Illington, the playwright James Forbes and the actor Holbrook Blinn and his wife Ruth Benson were all members of what Cobb in an account of his housebuilding activities called the Westchester County Despair Association. Adelaide and Rupert Hughes soon moved just twelve miles away and the Ben McAlpins and the George Dorans came soon after.

The Cobbs planned to build a new house on the property, but first they fixed up the barn to give them temporary living quarters. Because of the interruptions of the war and the scarcities it produced, they lived in the barn for four years. Their quarters there, however, as their daughter describes them, were quite attractive and comfortable:

> It was amazing what happened to that barn, which to start out with was nothing more than a plain, old, foursquare, upper-New-York-State barn, pushed up against a hillside so that it was two stories high in front and only one behind, which architectural pecularity gave it a certain air of being beleaguered, as though it were fighting with its back against the wall. It had no graces and few virtues except that it had been made originally of strong materials with honest workmanship. But now it received a new rakish roof, a circling of window boxes afroth with pink geraniums, a sassy balcony and in back, after Laura had had a long quiet conference with the earth and was informed by it of its requirements, which is always the way she finds out how to make a garden, the hillside was pushed back a few feet, leveled and paved and planted to make the most delicious little outdoor room imaginable.[2]

The bottom floor of the barn was made into a garage, furnace room, laundry room and servants' quarters; above were the living quarters, including three bedrooms and two baths. Comfortably settled in their barn, the Cobbs began the long process of picking a site for their house and agreeing on plans. In these decisions they had more than enough help from their neighbors, as Cobb makes clear in the humorous essays he wrote about their homebuilding experiences which were collected in the 1920 volume *The Abandoned Farmers.* In the early months of their life as landowners the dream house jumped from one location to another and sprouted and shed sleeping porches, vistas, sun parlors and even whole floors. Finally in early 1917 the plans were completed and the foundations dug, just in time for the American entry into the war. But, Cobb explains:

> Very soon labor was not to be had, or materials either. Take the detail of concrete. Now that the last war is over and the next war not as yet

started, I violate no confidence and betray no trust in stating that one of our chief military secrets had to do with this seemingly harmless product. We were shooting concrete at the Germans.[3]

So the Cobbs did not move into the main house at Rebel Ridge until after the publication of *Abandoned Farmers* in 1920. However frustrating Cobb presents the housebuilding situation in that book, however helpless he claims to be at the hands of nosy neighbors, imperious decorators and his determined wife, his real delight in his situation and in his new home is obvious. Elisabeth Cobb thought that the building of Rebel Ridge was one of the happiest periods in her parents' lives—happier than the years they spent living there.

In those days I used to watch my parents perched on a rock pile in the pouring rain, quite oblivious of wet, weariness, or weather, happily arguing about the proper place for the yet-to-be-broom-closet. Should it go here, or on maturer thought, there? I would be filled with amazement at them, amazement not unmixed with pity.[4]

Cobb also alludes to these sessions of castle building in the rain and Tony Sarg chose to illustrate one for the frontispiece to *Abandoned Farmers*. The bulging Cobb, cigar in mouth, eyes protruding, clutches an umbrella in one hand and points with the other, while his pretty wife, half the size of her husband, sits one step down from him on the unfinished foundation, holding her own umbrella.

Elisabeth Cobb also insists that Cobb's descriptions in *Abandoned Farmers* of his futile attempts to control his wife's extravagance in decorating and of his low-brow contempt for antiques were not an accurate picture of the situation, although it was a pose he maintained in conversation as well as in writing. Actually he had quite a fondness for luxury and joined Laura in her quest for antiques to fill the house. Some of the playful quarrels reproduced in *Abandoned Farmers* are no doubt real, but their outcomes are sometimes misrepresented. In the first essay he describes an early episode in their house search:

Having reached this conclusion I went to bed and slept peacefully—or at least I went to bed and did so as soon as my wife and I had settled one point that came up unexpectedly at this juncture. It related to the smokehouse. I was in favor of turning the smokehouse into a study or workroom for myself. She thought, though, that by knocking the walls out and altering the roof and building a pergola on to it, it would make an ideal summer house in which to serve tea and from which to view the peaceful landscape of afternoons.

We argued this back and forth at some length, each conceding something to the other's views; and finally we decided to knock out the walls and alter the roof and have a summer house with a pergola in connection. It was after we reached this compromise that I slept so peacefully, for now the whole thing was as good as settled. I marveled at not having thought of it sooner.[5]

Actually at Rebel Ridge Cobb turned the old ice house into a study for himself—and there is no record of a summer house with pergola on the grounds.

If anything, Cobb might have wished Laura more elegant and their house more extravagant. She told a reporter many years after his death,

Irvin loved beauty. He wanted it around him in his houses, in the silver and china and lace on his table and in his women. One day I was out gardening and he called for me to come for cocktails. When I appeared in dirty gardening clothes, he told me to go and put on something diaphanous and some expensive perfume and look like something he'd want to have cocktails with. Our Buff was precocious [which worried Irvin], but if someone told him she was pretty, that person would be his friend for life.[6]

In those years in the late teens Buff was in her teens also, and "precocious" and "pretty" are mild words to describe her. Dainty and vivacious like her mother, with her father's wide-spaced dark eyes, Buff soon became the belle of Westchester County and the barn house and later the big house swarmed with young people, as she describes:

Poor Irvin was soon fairly awash in a wave of large, noisy youths, who quite naturally thought him a senile old character to whom it was necessary to be courteous.... I quite agreed with them because I thought that he probably couldn't be much less than ninety years old and though a darling, a fragile one with weird antediluvian notions concerning the necessity of returning home at least twice a week before three in the morning. One had to indulge him, at least one had to pretend to indulge him, to the extent of taking off one's shoes when going upstairs and making the boys keep the drinks parked in the car....

My mother opened the house to my friends, doing for me what her mama and papa had done for her, and the place was always full of them. I can't ever remember sitting down to the table alone, nor hardly remember there ever being many older people among those present....

Laura tells me that once Dad was driven to appealing to her. "Look here," he expostulated. "I have a big house and six servants to run it and sixty acres—and I haven't any place to sit down or any place to go take a walk."

Dad, being no fool, did have his workroom detached from the main house and it seems to me that I only remember him in those days as a dim figure who occasionally emerged onto his little porch to yell something at a gardener and who was usually good for a touch.[7]

By the time Rebel Ridge was completed to the Cobbs' satisfaction in 1921, it was an impressive and beautiful estate. Two articles that year, one in *House and Garden* and one in *The Garden Magazine*, described its spacious layout and effective landscaping and supplied photographs. The house, of brick with sharp gables and several wings, had finally been built on a hill with a view that swept down to the spires of Ossinging and the distant Hudson River. The first view of the house from the drive showed it at the end of a grass alley with hemlocks and spruces on one side and redbuds, dogwoods and azaleas on the other. The alley ended at a walk which led through an arched stone entryway and across several terrace levels to the house. Cobb's study was on the other side, down a path edged with vinca winding one hundred and fifty feet through the trees. The ice house had been remodeled to resemble a miniature hunting lodge and several photographs from the time show Cobb standing on the porch his daughter mentions, wearing the voluminous smocks that he had adopted as working clothes.[8]

As his output makes clear, Cobb worked very hard during those years at Rebel Ridge. Cobb thought through a story for weeks or months before he tried to set it down. Mrs. Cobb explained to a reporter in 1916,

> Mr. Cobb works twenty-four hours a day and is forever living a story or dreaming it. He can be in a crowd without being of it.... I never break in on his thoughts. When he wishes to be silent I know he is working and I wait for him to speak first.... He works at writing as steadily and regularly as if he were a merchant.[9]

Cobb's attitude toward himself, his own writing and literature in general are curiously ambivalent during the teens. He was always willing to give interviews or write articles defining good writing or assessing other writers, but he remained humble about his own work and embarrassed by the praise he received. In 1913 he wrote in the *New York Press,* "These realists, Bennett, Galsworthy and Company, crawl along in a straight line. I'd rather go up the mountains and down the valleys.... I can't recall any examples of genius among present-day writers except Booth Tarkington and Gilbert K. Chesterton. In everyone else its good workmanship polished up."[10] Cobb always disparaged the writers who talked about writing in artistic terms and in the *Sun* in 1916 even criticized Conrad, whom he admired, for writing for other writers, not for the general public. He felt that setting and characterization are important but that they should be implicit in the narrative, not separate from it. He criticized O. Henry because his "characters don't live," calling that writer "a master of parlor tricks."[11] Questions about his own writing, however, frequently caused Cobb to retreat into his "I-am-just-a-reporter" defense. "I have no sense of form about the story I am going to write," he told a reporter from the *Post* in 1916. "Forms are 'bogus' so far as I have any consciousness about them. The story is a narrative told on a typewriter."[12] Cobb's mistrust about his own abilities is perhaps most graphically shown in a remark reprinted that same year. Bob Davis had asked Cobb why his output was so large. Cobb answered, "My boy, the public is going to wake up some day and dismiss me. This is too good to be true. I propose to take it now while they are not looking. It's now or never."[13]

The fact that Cobb's fame and prosperity in no way affected his humility was noted with satisfaction by his friends. Bob Davis, in 1917 in yet another tribute, said of him:

> Unlike most men who have risen from obscurity to a position of high eminence he still holds all his old friends; nor can the army of new ones crowd his cronies away from his fireside.... He is a kind of fat Pollyanna, at peace with all the world.... He wants to split all his happiness fifty-fifty. And he is a great listener to boot, which, in my opinion, is the greatest form of self-sacrifice.[14]

Bob Davis was probably too ready to accept the outer serenity which Cobb seldom shed as a mark of inner peace, but his assessment of Cobb's delightful company is certainly not unique. And his cronies, as Davis calls them, were as important to Cobb as he to them. Most of the friends that Davis would have been likely to include in this category were those who went on fishing or hunting trips with Cobb and the fireside he alludes to was as likely to be in the Maine woods as at Rebel Ridge.

The love of hunting and fishing that Cobb developed as a boy in Paducah never left him, but his early solitary tramps with the gun Dr. Saunders had given him were later replaced by convivial hunting parties. Several of Cobb's hunting companions agree that Cobb's later fondness for hunting and fishing was more a love of the all male company and the whiskey, food and stories they shared than an enthusiasm for the taking of game.[15] After Cobb moved to New York his expeditions became more and more elaborate. He and his hunting or fishing buddies—Bob Davis was the most frequent

Cobb standing on the terrace behind Rebel Ridge.
Photo reprinted by permission of Carol Sutton, Courier Journal and Times

member of his parties—travelled all over the continent in pursuit of the cameraderie of the campfire. During the teens and twenties Cobb shot ducks in the bayous of Louisiana, hunted deer in Texas and moose in Nova Scotia, taught the Maine guides a thing or two about campsite cuisine, fished the upper Mississippi River in Minnesota and returned as often as possible to the Bob White Hunting Lodge in North Carolina.

During the teens Cobb, Damon Runyon, Bozeman Bulgar and several other newspapermen bought a "pot-bellied" motorboat jointly and harbored it at Seaford on Long Island. They fished from it on the Sound in the summer and shot shorebirds from it in the fall, ducks and geese in the winter. Sometimes a sudden freeze would trap them and turn an afternoon excursion into a confinement that on at least one occasion lasted several days. Sharing the cramped quarters with Cobb only increased Damon Runyon's admiration for him, as his biographer attests:

> But when Cobb was along, what would have been a desperate situation turned into a delight. Damon said they would eat, drink and sleep and listen to the warmth of Cobb's voice telling stories. His fund of tale seemed to be endless, a continuity of entertainment, always flowing with imagination and tasteful variety from some infinite source.[16]

Early in the teens Cobb became a member of the Wyandanch Club on Long Island, one of the oldest sporting clubs in the United States. Although its members included millionaires, the club's accomodations honored self-reliance over luxury and members carried their own gear and mixed their own drinks. Even when such modern fripperies as indoor plumbing and electric lights were introduced into the pre-Revolutionary farmhouse that served as the main lodge, the old traditions of candlesticks at bedtime and china washstand sets in the bedrooms were continued. The tone was set by General George Washington Wingate, a courtly veteran of the Union Army who served as its president for decades, until he died in his nineties. In addition to the main lodge, there were individually owned "shooting boxes"—some of them mansions of two or three stories—at Wyandanch, and Cobb, along with such friends and co-members as Bob Davis and Owen Davis, the playwight, frequently joined parties at one or another of these. Cobb and the two Davises (who were not related) were unusual Wyandanch members because of their literary callings. Most Wyandanch members were businessmen and Cobb became acquainted with several captains of industry whom otherwise he might never have met. Two frequent hunting companions, at Wyandanch and later on their own estates, were Thomas J. Watson, founder of IBM, and Coleman DuPont, president of DuPont and later a United States Senator. Cobb later dedicated books to both these men.

Perhaps the closest such friend was Charles R. Flint, twenty-five years older than Cobb, who had made millions in shipping and munitions before they met. Flint had a keen sense of adventure that dominated his business deals and his hunting trips. Life for Flint was a game, one which he almost always won and pomposity and old age were the only things he feared. When he reached sixty he decided to delay the inevitable as long as possible by surrounding himself with younger, fun-loving men like Davis and Cobb. The younger men delighted in his hospitality, his good spirits, his hair-raising tales and his awe-inspiring reputation—the press had labelled him the "Father of the Trusts."

In 1923 Flint published his memoirs, *Memoirs of An Active Life,* to which Cobb wrote the Foreword and in which Cobb figures rather prominently. Flint reprints several pictures made on their hunting and fishing trips, most of them inscribed with flippant comments which probably reflect the tone of their conversations. A picture of Cobb and the two Davises, all dressed in elaborate hunting garb, is captioned, "Literature Let Loose on Long Island," and a picture of Cobb and Bob Davis, hamming, is tagged with the following exchange,

> "Yes, Robert, it was a small mouth, Red Eye Black Bass."
> "How much did he weigh, Irvin?"
> "Seven pounds, four and 3/4 ounces."
> "Any witnesses?"
> "Yes! Otherwise that Black Bass would have weighed 8, 9 or perhaps 10 pounds."[17]

Once Flint, Cobb and Bob Davis caught a six pound bass, stuffed a two pound fish into its stomach and sent it as a present to Theodore Roosevelt, a neighbor of Flint, with a humble note expressing the hope that he would enjoy the eight pound bass. Roosevelt responded with a polite note of thanks, but gave no indication that he was aware of the joke. Still, that was more response than Cobb and DuPont received in 1931 when they sent a box of game to president Hoover in the White House, labelled: "One dozen wild ducks. To be eaten, NOT referred to a Commission." The gift was never acknowledged.

It is interesting that Cobb was not intimidated by the wealth and Eastern establishment credentials of Flint and DuPont, while writers of Eastern background or education such as the Round Table regulars or H. L. Mencken or Scott Fitzgerald could make Cobb so uncomfortable with what he took to be their condescending attitude toward his origins that he soon preferred to avoid their company altogether. Cobb was probably oversensitive to the caustic wit of the Eastern literary set, but his friendships with businessmen and journalists show that he could relax with Easterners when he felt completely welcome. As the worlds of journalism and literature began to grow further apart in the late teens, Cobb found himself with more personal ties to journalism. He had always associated more with newspapermen and theater people than with authors; with a few exceptions, this tendency became even more pronounced after the war. His friendships with Flint, Watson, DuPont and others like them affected his attitudes toward business and government, and although Cobb identified himself with several liberal causes throughout the twenties, he never turned anti-establishment or radical in his philosophy like some other writers of that decade. His first-hand view of the war made him a patriot and further separated him from the literati. Cobb enjoyed success and soaked up praise and he was happy to please those who gave these to him. All of these factors probably were as important in establishing Cobb as a "low-brow" writer by the early twenties as his *Saturday Evening Post* connection and H. L. Mencken's judgments.

## Notes

[1]Cobb, *The Abandoned Farmers,* (George H. Doran, 1920), p. 75.

[2]E. Cobb, *Wayward Parent,* p. 172.

[3]Cobb, *Abandoned Farmers,* pp. 148-149.

[4]E. Cobb, *Wayward Parent,* p. 171.

[5]Cobb, *Abandoned Farmers,* pp. 23-24.

[6]Sutton, *Courier-Journal,* 4-26-64.

[7]E. Cobb, *Wayward Parent,* pp. 166-168.

[8]Clarence Fowler, "The Gardens at Rebel Ridge: Home of Irvin S. Cobb, Westchester, New York," *The Garden Magazine* (December, 1921), pp. 203-204.

[9]Lousville *Post,* Nov. 11, 1916; clipping, Louisville Free Public Library.

[10]New York *Press,* January 26, 1913; 3:1.

[11]New York *Sun,* November 26, 1916, 4:1.

[12]clipping, n.d., Brody collection.

[13]Louisville *Post,* July 22, 1916; clipping, Louisville Free Public Library.

[14]R.H. Davis, "Irvin S. Cobb: A Paducah, Kentucky, Gentleman," *American Magazine* (May, 1917), p. 4.

[15]Weiner, p. 99; Charles Ranlett Flint, *Memories of an Active Life* (New York: G. P. Putnam's Sons, 1923), p. 163.

[16]Weiner, p. 99.

[17]Flint, p. 163.

# Chapter Seventeen

In the months following Wilson's re-election in late 1916, developments in the European war made the neutrality Cobb had urged in that campaign less acceptable for both Wilson and Cobb. Wilson's peace note that December produced no concessions from either the Germans or the Allies. When the Germans resumed unlimited submarine warfare in February, 1917, the United States severed diplomatic ties. A few weeks later the publication of the Zimmerman telegram intensified the already strong anti-German feeling in the United States. As Wilson began to move away from his earlier neutralist position, he found himself in conflict with twelve isolationist senators led by Robert LaFollette of Wisconsin. This opposition became most intense over a bill Wilson requested allowing the arming of U.S. merchant ships against enemy attack. When the bill was defeated, Wilson armed the ships by executive order. On April 2, Wilson called for the declaration of war, which passed Congress on April 6.

Cobb supported Wilson in this course of action. His concern to protect Americans was as strong as ever, but neutrality no longer seemed an adequate protection. He wrote two articles for the *Saturday Evening Post,* published in April and May, 1917, in which he announced his changed viewpoint and urged Americans to support the war. Almost immediately Doran published the two articles in a slender volume called *"Speaking of Prussians—."* With Woodrow Wilson's permission, it was dedicated to him.

In *"Speaking of Prussians—"* Cobb claims only the authority of someone who has seen the European war at firsthand:

> I am in the advantageous position, therefore, of being able to recount as an eyewitness—and, as I hope, an honest one—something of what war means in its effects upon the civilian populace of a country caught unawares and in a measure unprepared; and more than that, what war particularly and especially means when it is waged under the direction of officers trained in the Prussian school.
>
> Having seen these things, I hate war with all my heart.... It is the most obscene, the most hideous, the most malignant—and sometimes

> the most necessary—spectacle, I veritably believe, that ever the eye of mortal man has rested on since the world began, and I do hate it.
>
> But if war has to come—war for the preservation of our national honour and our national integrity; war for the defense of our flag and our people and our soil; war for the preservation of the principles of representative government among the nations of the earth—I would rather that it came now than that it came later.[1]

Cobb urges his position not only with impassioned rhetoric but with memories of specific scenes and situations from his earlier trip, described in a far more partisan fashion than in his earlier articles. He explains the discrepancy this way:

> . . . now I am free to use weapons which I did not feel I had the right to use before that break did come. Before, I was a newspaper reporter, engaged in describing what I saw and heard—not what I suspected and feared. Before I was a neutral citizen of a netural country.
>
> I am not a neutral any more. I am an American! My country has clashed with a foreign power and the enemy of my country is my enemy. . . .[2]

In the second half of the book Cobb discusses the character and philosophical outlook of the German people, again supported by recollections of his earlier trip. He sees them as a race apart, cold-blooded, obedient to their commanders, dedicated to their own superiority among men and in the eyes of God. Cobb reports conversations with the representatives of the German Secret Service who escorted him on his earlier tour behind the German lines to the effect that Germany had earned the right to rule not only Europe but the entire Eastern Hemisphere and to force her superior culture on her new subjects. Although Cobb probably mistook bravado for conviction and inexperience for callousness, his book seems to be a sincere attempt to portray accurately his earlier reaction to the Germans, not to malign them deliberately for propaganda purposes. But Wilson could not have asked for a better piece of propaganda.

In spite of his sense of the necessity of Wilson's position, Cobb in the late spring of 1917 was still sensitive to—and repulsed by—the cruelest irony of war, that the quarrels of old men are resolved by the suffering of young soldiers and innocent civilians. His attempt to extract himself from his dilemma, to keep from being one of those old men sending teenagers off to horrible deaths, was sincere, characteristic and completely futile. Shortly after the first U.S. troops began to cross the Atlantic he tried to enlist. Even as a young, slender man in 1898 he had been rejected for his flat feet and poor lungs, so he knew no ordinary enlistment officer would consider him with twenty extra years and sixty extra pounds. So he decided to go straight to President Wilson and see if a special exception could be made, if perhaps a post could be found for him in Military Intelligence. Wilson turned him down very tactfully, assuring him that he would be much more useful to the war effort as a correspondent for the *Saturday Evening Post.* Cobb quotes him as saying:

> You forget this foolishness and go on back. You can be of some account to your country over there, writing about our effort, our spirit, our boys—most of all about our boys; writing stuff for the mothers and daddies and sisters and wives and daughters to read. That's where I'm telling you to go. No, that's where I am ordering you, as a loyal citizen, to go.[3]

His Paducah sense of duty mollified, Cobb began to make arrangements for his second trip to the war front as a correspondent. He did not leave until January, 1918; in the meantime, he wrote "The Thunders of Silence," a scarcely veiled attack on Senator LaFollette that was published in the *Saturday Evening Post* in February, 1918, and later issued by Doran as a separate volume. The Congressman depicted in the piece, Jason Mallard, is called a "pacificist demagogue." As Cobb describes him,

> He fought against and voted against the breaking off of diplomatic relations with Germany; fought against the draft, fought against the war appropriations, fought against the plans for a bigger navy, the plans for a great army; fought the first Liberty Loan and the second, he fought, in December last, against a declaration of war with Austro-Hungary.[4]

But, in Cobb's fanciful account, Congressman Mallard's influence is destroyed by newspapers reporters. Realizing that Mallard is motivated by "vanity" and "love of notoriety," they make a pact to print no mention of him at all. Mallard becomes so desperate at this vacuum of publicity that he finally commits suicide.

Before Cobb's first trip to the war he had looked upon the experience as a big adventure—or at least that was the impression he tried to give Laura. The dangers of that trip became apparent only after he reached Europe. But both Laura and Cobb knew that this trip was no adventure, that the possibility of his being killed was as great as if he had managed to go as a soldier. Not only would he be vulnerable to German bombs and gunfire on the continent; first he had to cross the submarine-infested Atlantic. The Cobb's travelled from their barn in Ossinging to stay at the Algonquin Hotel the night before Cobb was to sail. Frank Case got up to see them off and Cobb recalled looking back over his shoulder to see Case "blinking and wiping his eyes." Elisabeth Cobb's memory of her father's departure is also grim:

> He sailed away on a bitter cold morning in January and Moie and I went down to the docks to see him off and stood shivering there, though only half from cold, for a long time while his papers were scrutinized and his luggage got aboard. I remember the shock of seeing that his ship was camouflaged and realizing that it was thus strangely striped and stippled because it was going into most perilous places and with my father aboard it.... He made us laugh even then, though, by coming off the ship grinning at the spectacle he made in a life belt. "I sure boil over the top of this thing like a charlotte russe, don't I?" he asked.[5]

Of the convoy of twelve ships in which Cobb crossed the Atlantic, four were sunk by submarines and Cobb's ship, *The Baltic*, was in sight of *The Tuscania* when that ship was torpedoed off the coast of Britain. In accordance with usual wartime practices the passenger lists had not been made public and Cobb's family in New York and Paducah did not know which ship he was on. When he was able to telegraph his wife and his mother of his safe arrival in Britain on February 9, the news made the Louisville *Courier-Journal*. Manie Cobb expressed her relief to the reporter that he had not been on the *Tuscania*. The *Courier-Journal* articles explained that Cobb was on a mission for the *Saturday Evening Post* "and probably the United States government." Cobb's first *Post* article of his trip described the experience of standing on the deck of his speeding ship, watching the receding *Tuscania* founder and sink with two hundred American soldiers on board.[6]

Cobb's second set of war dispatches, published by Doran in 1918 as *The Glory of the Coming,* is similar to the first set in its personal tone and its emphasis on Cobb's experiences and conversations. It differs, as might be expected, in its wholehearted identification with the Allied effort. No longer are the French refugees, who figure as prominently in this account as the French and Belgian homeless did in the earlier one, merely pitiful victims; now Cobb sees courage in their actions and gratitude on their worn faces. While Cobb and his companions of his first trip were anxious to display their civilian clothes in hopes of protection from both sides, now they are proud of the American khaki uniforms they wear. Cobb also claims the uniforms—or more specifically the trenchcoats that covered up their undecorated sleeves—served a practical purpose as well: sentries viewing portly, middle-aged men in such indeterminate but official garb assumed they were officers and waved them on.

Cobb's greatest adventure during the trip was made possible by just such a ruse. In late March he and two other reporters also working out of Paris, Raymond Carroll and Martin Green, decided to go to the battlefront at Noyon where a massive German attack was being received by French and British troops. Although the attitudes of the combatants toward newspaper reporters had relaxed somewhat, there were no provisions for permitting them to view such battles at close hand. Thus Cobb, Green and Carroll were the only American journalists to give eyewitness accounts of the scene. They managed this coup by convincing an American soldier with a Model T Ford whom they fortuitously found in Soissons to drive them to the front. They were careful to drive as close as possible to the ragged line that separated the British troops on the left from the French troops on the right, hoping that each side would assume that they had been authorized by the other. Due either to such a misconception or to the official-looking appearance of the passengers, the car was not stopped and Cobb was able to file his stories of the battle. Although the Germans were succeeding in their efforts to push the British back, Cobb insists in his account that the British troops were not demoralized and the retreat was a tactical one. He quotes a British soldier:

> In wave after wave the Germans came on, marching close together in numbers incredible.... I saw them caught by our machine gun fire and piled up, heap on heap...they kept on coming. They climbed right over that wall of their own dead.... When our line began to move on, further to the west, we got orders to evacuate the station. [The soldiers] didn't want to go.... I'm told by reliable witnesses that their officers had almost to use force against them—not to make them keep on fighting but to make them quit fighting.[7]

Because of the usual mail and printing delays, Cobb's stories about the Picardy offensive were not printed in the *Saturday Evening Post* until late May and early June, as similar German attacks were being repulsed by American troops at Cantiguy and Chateau-Thierry. Cobb did not see these battles, but he encountered many American soldiers in the trenches and proudly reported on their behavior in bombing raids and local skemishes. He had no trouble striking up conversations; in fact, he was frequently mobbed. Many of the soldiers had read his earlier articles on the war and more recognized his portly figure and rosy, jowled face.[8] The soldiers Cobb describes are wise-cracking, confident and respectful.

They may be cowpunchers from Wyoming, rural blacks from Georgia, or small town boys from Ohio, but all are relaxed in their new roles, keeping up with baseball back home and looking out for refugees. Cobb's earlier fears that the war would somehow taint the American character, would turn these teenagers into Prussian machines or Belgian defeatists, disappears and his pride and confidence shines through his reports. He quotes a private who interrupts a captain's reference to "No Man's Land" with,

> It might a-been No Man's Land oncet, Cap'n, but frum now on it's goin' to be all Amurikun clear out to them furtherest wires yonder.

And, as Cobb explains,

> That night just after dust forty-five of our boys, with twice as many Frenchmen, went over the top at the very point we had visited, and next morning, true enough and for quite a while after that, No Man's Land was "All Amurikan clear out to them furtherest wires."[9]

These mothers and sisters back home whom Wilson had urged Cobb to write for must have been encouraged by Cobb's presentation of the nonchalantly invincible American soldier.

Cobb's later dispatches cover topics more removed from the battlefront. He writes of the army fliers ("today the knights-errant of the army"), of the behavior of Londoners during the air raids, of the supply problems of the Allies and always, of the hideous changes war made in the landscape. Several of his stories describe with contempt the meddling do-gooders who swarmed from the United States. Cobb was careful to exempt from his scorn workers in the Red Cross, the Salvation Army, the Knights of Columbus, the Y.M.C.A., or in any group of amateurs who were willing to endure filth and discomfort in order to help the soldiers. He singles out for praise a group of Smith College girls who were working among displaced peasants in France. For any such volunteers there was plenty that needed to be done.

> But for the camouflaged malingerer, for the potential slacker, for the patriotic but unqualified zealot, for the incompetent one who mistakes enthusiasm for ability and for the futile commission member there is no room whatsoever. This job of knocking the mania out of Germania is a big job and the closer one gets to it the bigger it appears. We can't make it absolutely a fool-proof war, but by a proper discrimination exercised at home we can reduce the number of Americans in Europe for whose presence here there appears to be no valid excuse whatsoever.[10]

Cobb sailed back to the States on the *Laviantha* in June of 1918. He had not been able to write his family of his plans, so Laura had no warning for the telephone call he made to her from the New York dock. Elisabeth Cobb describes his homecoming this way:

> "Hello," he said. "Hello, Loll."
> "Hello," said she. "Who is this?"
> "Why, it's me," he said. "It's Irvin."
> "Irvin who?" asked Laura.
> "Your husband."
> "I'm, sorry," said Laura. "I'm afraid I don't understand who you are."
> "Look here, woman," he roared. "Just how many Irvins are you married to, anyhow?"
> So she dropped the receiver and began to weep with excitement and they were cut off and Dad could not get her back, but just went on up to Grand Central and caught a train to Ossining, still not sure whether his wife knew that he was home or not.[11]

On June 23 a syndicated article appeared in the Chicago *Tribune,* headlined "Irvin S. Cobb Is Home with News About War." Cobb had told the reporters that met his ship in New York that "the world will listen to Woodrow Wilson."

Probably in an attempt to prevent an illness like that which followed his first trip to the warfront, Cobb spent most of the summer of 1918 in relative inactivity. Many of the *Saturday Evening Post* articles collected as *The Glory of the Coming* were written after he returned. They continued to appear in the *Post* through November of that year. The Cobbs also engaged in farming on a fairly elaborate scale at Rebel Ridge that summer, with vegetable gardens, horses, cows and chickens. It was as bucolic a refuge from the war as Cobb could have wished, although he probably enjoyed playing golf with his Westchester County friends more than gathering eggs.

In September, Cobb's tranquility was shattered by an event much closer to home than Belleau Wood. Charles Chapin, the slave-driving editor Cobb had worked under at the *Evening World,* murdered his wife Nellie. In the chilling autobiography the unrepentent Chapin later wrote in prison, he explains that what he had originally planned as a murder-suicide was completely necessary. Chapin had always lived extravagantly; when Cobb first knew him Chapin's extravagance was due to expectations of inheriting the millions of his eccentric and finally insane uncle, Russell Sage. Sage died while Cobb was still at the *Evening World* and Cobb tells how he was commissioned to write and then twice to revise Sage's obituary on the afternoon of his death, as rumors made it appear advantageous to Chapin to declare Sage, first, of perfectly sane mind, later, so mentally incompetent as to be incapable of making a will and, finally, sane again. The revision didn't help; Chapin's legacy was pitifully small. His disappointment was cushioned at first by his success on the stock market, but a series of unwise gambles and subsequent reversals brought him finally in 1917 to the point at which he was not only deeply in debt but also had lost securities legally entrusted to him by several relatives.

Suicide seemed the only answer and, at least to Chapin, it was unthinkable to leave his luxury-loving wife behind to suffer and perhaps starve without him. First, Chapin ordered a double tombstone, with both their names engraved but no death dates, erected at his funeral plot. Then he procured some guns. Chapin describes several earlier occasions on which he considered the murder-suicide but postponed it; finally, on the night of September 16, he waited until his wife was sound asleep and then shot her. She did not die immediately and Chapin sat beside her until she did, over two hours later. Chapin insists that the delay was out of compassion and that her death, when it came, so crazed him with grief that he lost the ability to shoot himself and instead wandered through the streets of New York for almost twenty-four hours, a gun in each pocket.[12]

During some of those hours—as soon as he could get to New York City after the news of the murder reached Ossining—Cobb was sitting with his former colleagues in the *World* office anxiously waiting for reports from the city-wide manhunt.[13] Early on the morning of September 18, Chapin walked into a precinct police station and confessed. Cobb was one of several friends who rushed to his prison cell to offer their help. Chapin was astonished to discover that he was not allowed to plead guilty and distressed to realize that his sanity was questioned. After four months of hearings, Chapin was declared "legally sane but medically insane" and was permitted to forego a trial in exchange for a life sentence at Sing-Sing.

Cobb deals very harshly with Chapin and his crime in *Exit Laughing*. It is not clear whether embarrassment or modesty kept him from acknowledging there the many services he performed for Chapin after he was sent to prison. Each month Cobb sent Chapin a check—the largest allowed—for pocket money. When the fastidious Chapin complained about the fit of his uniforms, Cobb arranged to have special ones made by Chapin's old tailor.[14] And when Chapin turned to gardening, spending some of the money Cobb had sent him on seeds and bulbs for beds in the prison yard, Cobb wrote an article about Chapin's beautification program (without indicating his own interest) that brought in contributions of rose bushes and rare plants from all over the world. As the spokesman for a group of philanthropists, Cobb talked to Governor Al Smith about a parole for Chapin—but Chapin declined the assistance. In the mid-twenties Cobb wrote a series of short stories about a hard-boiled editor named Ben Alibi who resembled Chapin in many ways. He was careful to get Chapin's approval before the stories were published.[15] Chapin died, in prison, in 1930.

## Notes

[1]Irvin S. Cobb, *"Speaking of Prussians—"*(New York: George H. Doran Co., 1917), pp. 12-13.

[2]Cobb, *Prussians,* p. 13.

[3]Cobb, *Exit Laughing,* pp. 305-306.

[4]Irvin S. Cobb, *The Thunders of Silence* (New York: George H. Doran, 1918), pp. 11; 16.

[5]E. Cobb, *Wayward Parent,* pp. 173-174.

[6]Irvin S. Cobb, *The Glory of the Coming* (New York: Geroge H. Doran Co., 1918), p. 34.

[7]Cobb, *Glory of the Coming,* pp. 124-125.

[8]Knightly, p. 127.

[9]Cobb, *Glory of the Coming,* pp. 54; 57.

[10]Cobb, *Glory of the Coming,* p. 278.

[11]E. Cobb, *Wayward Parent,* p. 174.

[12]Chapin, pp. 265-316.

[13]*Motion Picture Herald,* March 25, 1944; clipping, Louisville Free Public Library.

[14]*Motion Picture Herald,* March 25, 1944.

[15]Letter, Irvin S. Cobb to John Wilson Townsend, February 22, 1925, Crabbe Library, Eastern Kentucky University.

# Chapter Eighteen

The *Post* articles from Cobb's second war trip that reached the widest audience were two published under the running title of "Young Black Joe" and combined into a single chapter in *The Glory of the Coming*. These described the activities of Black American soldiers in Europe, particularly those of the New York Regiment commanded by Colonel Bill Hayward which in May and June of 1918 was under siege just north of Sanite Menehould. Most of the other correspondents noted the black soldiers only in passing, or, worse, transferred stock racist jokes to the battle situation and used references to the black soldiers to give their columns comic relief. Cobb introduced some dialect humor into his account, also, although the black soldiers are seldom the butt of the jokes. What made his account so different from those of other journalists, however, is that he saw the black soldiers under fire, was impressed with their bravery and discipline, and described their behavior with an eloquence fired by the perspective of a Southern background. Black newspapers all over the country reprinted the articles after they ran in the *Post* in August, 1918, as did such large metropolitan newspapers as the Louisville *Courier-Journal*. Cobb discovered, to his amazement, that he had become a hero to blacks all over the country and when he embarked on another lecture tour in the fall of 1918, he was met all along the way by black porters, railway workers and passers-by who wanted to shake his hand and thank him for the articles.

Because of this appreciation and good will, Cobb was asked to join Theodore Roosevelt as a chief speaker at the Circle for Negro War Relief Benefit held at Carnegie Hall on November 2, 1918. Before an audience of two thousand Cobb said, "The color of a man's skin hasn't anything to do with the color of his soul. The value of your race has been proven over there and [your] value here at home is unquestioned."[1]

While Cobb was visiting his mother that Christmas he received a tribute from the blacks of Paducah that he calls his "greatest thrill" in *Exit Laughing*. The chapter in that autobiography describing the event was itself printed separately in 1941 under the title "Glory, Glory, Hallelujah!" and given wide circulation.

Cobb was informed of the celebration planned in his honor by a committee of important Paducah blacks—a lawyer, a physician, an undertaker, a grocer and a barber—who waited respectfully in his mother's kitchen while the black cook, Mattie Copeland, fetched him. They told Cobb that all the black community wanted to meet together at the largest church in town, the Washington Street Colored Baptist Church, to show their appreciation to him if he would agree to attend and to say a few words about the black soldiers at the warfront. Cobb accepted, but turned down the offer of a ride to the church in the undertaker's carriage behind two white horses, preferring to walk instead.

Cobb's description of the celebration is as interesting for what he did not find remarkable about the day as for what he did. The inequities and taboos of the relationships between the races in Paducah were understood perfectly by both blacks and whites, and both Cobb's hosts and Cobb himself planned their activities for the day with no apparent fear of offending the other race and with no such unpleasant result. Cobb thought it appropriate to ask six white men to accompany him to the church, four his own age and two older veterans of the Civil War, one Unionist and one Confederate, who wore their uniforms to the celebration. The blacks, of course, had not been so indelicate as to ask Cobb to eat with them and no one seems to have thought it in poor taste that Cobb asked his six white guests to his house for a huge noonday dinner cooked by Mattie Copeland before they proceeded to the church for the service. (Cobb does note with proud amazement that Mattie managed to wash the dishes and still make it to the church on time.)

As the seven white men entered the black district of Paducah, they were met by practically the entire black population of the town, many in lodge uniform or choir robes. Cobb and his party passed to the head of the parade and all marched to the church to the music of a brass band. Every available space in the church was filled, including the window ledges; adventurous youths even stretched out on the roof and watched through the ventilator openings. Many of the black faces Cobb could see from his podium seat were familiar to him: Donie Rucker, his old nurse; craftsmen and handymen who had served his family over the years; men who guided his hunting trips or cooked his catch.

The ministers of each of the six local black congregations spoke first, as the anticipation of the audience grew and its emotional response became more vocal. Then the eloquent lawyer Etheridge rose to introduce Cobb and to highlight the subject: the importance of the black soldiers to the war effort. The mood and the response became even more intense and Cobb stood up to speak. He remembers the effect it had on him:

> I know of nothing more hypnotizing to the eye, or paradoxically, more stimulating to the tongue, than for a speaker to stand before a great audience every member of which, in perfect harmonious unison with very other member, is thrusting his or her tense body from side to side and at each completed swing joining in a medley of restrained grunts, small panting sounds and muffled fervent exclamations.... The very walls seemed to be keeping pace with us.[2]

Cobb began with a brief history of black military service in his country, telling of Crispus Attucks' noble death in Boston and of heroic black soldiers in the Civil War. He then described the exploits of the Tenth Cavalry in Cuba and Hayward's regiment in France. As he talked, the audience responded with "Amens," "Hallelujahs," and more specific interjections. Donie Rucker called out, "Tha's my chile! I learn' 'im his letters! Harken an' heed!"

The final part of Cobb's speech was the description of a black Paducah native, Sgt. William Kivil, who had been decorated for bravery on a French battlefield. Cobb judged his audience perfectly, however, and postponed referring to Kivil by name until the very end of his speech, dwelling first on his bravery, his character, personal memories of his boyhood in Paducah and the praise given him by his officers in France. The audience, who were of course already acquainted with Kivil's achievement, shouted "Name the boy!" each time Cobb's voice paused. When all present sensed the climax at hand, the shout became "Praise Gawd, he goin' name 'im now!" Cobb pronounced Kivil's name, Kivil's grandmother fell over in a cataleptic trance and the choir burst into "Mine Eyes Have Seen the Glory of the Coming of the Lord." When Cobb managed to escape from the mob who rushed forward to congratulate him, he went home to bed, where, he says, it took twelve hours' rest to recover the strength drained from him by the exhilaration of the afternoon.

Cobb's stay in Paducah was only a stop on the extended lecture tour he made in the fall and winter of 1918-1919, talking of his latest trip to the front. When he returned to New York in March of 1919, he found that the National Association of City Editors, of which he was a member, was using his name without permisson in their "Appeal to Fight Bolshevism." An article in the New York *Times* quoted his threat to resign if the president of the organization, C.P. Steen, didn't step down or end the campaign; "Steen chose to do the latter."[3] Cobb made the news in another liberal stand that August by delivering a speech supporting the Actor's Equity Association, then on strike.

Cobb was constantly in the public eye that year of 1919, and he made friends and enemies in unexpected places. On January 6 he was made a Chevalier of the French Legion of Honor for his services to France during the war, an award which annoyed some journalists such as Burton Rascoe, who sneered in the Chicago *Tribune* that perhaps Cobb deserved it because "after he had whitewashed the Germans, he so industriously smudged them with ink as to lessen their morale in the Argonne and at Chateau-Thiery."[4] The honorary degree Cobb received from Dartmouth that June also raised some eyebrows. The two most formidable enemies Cobb made in 1919, however, were Woodrow Wilson and H. L. Mencken.

The friendship between Cobb and Wilson ended swiftly when Cobb publicly criticized the makeup of Wilson's commission to the Paris Peace Conference, and Cobb compounded the injury when he chose to attack the League of Nations during his lyceum tour of the winter 1919-1920. Wilson considered such independent opinions in his friends to be disloyalty bordering on treason, and afterwards, in Cobb's own words, Cobb "couldn't have got into the White House with burglar's tools."

If Wilson was disturbed by Cobb's political independence, Mencken was offended by his patriotism. Until Cobb's second trip to the warfront, Mencken's attitude toward the Cobb books he reviewed in *Smart Set* was sometimes warm, sometimes disparaging, but always cordial. He praised *Back Home* in 1913 and *Roughing It Deluxe* in 1914, but found *Cobb's Anatomy* and later *Speaking of Operations* to be less funny than their fans claimed.[5] His negative remarks about *Speaking of Operations* brought in such a large and heated response that Mencken dealt with the book more fully the next month. He refused to retract his statements but joked that he thought many of the letters had come from Robert H. Davis and offered a jovial list of traits that he and Cobb shared:

> Besides [some] friends in common, we also have many interests, aspirations and vices in common. Both of us are too fat; both of us prefer malt liquor to the juice of the grape; both of us are old newspaper men; both of us are unlucky at all games of chance; both of us have written very bad books; each of us is the original Joseph Conrad man. Nevertheless, despite these points of contact and amity, I cling

tenaciously to the theory that *Speaking of Operations* is a fifth rate piece of writing and go before the jury maintaining firmly that I myself have never written anything worse.[6]

This is hardly a review to make an author beam, but the tone of its criticism is that which one crony reserves for another and it would not have been surprising if Mencken's next consideration of Cobb had been filled with praise. Instead, in 1918 Mencken wrote his friend George Sterling:

My next critical book, if I ever do one, will examine the corpses, including Irvin Cobb, who was born dead. A good place for the monument is in front of the Curtis Building in Philadelphia.[7]

That book appeared in 1918 as *Prejudices: First Series* with a vicious chapter, "The Heir of Mark Twain," devoted to Cobb.[8]

Clearly external events had more to do with the change in Mencken's attitude toward Cobb than the literary merit of anything Cobb had written in the meantime. Mencken made no secret of his early hope that Germany would defeat France and Great Britain; he reacted to the sinking of the *Lusitania* with a jubilant "The war is in its last stage! Deutschland uber Alles!"[9] In 1916 when he wrote the *Speaking of Operations* review he would have been gratified with both the inaccurate reports that Cobb was pro-German and Cobb's actual dedication to keeping America out of the war. This harmony of interests was destroyed, however, when Cobb began to urge American involvement and to describe the faults of the Prussian character. While the glowing patriotism of Cobb's war stories made his popularity skyrocket, Mencken's position became quite uncomfortable and his readership sank. Although he and George Jean Nathan managed with a struggle to keep the non-political *Smart Set* going, the Baltimore *Sun* gave him no assignments. Mencken compensated for the damage his unpatriotic attitudes had caused him by attacking those who cheered the war effort.[10] He wrote his friend Fielding Hudson Garrison in November, 1919:

One does not ask an intellectual, in time of war, to stand against his country; one expects him to stand with his country—*but like a gentleman.* For example, like Lansdowne, like Arnold Bennett and like Anatole France, not like D'Annunzio, Kipling and Irvin Cobb.[11]

The *Prejudice* volume made no reference to Cobb's "ungentlemanly" conduct during the war. Instead Mencken expressed mock horror at Cobb's literary reputation:

> Nothing could be stranger than the current celebrity of Irvin S. Cobb, an author of whom almost as much is heard as if he were a new Thackeray or Moliere. One is solemnly told by various extravagant partisans, some of them not otherwise insane, that he is at once the successor to Mark Twain and the heir of Edgar Allan Poe. One hears of public dinners given in devotion to his genius, of public presentations, of learned degrees conferred upon him by universities, of other extraordinary adulations, few of them shared by such relatively puny fellows as Howells and Dreiser.... Men pledge their sacred honor to the doctrine that his existence honors the national literature. Moreover, he seems to take the thing somewhat seriously himself. He gives his *imprimatur* to various other authors, including Joseph Conrad; he engages himself to lift the literary tone of motion pictures; he lends his name to movements; he exposes himself in the chatauquas; he takes on the responsibilities of a patriot and a public man.... Altogether, a curious and, in some of its aspects, a caressingly ironical spectacle.
>
> In the actual books of the man I can find nothing that seems to justify so much enthusiasm, nor even the hundredth part of it. His serious fiction shows a certain undoubted facility, but there are at least forty other Americans who do the thing quite as well. His public bulls and ukases are no more than clever journalism—superficial and inconsequential, first saying one thing and then quite another.[12]

The rest of the article continues in this manner, dismissing Cobb as a humorist in the Bill Nye vein. Mencken finds only two things in the Cobb canon to praise, the comic story "Hark from the Tomb" (although he insists Lardner, Ade and Owen Johnson have done better) and the goldfish image in *Speaking of Operations*.

This attack was very painful to Cobb—five years later his Kentucky friend John Wilson Townsend was still commiserating with him about it[13]—but it had little effect on the public response to Cobb at the time. Cobb was a hero and Mencken was a renegade, so few people were buying Mencken's opinions in 1919. The general reading public continued in this assessment of the two men through the next decade, but a revolt was brewing among intellectuals and academic critics that would elevate Mencken's opinions and practically eliminate Cobb from the field of serious literature by the mid-twenties. This revolt—and Mencken's reinstatement as an admired spokesman on literary matters—was aided by the disillusionment with the war effort and politics in general which set in after the Armistice.

Mencken's original target in the early teens was the New Humanists, a group of critics headed by Paul Elmer More and Irving Babbitt, traditionalists who sought a portrayal of uplifting human ideals in literature. Mencken's insistence that literature should portray life as it is, not as it ought to be, was not out of line with Cobb's own thinking, as is indicated by Mencken's 1918 assessment of *Back Home* as "unfailingly persuasive" and "altogether attractive."[14] The war, however, complicated Mencken's original divison of contemporary writers into mannered genteel traditionalists and praiseworthy realists, and all patriots were out. Mencken wrote in 1925:

> The war, indeed ruined all the literary patriots. The art of letters demobilized almost as quickly as the art of money-lending and so left them high and dry. It would be curious to make a list of the more florid of them: Owen Wister, Robert W. Chambers, Irvin Cobb and so on. Not one of them is taken seriously today. All of the men who are talked about now were missing when the roll was called by Dr. Creel: I point to Cabell, Sinclair Lewis, Eugene O'Neill—and Dreiser.[15]

It is not clear whether Mencken is taking credit for having brought about this state of affairs.

Of course, Mencken's statement about Cobb's not being taken seriously is true only of a small group of critics and literati. Cobb was highly praised in two books published in the early twenties, Blanche Williams' *Our Short Story Writers* and Thomas L. Masson's *Our American Humorists*. The general public continued to take him very seriously indeed. In 1925, the same year that Mencken published this dismissal, an article in the Louisville *Herald* called Cobb the highest paid short story writer in America, citing his price per story as $3,500 to $4,000.[16]

Probably the most important effect of Mencken's criticism and other similar jibes was that on Cobb's opinion of himself. Cobb had always been humble about his talents, but the example of such earlier reporters-turned-fiction-writers as Mark Twain had encouraged him to exert himself to produce literature. The message that came through from Mencken and his disciples was to stop trying, that he was a hack and a humorist who pleased the boobs but who could never make it with the readership that mattered. American literature, which had seemed so democratic a profession before the war, suddenly was a class system and the upper class was closed to those unblessed by the appropriate critics. Cobb and his colleagues at the *Saturday Evening Post* (Lewis was no longer one of their group) were consigned to the lower class that turned out trash for the masses.

In 1926, Cobb wrote:

> Once I considered the advisability of trying to break into the ranks of the Younger Intellectuals, figuring it might give me prestige to live among the elect. But I couldn't make the grade. In the first place, I wasn't old

> enough—the average age of a Younger Intellectual being, I should say, about fifty-five and, in the second place, I labored under the fatal disability of liking so much of the stuff that is written by Americans and so many of the folks who are writing it.
>
> You cannot enroll with the younger intellectuals if you look with an eye of favor on the domestic literary output. You cannot be expected to be even so much as an image bearer in their lodge; you already are blackballed before you apply. If a book or a poem or a play is popular it cannot be art because true art is over the head of the mob—that is the first verse in their litany.[17]

If true art was by definition unpopular, then Cobb was hopelessly inartistic, because his popularity continued. If everything Cobb did had not been received with such enthusiasm, he might have been more careful with his editing and more restrained in his output. Had he, like Dreiser and Lewis, retired from journalism and the weeklies to devote himself to major fiction, he might have produced a work that received the blessing of Mencken and his disciples. The chance was a tenuous one, however and the rewards of such a choice dubious. A man less in need of constant reinforcement than Cobb and one less aware of the four women who depended on his support, might have hesitated before making such an attempt. Cobb never even considered such a line of action and only two volumes of the sixteen he published between 1919 and 1935 contain any attempts at serious fiction. The others include his war reporting, humorous personal essays and comic stories. He also began the more serious autobiographical account of his early experiences as a newspaper reporter which were later collected by Doran in the volume *Myself to Date.* A few months before Mencken questioned Cobb's place in literature in *Prejudices,* one of these accounts had appeared in *American Magazine* entitled "I Admit I Am A Good Reporter."[18] This remained Cobb's only positive conviction about his professional accomplishments.

The development of Cobb's reputation in the teens might be outlined in this way: by 1912 he was famous as a great reporter and a great humorist. At mid-decade he appeared to be on his way to being hailed as a major writer. But the events of the late teens intervened—the war, Cobb's highly successful lecture tours, the reevaluation of contemporary literature—and when the smoke cleared, Cobb's chances to become a major writer were over. Instead, he was a celebrity and he remained a celebrity for the next two decades.

The warmth with which the American public still responded to Cobb as a personality and an authority on public matters is shown by an account in the Houston *Post,* August 4, 1920, of the lecture stop Cobb made there:

> The casual and delightful humor of Mr. Cobb... kept 3500 people in an interested and appreciative state of close attention Tuesday night, at the city auditorium for two hours. He talked on "Made in America" and keyed his remarks with a strong plea for America first and last by all loyal Americans, but held consistently to a lighter touch of thought which brought frequent applause.[19]

The humor which Mencken found uninspired gave Cobb the opportunity to have his views understood and accepted by surely a larger percentage of the population than that reached by any other writer of his time. The seriousness with which the public accepted him as an authority on matters of government is perhaps shown by the astonishing fact that, at the 1920 Democratic Convention in San Francisco which he was covering as an ordinary member of the press corps, he received one half vote from Kentucky for president—and a whole vote from the state of Washington.[20] He also received several votes for Vice President. For a time H. L. Mencken's displeasure must have seemed rather insignificant.

## Notes

[1]New York *Times,* November 3, 1918, 12:1.

[2]Cobb, *Exit Laughing,* p. 441.

[3]New York *Times,* March 18, 1919, 4:2.

[4]Chicago *Tribune,* January 11, 1919; clipping, Louisville Free Public Library.

[5]*Smart Set* (February, 1913), pp. 155-157; (October, 1914), p. 158; (February, 1916), p. 157.

[6]H. L. Mencken, "The Great American Art," *Smart Set* (March, 1916), p. 309.

[7]Carl Bode, *The New H. L. Mencken Letters* (New York: Dial Press, 1977), p. 85.

[8]H. L. Mencken, *Prejudices: First Series* (New York: Alfred A. Knopf, 1919), pp. 97-104.

[9]Edgar Kemler, *The Irreverent Mr. Mencken* (New York: Little Brown & Co., 1950), p. 90.

[10]Douglas C. Stenerson, *H. L. Mencken* (Chicago: University of Chicago Press, 1971), p. 177.

[11]Forgue, ed., *Letters,* p. 160.

[12]Mencken, *Prejudices,* pp. 97-98.

[13]Letter, John Wilson Townsend to Irvin S. Cobb, August 23, 1924, Crabbe Library, Eastern Kentucky University.

[14]Smart Set (February, 1913), p. 155.

[15]H. L. Mencken, *The Bathtub Hoax and Other Blasts and Bravos from the Chicago Tribune,* ed. Robert McHugh (New York: Alfred A. Knopf and Sons, 1958), p. 83.

[16]July 1, 1925; clipping, Louisville Free Public Library.

[17]Cobb, *Some United States,* p. 106.
[18]American Magazine, August 1919.
[19]Clipping, Louisville Free Public Library.
[20]New York *Times,* July 6, 1920, 4:1.

# Chapter Nineteen

During the early twenties Cobb found his reputation as a man to be listened to on public matters very useful as he fought two developments in America that seemed to him to threaten the freedoms defended in World War One: prohibition and racism. His stand against prohibition was vocal from the passage of the Volstead Act, although he did not exchange jokes for actions until the second half of the decade. If prohibition at first seemed a laughing matter, however, Cobb saw the resurgence of the Ku Klux Klan as a matter demanding his serious attention from the beginning, especially when the Ku Klux Klan organizers threatened to take over Paducah. The Paducah *News-Democrat,* still owned by Urey Woodson, was opposed to the Klan, and Woodson watched with apprehension as Klan fever spread outward from Louisiana and other points in the Deep South towards Kentucky.[1] Woodson and Cobb discussed the phenomenon during Cobb's visit home at Christmas in 1922 and Cobb offered to write an editorial for the hometown paper attacking the Klan. By the end of their discussion the plan had ballooned and it was announced that Cobb would serve as managing editor for the paper on one day, December 30, 1922.

Woodson set the stage for Cobb's editorial the day before. Among the announcements of Cobb's one-day take-over and an editorial praising Woodrow Wilson's personal sacrifice for world peace, he placed two articles about the Klan: one a description of arrests and confessions related to Klan murders in Louisiana and the other a report that Klan organizers were having more difficulty finding members in Western Kentucky than they had expected.[2]

Cobb thus was able to declare a victory. The front page headlines for his editorial read "Praise God from Whom All Blessings Flow, For the Ku Klux Has Failed in Paducah." The article itself developed this theme at a fever pitch:

> The Ku Klux Klan does not belong in Paducah—thank God! It does not belong in any community whose people believe in fair play, in religious

Irvin S. Cobb, September 1922
Photo reprinted by permission of Louisville Courier Journal and Times

> liberty, in tolerance , in law and order and decency. It does not belong anywhere under the American flag. It is damnable outrage that it should now exist in this country.

Cobb attacked the Klan with the traditional orator's gambit of espousing the ideals it claimed to support while insisting that they could best be reached in other ways:

> I believe in the tenets of the Christian religion. I believe in the tenets of all religions whose sponsors preach honesty, charity and forbearance and the right of every man to worship his god or gods according to the dictates of his own conscience.
>
> As a Southern man, the son and grandson of Southerners, I believe with all my heart in white supremacy. I do not believe in a campaign of terror and violence aimed against black men. If a negro disobeys the law or wilfully disregards it the law itself is for his punishment.
>
> I believe in the protection of our pure womanhood. I do not believe though that men who ride in masks to perform their self-appointed functions are the proper guardians of womanhood....
>
> I believe in Just Laws and Liberty. But I have never read the law which authorizes a midnight mob to execute the mandates of that or any other law. And I do not hold Liberty so cheaply that I would use her holy name as my excuse for denying freedom of thought or action to my neighbor.... I believe with all my heart in Free Public Schools.... I believe in making them free and keeping them free from the meddling interference of any sect, any race, any specialized group. [Catholics and Jews shouldn't push their ideas] and by the same token Catholic children and Jewish children are entitled to exactly the same measure of protection in their religious beliefs from meddlesome or over-zealous Protestants....
>
> Taking it all by and large, I figure that in all the broad essentials I am qualified to make a first rate Klansman. We do not differ in our principles but only in our plans for applying them.

Cobb ended his editorial by objecting to the Klan's use of the word "Knights" for themselves; the organization might better be called "The Masked Brotherhood of Bigotry, Bravado, Bluster and Bunk."[3]

It is not clear whether, as Cobb judiciously claims, the battle against the Klan had already been won or whether Cobb's attack helped turn the tide. Cobb's influence came not just from his words but from the combination of reverence and affection with which Paducahans viewed him. Dr. John Weber, pastor of the Broadway Methodist Church in Paducah, wrote a tribute to him published in this same December 30 issue:

> This has been a great week with the Paducahans.
>
> Her favorite son, Irvin S. Cobb, is back home with the folks giving

> and receiving honor from all Paducah....
>
> Paducah's attitude is more than pride—Love enters large in making it up. He is a loveable man and all Paducah loves him.[4]

This love is shown in the advertisements which line the pages of this special issue: most of them refer to Cobb by name, featuring portraits of him with colorful quotations or even endorsements of the product featured. Paducahans seemed to understand that in his Klan editorial Cobb was not lecturing them as an uppity son but as a loving brother. Whatever the cause, the Klan made no more progress in Paducah.

If the Klan editorial was typical of Cobb at his most vehement, the remainder of the December 30 issue featured Cobb as gentle humorist and local boy who made good. Cobb brought in several old friends as staff members and they all seemed to enjoy themselves spoofing typical newspaper stories and making jokes at each others' expense. Matthew J. Carney, who had grown up in Paducah as a slightly younger contemporary of Cobb's, agreed to come back to Paducah from New York City, where he was then president of Union Carbide, to serve as drama critic, reviewing the two theater programs then playing in Paducah. His effort led Cobb to conclude in another column, "Matt Carney draws one of the largest salaries paid to an executive in the world. But as a drama critic he is still a bust."

Cobb's sister Manie Howland wrote an article on Marilyn Miller, a New York actress who had once lived in Paducah. E.A. Jonas, the associate editor of the Louisville *Herald,* wrote an admiring tribute to Cobb, bringing forth the Cobb's rejoinder, "The acting managing editor has but one small criticism.... Mr. Jonas didn't go quite far enough." Urey Woodson remembered the day Cobb had left for New York in 1904, quoting from the *News-Democrat* article about his departure.

The most complicated series of jokes in the paper involved Cobb's Paducah hunting buddies. Cobb wrote a long editorial purporting to expose the inepitude of the quail hunting of Dr. Philip Stewart, George Goodman and W. J. Gilbert. They talk about shooting quail, they eat quail at the tables of others, but, Cobb claims, he himself has never actually seen one of them kill a quail. This article was balanced by "A Card to the Public," signed by William Jackson Gilbert, in which he insists "I have never been a quail shooter as my profession is that of a druggist" but notes "I couldn't miss Mr. Cobb if I shot at him." Another article announced that Goodman and Gilbert were leaving by train for Louisiana, where they would join B. B. McAlpin, P. M. Atkins and Mike Hogg on a ten day boat trip to shoot ducks in the bayous from Louisiana to Texas. The article noted that Cobb was invited to join them "and he probably will accept the invitation."

Cobb summed up his experience in getting out the paper in an article entitled "Hail and Farewell":

> The acting managing editor of the *News-Democrat* has learned, as a result of his one day's work at his old job, these two things:
>
> First—In the eighteen years since he went away they have learned a lot in this town about getting out a newspaper.
>
> Second—And he has forgotten a lot.[5]

It was a crazy way to attack the Klan. Only Cobb would have thought of it or made it work.

Cobb's interest in suppressing the Klan continued after he had "saved" Paducah. Often he lamented about its effect on the image of the South in the rest of the country. Before the New York Southern Society in 1923 he said:

> I believe the men and women of the new South should strive hard to free themselves of overmuch partisanship and provincialism and, by taking a broader viewpoint, learn to look at this country nationally instead of sectionally. For one I'm getting doggone good and tired of having these Northern people thinking that the only burning issues the South has lately contributed to the country are the boll weevil and the Ku Klux Klan.[6]

Like many Southern critics of the Ku Klux Klan in his day, Cobb saw the twentieth century Klan as much more reprehensible than the nineteenth century Klan had been. In a speech in 1924 at a luncheon honoring Cardinal Hayes given by the Catholic Actors Guild of America, Cobb deplored the Klan and insisted that his father, a Klan member in the seventies, must have been "turning in his grave because the name was stolen to propogate religious intolerance and bigotry."[7]

In 1922, the year of his campaign against the Klan in Paducah, Cobb wrote his first novel, *Jeff Poindexter, Colored,* using as his main character Judge Priest's clever black servant. The book uses the typical plot of a P.G. Wodehouse novel (Cobb described the novel to Townsend as "sort of a Jeems Yellowplush in black"), with Jeff on loan to a dizzy young fop in New York, who gets into complicated jams with shysters and girls that only Jeff can get him out of. Cobb maintains the comic tone and pace very well, although there are some indications of Cobb's goal, as explained to Townsend, "to show the psychology of the modern Southern negro without either idealizing him or burlesquing him."[8] Jeff, who tells the story, meditates from time to time on racial misunderstanding:

> There's a whole heap of white folks, mainly Northerners, which think that because us black folks talks loud and laughs a plenty in public that we ain't got no secret feelings of our own.... Which I reckon is one of the most monstrous mistakes in natural history that ever was.... All what [white employers] gleans about [a black servant]—his real inside emotions, I means—is exactly what he's willing for 'em to glean; that and no more. And usually that ain't much.... In times past they has met up with so many white folks which takes the view that everything black men and black women done... was something to joke about and poke fun at. Now, you take me. I is perfectly willing to laugh with the white folks and I can laugh to order for 'em., if the occasion appears suitable, but I is not filled up with no deep yearnings to have 'em laughing at me and my private doings.[9]

It seems a rather trivial setting for preaching the common humanity of man and Cobb never ventures into criticism of the social order, yet there are signs that Cobb felt *Jeff Poindexter* was as strong a statement of racial equality as the traffic would bear. That same year, 1922, Walter White, then a staff member of the NAACP, submitted to Doran the manuscript of a novel describing the grim effects of racial prejudice on the life of a black doctor. Doran asked Cobb for his opinion. Although agreeing with Doran about the power of the book, Cobb urged that Doran only accept it for publication if it were changed radically. As it was, he felt, it would lead to racial violence, death and destruction across the South. White dismissed Cobb's advice as racist and took the book to H. L. Mencken, who encouraged White to seek another publisher. Knopf brought out *The Fire in the Flint* in 1924.[10] The riots Cobb had feared did not materialize. It is ironic that Cobb's sensitivity to racial tensions led him to discourage White, while Mencken, an avowed racist who placed both blacks and Southern whites at the bottom of his social totem pole, became a hero in White's eyes.

Even though maintaining the public's respect for his views on public issues remained very important to Cobb and the decline in that respect after the mid-twenties hurt him terribly, he apparently made no connection between that decline and the frivolousness of some of his activities. After all, he had written humorous articles and sports stories and told jokes after formal dinners in the teens and no one had felt those endeavors detracted from his authority as a war correspondent. But the public mood was changing; Americans began to demand that the fiction writers they took seriously be somber (or frantic) social critics and that public spokesmen be equally humorless experts in their field. While earlier commentators had marveled at Cobb's versatility, in the twenties critics seemed to want to categorize him according to only one or two of his interests. Most classified him as a humorist or a lecturer or a sportswriter.

In 1921, the *New York Times* asked Cobb to cover the World Series in a series of articles syndicated elsewhere. (He had also covered the series for the *Times* in 1917.) That July Cobb had written a series of articles for the *Times* on the Dempsey-Carpentier bout that some sportswriters fifty years later still claimed was the greatest sports story ever written.[11] His description of Dempsey's blow in the fourth round that ended the fight goes like this:

> The thud of its landing can be heard above the hysterical shrieking of the host. The Frenchman seems to shrink in a good six inches. It is as though that crushing impact had telescoped him. He folds up into a pitiful, meager compass and lies on the floor...as though even in the stupor following that deadly collision between his face and Dempsey's fist, he would protect his vulnerable parts....[12]

The gradual lessening of Cobb's authority may have another cause. Cobb's sports stories have a strong voice; even his Little Man articles present a recognizable personality that readers may identify with. While Cobb did not abandon such writing in the twenties, however, he entered some new fields that obscured or narrowed the presentation of the personality behind his work.

The most obvious such endeavor was the joke column and the joke books. Although famous for his stories, Cobb as a speaker had never been just a stand-up-comic—he had tied his jokes to some central point or theme and thus retained his personality. His earlier humorous newspaper columns had been wells of comic invention. In 1922, however, he started a new syndicated newspaper column, "My Favorite Stories," that printed a joke a day with little lead-in and no point beyond the punch line. There is rarely a reference to some incident or situation in his own life to set up a story; slightly more frequently, a mention of some friend or celebrity who told the joke or figures in it. Mostly, however, the jokes are impersonal and give no reader any reason to think of Cobb other than as a collector of funny stories.[13] The column ran for over seven years and led to two equally impersonal joke collections: *A Laugh a Day Keeps the Doctor Away*

(1923) and *Many Laughs for Many Days* (1925).

Cobb's connection with the movie industry and the new medium of radio may have also helped to trivialize his image in the early twenties because they emphasized Cobb's celebrity, not his talent. Silent movies with their brief subtitles were not the best showcase for a writer whose strong points were human understanding and facility with language, and none of Cobb's silent movies are landmarks in film history. Their popularity—or Cobb's fame—brought him many movie contracts, however. Shortly after his return from the war in 1919 he wrote *The Face in the Dark,* a melodrama which starred Mae Marsh. In 1920 his *Life of The Party,* adapted by someone else, was filmed with Fatty Arbuckle. In the spring of 1921 Cobb was hired to write the scenario and subtitles for *Peck's Bad Boy* starring Jackie Coogan. The New York *Times* panned it, suggesting that perhaps "Mr. Cobb sought to satirize the picture by putting absurd words into the mouth of an incredibly mechanical five year old," but the public loved it.[14]

The making of *Boys Will Be Boys* in 1921 was the first time the talents of Cobb and Will Rogers were joined professionally, although their friendship had been growing since 1915. Cobb's story based on his father's love of taking children to the circus had been turned into a play by Charles O'Brien Kennedy with Cobb's help in 1919. It enjoyed a two-month run on Broadway. The movie version of Kennedy's play starred Rogers as Peep O'Day, the idealized Joshua Cobb.

Edward G. Robinson, who had earlier played in Cobb's stage drama *Under Sentence,* made his movie debut in 1921 in *Fields of Glory,* filmed from an original Cobb script. Afterwards Robinson was happy neither with the author nor the genre.[15] Cobb also wrote two other movies filmed that year, *Pardon My French* and *Five Dollar Baby.* In late 1923 Cobb played his first dramatic screen role since his *Arab* walk-on in *The Great White Way,* a movie nominally about a boxer but publicized for all the Broadway celebrities it featured playing themselves. Damon Runyon and Arthur Brisbane also appeared, as well as the entire Ziegfeld Follies chorus. The New York *Times* commented,

> Mr. Cobb took the occasion in a sporting way, possibly a bit nervous because of his plus fours and his light-hued golf hose, filled with well-rounded calves and quite small around the ankles.[16]

Radio was still in its infancy when Cobb agreed to be one of the featured performers on the *Everready Hour,* which debuted on December 4, 1923, three years before the formation of the first radio network. The *Everready Hour,* sponsored by the battery company, was the first variety show on radio featuring a host of stars each week. Eddie Cantor, Weber and Fields, John Drew, George Gershwin, Will Rogers, and Elsie Janis were among the other regular performers, in addition to a concert orchestra, a string quartet, and a jazz band.[17] Needless to say, Cobb was not hired to speak out on public issues or to give readings of serious literature, but to play the comic Southerner and fat man. It is no wonder the public sometimes forgot that he did anything else.

In emphasizing these trends in the early twenties that led to the later changes in the public's perception of Cobb, however, it would be misleading to ignore the attention that Cobb was still devoting to fiction writing and the praise he was still receiving. In 1922 Hildegarde Hawthorne writing in the New York *Times* praised Cobb's new collection *Sundry Accounts,* especially the story "Darkness," originally printed in the *Post* in 1921:

> This is a psychological story, and there is nothing funny about it. It is a grim and perfectly done picture of a human being in the grip of a dreadful fear, crushed under the conviction of sin.... he is a good and careful writer, and he is skillful at drawing unusual and rococo figures. He also has a strong sense of plot.

But Hawthorne sounds a note heard frequently in the twenties:

> Mr. Cobb writes a great deal, perhaps too much. Something of the bubbling spirit that was his is missing from his later work.[18]

A reviewer in the Boston *Tribune* put it this way in 1922:

> We wonder if Mr. Cobb is not spreading himself out a little thinly these days when his work is in such great demand.[19]

This great demand is shown by the fact that Cobb was the greatest prize Ray Long caught in his celebrated raid on the *Saturday Evening Post* which brought Cobb, Peter B. Kyne, Mary Roberts Rinehart and other writers to the staff of Long's *Cosmopolitan* with contracts and salaries far more generous than those Lorimer had paid at the *Post.* Lorimer was incensed and hurt at their defection, not merely because he found it disloyal but because he felt that *Cosmopolitan* was at least a step below *Post* in quality.[20]

One of the first stories Cobb wrote after he joined Long's staff at *Cosmopolitan,* "Snake Doctor," is often considered one of his best; it won the O. Henry Memorial Prize on March 24, 1923. Cobb's story, whose title refers to a Southern name for the dragon fly, tells of a swamp-dweller driven by fear and jealousy to kill his innocent wife who dies himself of a barbed wire scratch he imagines to be a venomous snake bite. It is ironic that (when it came to Cobb) this distinguished award was already tainted by the shrinking reputation of O. Henry, for whom it had been named. The comparison between the two writers made in *Brentano's Book Chat* that November was not meant to flatter Cobb:

> Mr. Cobb is also the most notable of O. Henry's vanishing disciples.... The essence of O. Henrianism, obviously, is a well-set stage, with spots neatly marked by crosses where villains shall die and lovers embrace. One knows when Mr. Cobb says a man has a mole on his nose that he is not merely describing a facial blemish. To Chekhov, de Manpassant, Bunin, Bercovici a mole is a mole; to Sinclair Lewis and P. G. Wodehouse, it is a thing of laughter; to Cabell it is a *greas* and to Sherwood Anderson a great and utter grief. But to Mr. Irvin Cobb a mole is a milestone in a labyrinthian plot. Fate resides in that mole.... High plot, and balanced endings, and persons getting what is coming to them, and the fruit determined in the seed—that is refined O. Henrianism as mostly highly polished in Mr. Cobb.[21]

Also in 1923 Doran brought out *Snake Doctor and Other Stories,* a highly uneven collection which Cobb dedicated to Ray Long. That same year the Review of Reviews Corporation, in cooperation with Doran, brought out a ten volume *Works of Irvin S. Cobb* which included most of the Doran books (some in combined form) and featured an embossed signature on the cover of each volume.

## Notes

[1]George Brown Tindall traces this new upswelling of prejudice to Tom Watson's attacks on Blacks, Catholics and Jews during the teens and to the 1915 movie *The Birth of a Nation.* The prejudices of Watson, D. W. Griffith, and "Colonel" W. J. Simmons, the organizer of the "new" Ku Klux Klan, found a sympathetic reception in the minds of white southerners confused and threatened by the postwar situation of "urban booms and farm distress." George Brown Tindall, *The Emergence of the New South 1913-1945,* vol. X of *A History of the New South,* ed. Wendall H. Stephenson et. al. (LSU Press, 1967), pp. 184-192.

[2]Paducah *News-Democrat,* December 29, 1922, 4:1.

[3]Paducah *News-Democrat,* December 30, 1922, 1:30.

[4]Paducah. *News-Democrat,* December 30, 1922, 1:2.

[5]Paducah. *News-Democrat*, December 30, 1922; 4:1.

[6]December 12, 1923; dinner program with speeches in Paducah Public Library.

[7]Burkhalter, p. 42.

[8]Letter, Irvin S. Cobb to John Wilson Townsend, no date, Crabbe Library, Eastern Kentucky University.

[9]Cobb, *Poindexter,* pp. 116-117.

[10]Walter White, *A Man Called White: The Autobiography of Walter White* (New York: Viking Press, 1948), pp. 66-68.

[11]Dick Cavett Show, early 1979.

[12]Louisville *Evening Post,* July 5, 1921; clipping in Louisville Free Public Library.

[13]Kentucky Library, Western Kentucky University, has a near-complete run of these columns.

[14]New York *Times*, March 25, 1921, 9:2.

[15]Edward G. Robinson, *All My Yesterdays: An Autobiography* (New York: Hawthorn Books, Inc., 1973), pp. 61-62.

[16]New York *Times*, January 4, 1924, 10:1.

[17]Frank Buxton and Bill Owen, *The Big Broadcast: 1920-1950* (New York: Viking Press, 1972), p. 79.

[18]New York *Times,* May 14, 1922, 14:1.

[19]Clipping, Brody collection.

[20]Burton Rascoe, *We Were Interrupted* (Garden City: Doubleday & Co., Inc., 1942), p. 86.

[21]Clipping, Louisville Free Public Library.

# Chapter Twenty

The incredible pace Cobb maintained to be a writer, a lecturer, a comedian and a watchdog for justice all at the same time had a bad effect on his health. In the spring of 1921 he began to suffer chest pains. A doctor he consulted found nothing wrong but put him on a diet, an experience Cobb described that year in the humorous book *One Third Off*. (The title is wishful thinking: the thirty-nine pounds Cobb lost dropped him barely below two hundred pounds.)

By February of 1922 he had forgotten the diet and was pushing himself to do yet another lecture tour, this one in New England, when he came down with influenza. His daughter explains his behavior and its aftermath:

> Refusing to cancel a single engagement, or even to go to bed in between them, he doggedly continued his tour, living for several days on handfuls of aspirin, to which it was afterward discovered that he was allergic, and priming himself for travel and talks by nips from a flask of bootleg whisky. He found that he was not relishing his food very much, so one night, to perk up his appetite, he supped off a large helping of pickled pigs' feet. He said afterward that he had figured that if pickled pigs' feet didn't cure him of what ailed him he'd call in a doctor. Strangely enough, they were no cure-all, so the next day, again putting off the dread moment of asking for medical advice, he had some more aspirin, some more whisky and two dozen of those outsize New England oysters.
>
> The Boston physician who finally examined him, and gave him at the most but a few hours to live, said that his liver had turned into as hard a rock as any you could find on a Massachusetts hillside. He said that the Pilgrim Fathers could have landed on him. A blood vessel had burst. . . .[1]

Stories in the New York *Times* on three consecutive days kept the public informed of Cobb's condition as doctors struggled to save his life.[2] He remained in Boston for three weeks, and according to Elisabeth Cobb, "when he was brought home on a stretcher, he was still whiter than the pillow under his head, dead-white, gray-white, sick-white—that ruddy "high-complected' man. . . ."[3] As one might expect from Cobb, he turned the experience into a *Post* article called "But I Kept My Teeth!"

One of the strains on Cobb's life had been his beloved Rebel Ridge and the commuting it required; the next month after his attack in Boston it was advertised for sale. By 1923 the Cobbs were living in Manhattan in an apartment at 830 Park Avenue which the family maintained, sometimes in conjunction with other homes, until 1936.[4]

The move did nothing to slow Cobb down. The time he saved in commuting he probably spent in his expanded social life. He had socialized in Westchester, of course, and frequently had stayed overnight at the Algonquin in order to make a dinner or an appointment in Manhattan. But now that he was a city-dweller again he was able to enjoy the company of his New York friends much more often.

A new pleasure for Cobb was escorting his attractive daughter around town. Buff was twenty when they moved to Park Avenue, and she dazzled Manhattan as she had Westchester County. Frank Case's daughter Margaret remembers "my chief concern was whether I would be cut in on as often as Connie Bennett or Buff Cobb. . ., or whether—oh, heaven!—I could get as many stags trailing me around the floor as those two girls had."[5] The Cobbs commissioned artist Wayman Adams to paint a joint portrait of father and daughter which was reproduced in the *Times* in March and featured in the June, 1923, issue of *Hearst International Magazine* as "Art of the Month."[6] Newspaper photographers seemed fascinated by the faces of the big, homely man and the petite, pretty daughter who yet looked so much like him. One of several joint pictures of the two of them, published in the New York *Times* in January, 1923, shows them in elaborate Arabian costumes at the Illustrators' Ball. Laura, who loved small parties but hated gala affairs, was probably quite glad to remain at home.

The Park Avenue apartment was the scene of Buff's wedding, on February 12, 1924, to Frank M. Chapman, Jr., a hopeful young opera singer.[7] Frank Chapman, Sr., was an ornithologist, and in his bridal toast Cobb claimed that the book he had read while walking Buff as a colicky baby was Chapman's *American Birds*.

Living in Manhattan meant that Cobb could spend a lot more time with his friends at the Algonquin Hotel. The regulars whose company he enjoyed most there were those of his own generation: Burton Rascoe, Carl Van Vechten, Fannie Hurst, Gertrude

Atherton, Heinrik Van Loon, Joseph Hergescheimer, and Frank O'Malley. His attitude toward the younger, penurious set that ordered hamburgers or pie from the round table at rear center was amused but aloof; their manners weren't very good but they were just kids. Alexander Woollcott, Robert Benchley, Harold Ross, and Dorothy Parker sometimes admired his wit, as when he scored a hit on the long-faced FPA by reacting to a mounted moose head, "My God, they've shot Frank Adams!," but more often they made fun of his Southern accent and old-fashioned ideas. Frank Case, who loved all his regulars as children, was continually trying to smooth relations between the Round Table group and the rest of his clientele. He tolerated Woollcott and company out of kindness; he made very little money from them, and the tourists who came to see celebrities were far more interested in Cobb and his friends.[8]

Cobb's cronies at the Lambs' and the Friars Club also welcomed him back, although Prohibition had dampened their merriment some. As Cobb puts it, the bar at the Lambs' was "given over to soft drinks, confectionery, and vain regrets." Cobb became especially interested in the plight of the only female member of the Friars Club, Nellie Revell. Revell, a widowed police reporter and sports writer, had been bedridden since an automobile accident in 1920 crumpled her spine. Cobb joined the rest of the Broadway regulars in making regular visits to Revell in her hospital room. Revell joked that she had received over 1,000 copies of *Speaking of Operations* from well-wishers. She wrote an autobiography, *Right Off the Chest*, to which Cobb wrote the introduction, calling her "blithe, brave, witty, wholesome, kindly, sweet-savored, indomitable,... the bravest living creature I have ever met in my life."[9] On May 25, 1924, the doctors judged her able to leave the hospital in a wheelchair for the first time, and the Friars Club threw a dinner for 1200 in her honor. George M. Cohan presided, Eddie Cantor directed the variety show, and Cobb and Will Rogers were among the featured speakers.

Cobb and Bob Davis had of course continued their friendship during Cobb's years at Rebel Ridge; with Cobb back in New York City, they were together even more often. Davis had visited Paducah with Cobb at least once during the teens, and the correspondence he subsequently entered into with Cobb's mother provides an interesting sidelight on the friendship of the two men. On March 6, 1922, Davis wrote Manie Cobb to assure her that Cobb was recovered from his Boston illness. He promised to come to Paducah with Cobb that Christmas, saying he could already picture "the sisterly Miss Ruby approaching with a pitcher of milk in one hand

and a bottle of homebrew cherry brandy in the other."[10] Manie's letters back are sprightly and continue Davis' jokes. When Davis couldn't make it that Christmas after all, she sent him a box of "scaly bark hickory nuts."[11]

Davis understood perfectly what a mother wants to hear about, and his letters talk mostly of Cobb. In the summer of 1923 he wrote, "We have had a splendid summer together. We fished and played and slept and banqueted all over New England and Canada. . . . Just now we are having a terrible argument over who looks best in a golf stocking." In January 1924 Davis wrote that Cobb "was with us again last night. We had a lovely dinner and a house of good people. Tomorrow night we are going down to Wyandach to get two nights of quiet. My wife never cares where I go as long as I'm with him."[12]

Except for the men's hunting trips, the Davises and the Cobbs entertained each other as families. Madge Davis and Laura got along well, and Laura enjoyed Bob Davis's company. Often Bob Davis did the cooking when they got together; his specialities were game recipes of all kinds and Indian curry.

It was useful to have a great editor practically in the family when Buff Cobb Chapman decided she wanted to be a writer. In April of 1924 Cobb gave Buff's first fiction effort to Davis for comment, asking him to give his views to Cobb first "before you communicate with the kid."[13] Davis sent it back three days later (to Cobb) with the critique "A peach up to the last two pages. There it flops. . . . If she attempts anything subtle or occult, good night. It is Buff's function in literature to be sane and wholesome, otherwise she ain't your offspring—which she is." Davis agreed to pay one hundred dollars for the story when revised.[14]

Two friends who became very important to Cobb after he returned to Manhattan were O. O. McIntyre and Will Hogg. McIntyre and Cobb first met in the mid-teens as a result of one of Cobb's astounding acts of charity. Almost ten years after Cobb left Paducah, a gangling, shy youth named Odd McIntyre left Plattsburg, Missouri, to make it as a New York newspaperman. McIntyre was struggling in his first job when Cobb made his triumphant 1914 return from the war front, but his father back in Missouri had illusions about his son's success and the size of the New York newspaper world. He had written his son, "I suppose you know Irvin S. Cobb. I think he knows how to tell a story. If he's ever out this way, ask him to look me up." It didn't seem a likely occurrence—until Cobb announced a western tour that would take him through Missouri. McIntyre hated to have his father realize how unimportant he was, so he wrote Cobb an apologetic letter telling him the situation and asked him please to visit his father if he went through Plattsburgh.[15]

And of course Cobb did all that was asked of him and more. The elder McIntyre met him at the station and proudly escorted him to his house, where he had invited all his friends to meet the celebrity. Cobb had still not met Odd, although he must have found out somewhere to pronounce his name "Ud," for all his fabricated stories about the good times and great successes with Odd in the city were accepted unquestioningly by the Plattsburgh citizens. Odd McIntyre thanked him in person after his return, and they became good friends.

McIntyre later became almost as famous as Cobb as the writer of a syndicated column, "New York Day by Day," which ran from 1916 until he died in 1938. For twenty-two years he pictured himself as a newcomer to the town, a yokel from the sticks who wasn't used to city ways and wasn't sure he wanted to be. At his death, the column was published in 379 daily and 129 Sunday newspapers, one of which was available in every large town and city in the United States. His view of New York turned out to be that of most of the nation, and Americans loved hearing about the wicked city and the wholesome countryside from him.

When Cobb first met him McIntyre was far more sociable than he later became, but he always was an odd, prickly personality who did not make friends easily. He was a hypochondriac whose conversion to Christian Science in 1918 only drove his fears inward without removing them. Visitors to his home, of whom there were very few, understood that sickness and death were taboo subjects. Even his wife dared not broach the subject of the signs of illness already evident in him in the twenties.[16]

Yet with someone he really trusted, such as Cobb or Bob Davis, he was a delightful conversationalist in the story-telling tradition they all felt comfortable in. Before his paranoia overcame him, he liked to venture out to Broadway and eat with the crowd at Dinty Moore's or Lindy's. From those days he retained such unexpected friends as Jack Dempsey, George Gershwin, and Al Jolson.

McIntyre's closest friend was Will Hogg, the charming, aggressive, millionaire son of the late Governor James Hogg of Texas. Hogg met both Cobb and McIntyre sometime in the teens and immediately became an important part of their lives. Cobb knew Hogg best as a traveling and fishing companion for a brief fifteen years before Hogg's death in 1930, yet he chose to open and close his autobiography with memories of Hogg, praising his generosity, his wisdom, and his delightful company and calling him "the most lovable human being I ever knew."[17]

McIntyre's adoration of Hogg was, if possible, greater than Cobb's, because Hogg had done so much for McIntyre. What Hogg did, basically, was to start running McIntyre's life for him, with such expediency and charm that McIntyre was pleased. Hogg's New York apartment (he also maintained a home in Houston where his New York friends often visited) was on Park Avenue, and he and Cobb became neighbors after Cobb's return to Manhattan. The McIntyres, typically, were still living in the Ritz-Carlton Hotel. Hogg and Cobb got into the habit of meeting them at the hotel for breakfast each morning until Hogg decided that the McIntyres needed an apartment of their own. McIntyre demurred; they were comfortable and finding an apartment would be too difficult. But the more uneasy McIntyre became, the most adamant Hogg grew. He picked out an apartment for them and made it possible for them not to agree.

Hogg managed many other events in their lives the same way. He took them to Florida one year, to Europe the next. His interest and his confidence gave McIntyre an important sense of security, and the McIntyres became so dependent on Hogg that they bought a house in Houston, planning to be together in retirement. Hogg died suddenly after an operation in 1930, however, and McIntyre never retired.

Another friend Cobb met frequently at the McIntyre apartment was Will Rogers. Rogers and Cobb were introduced by a theatrical acquaintance in 1915; Rogers was doing his roping act at the Ziegfeld Follies then. They shared many traits in common: both were from rural backgrounds, both preferred country values, both sometimes hid their intelligence behind a mask of ignorance, both loved the masculine company of a campground fireside. At the end of the teens Rogers moved his family to California so that he could continue the movie career he had begun in the east, but after some movies he tried to produce himself failed, he returned to New York alone in 1921 to star in the Follies again. Shortly after Cobb's return Rogers started a newspaper column for the same syndicate that published McIntyre and Cobb.[18]

Charles M. Russell, the distinguished western painter and the fifth man whom Cobb cherished in his closest circle of friends, did not make Cobb's acquaintance until 1919, although he had met Rogers fifteen years earlier. Rogers and Russell met by chance in

1904 on a train to New York. Both were shy, unpolished kids with big dreams of success in the city. Russell brought along several of his canvases of western scenes; Rogers had his lariat. They met for lunch several times in the city and remained friends. Russell's fame came much more quickly than Rogers'; by 1911 his yearly trip to New York produced a one-man show at an important gallery.[19]

Cobb apparently never saw one of Russell's early New York shows. He had loved all things pertaining to the American Indian since he had collected arrowheads as a child, however. Seeing some of Russell's paintings of Indians in a gallery in San Francisco in 1919, he stayed there admiring the paintings until the shop closed. Later he wrote Russell an admiring note. In return he received one of Russell's famous illustrated letters, with exquisite watercolor sketches bordering the message. Russell thanked him for his letter and explained that he had heard Cobb's lecture in San Francisco:

> both halfs of me heard your talk and the better and the bad both enjoyed it. I would have liked to have shaken your hand.... I'm sort a shy about bargin in on strangers.... a compliment from you ain't scratched on sand but gouged in granit.

Page one of the letter is illustrated with two Indians and the sign language for "friends;" page two has a double self-portrait of Russell dressed as an eighteenth century colonist and a nineteenth century dandy. He invited Cobb to visit his camp in Montana any time and ended, "I can't say friend caus we ain't smoked yet."[20] The next year when Cobb was on a train from the West Coast to Chicago he suddenly remembered the invitation and got off the train in Great Falls, Montana, to meet Russell.

Cobb returned to Russell's home in Montana several times, taking his family with him. Russell's big log cabin, called "Bull Head Lodge," was located on Lake McDonald in what became Glacier National Park, an area of ruggedly beautiful mountains and clear, cold water. Rogers introduced Russell to such Hollywood figures as William S. Hart and Douglas Fairbanks, Jr., and they too were invited to Bull Head Lodge and regaled with Russell's famous stories.[21]

One especially memorable trip to Montana for Cobb came in the summer of 1925. Buff and Laura were with him. Russell was a friend of and apologist for the Indians of the Old West, especially the Blackfeet Indians of Montana, and he despised the tourists who patronized them. The Indians accepted Russell as a friend and gave him the Indian name "Antelope" because the pale reinforced seat on the back of his riding breeches reminded them of the rump of a pronghorn. Russell had recognized Cobb's genuine interest in Indians and vouched for him to the tribe, thus giving Cobb the opportunity to get a much more accurate understanding of the Blackfeet—and a lot of new items for his growing collection of Indian paraphernalia. In 1925 Cobb was made an honorary member of the Blackfeet Confederacy, with the Indian name "Fat Liar," the retort made on an earlier visit by an old woman to Cobb's attempted compliment.[22]

In *My Wayward Parent* Elisabeth Cobb describes her father's ideal heaven as "a campfire in the woods, with Bob Davis getting the dinner, and he and the two Wills and O. O. McIntyre listening to Charley Russell tell stories."[23] It makes an interesting picture: Davis' amiable, frog-like face intent on the pot he is stirring, while the firelight illuminates the relaxed portliness of Cobb and Hogg, McIntyre's nervous angularity, and the lanky, lean forms of Rogers and Russell, who looked much alike, although Russell's face was more conventionally handsome, lacking Rogers' lopsided grin. Cobb never achieved this ideal on earth, however; for one thing, McIntyre would never willingly have sat on the ground in the woods, and, although Cobb camped with each of the other four, there was too little time before Russell's unexpected death in 1926 to get all six together at the same time. The picture of the five writers listening to the artist talk is quite accurate, however: both Rogers and Cobb claimed that Charley Russell was the best story-teller in America.[24]

## Notes

[1]E. Cobb, *Wayward Parent,* p. 156.

[2]New York *Times*, February 20, 1922; February 21, 1922; February 22, 1922.

[3]E. Cobb, *Wayward Parent,* p. 156.

[4]Letter, Irvin S. Cobb to John Wilson Townsend, September 13, 1934, University of Kentucky Library.

[5]Harriman, *Blessed,* p. 111.

[6]clipping, Louisville Free Public Library.

[7]wedding invitation, Crabbe Library, Eastern Kentucky University.

[8]Harriman, *Vicious Circle,* p. 32.

[9]Nellie Revell, *Right Off the Chest* (New York: George H. Doran Co., 1923), p. viii-ix.

[10]Robert H. Davis to Manie S. Cobb, *March 6, 1922:* Davis Collection, New York Public Library.

[11]Manie S. Cobb to Robert H. Davis, January 23, 1923; Davis Collection, New York Public Library.

[12]August 29, 1923; January 24, 1924; Davis Collection, New York Public Library.

[13]Irvin S. Cobb to Robert H. Davis, April 20, 1924; Davis Collection, New York Public Library.

[14]Davis to Cobb, April 23, 1924, Davis Collection, New York Public Library.

[15]Charles B. Driscoll, *Life of O. O. McIntyre* (New York: Greystone Press, 1938), p. 298.

[16]Driscoll, pp. 18-19.

[17]Cobb, *Exist Laughing,* p. 556.

[18]Richard Ketchum, *Will Rogers: His Life and Times* (New York: American Heritage Publishing Co., 1973), p. 27.

[19]Shannon Garst, *Cowboy Artist: Charles M. Russell* (New York: Julian Messner, Inc., 1960), pp. 161-172.

[20]The letter is in the Brody collection.

[21]Harold McCracken, *The Charles M. Russell Book: The Life and Work of the Cowboy Artist* (Garden City, N.J.: Doubleday, 1957), p. 212.

[22]Irvin S. Cobb, *This Man's World* (New York: Cosmopolitan Book Corp., 1929), p. 110.

[23]E. Cobb, *Wayward Parent,* p. 201.

[24]McCracken, p. 212.

Irvin Cobb, his mother Manie Saunders Cobb, and his sister Reubie Cobb, probably in 1926.
Photo reprinted by permission of Paducah Public Library

# Chapter Twenty-one

1926 was a significant year for Cobb in many ways. On April 30 he celebrated his fiftieth birthday in Paducah, with an elaborate banquet at the Woman's Club. Cobb's mother was present; his wife and daughter were not. Bob Davis was the chief speaker, and, through the generosity of Matthew Carney, each guest was presented with a leather-bound copy of *The Story of Irvin S. Cobb,* a reverential biography by a Paducah newspaperman, Fred S. Neuman.

But adoration in Paducah could not assuage the pains of turning fifty. Cobb no longer had the vision and self-confidence he had displayed ten years earlier in his essay "Looking Both Ways from Forty." At fifty Cobb found more pleasure in looking back than in looking forward. In 1916 *American Magazine* had wondered what new developments lay ahead in Cobb's career; in 1926 critics assumed that his career was past development. A review of his 1926 collection *Prose and Cons* in the New York *Times* shows the tone:

> A good many...regret that Mr. Cobb became a funny man. They believe that a good short story writer—one that might have met with success in something quite out of the reach of popular fiction—has been obscured and lost.[1]

In ten years Cobb had changed from the man who could do anything to the man who had done practically nothing except spread a few laughs. Cobb's depressions grew more frequent, and he tried more and more to surround himself at all times with fun-loving friends.[2]

Prohibition was also getting on Cobb's nerves. He had denounced it as wrong-headed Puritanism from the start, of course, but the relative honesty of the controls in the early years and the available supplies of good bootleg stocks made it bearable. By mid-decade, however, the growing corruption of the law and the danger of being poisoned by adulterated liquors were creating an intolerable situation as far as Cobb was concerned. This change in attitude was accelerated by the Earl Carroll trial.

Earl Carroll was a Broadway figure with whom Cobb had been acquainted for many years. He was a good friend of the McIntyres and Will Hogg. When Carroll decided in the teens to emulate Ziegfeld's success with an imitation Follies called Vanities, Hogg was one of his chief backers, and the McIntyres were given front row seats for that and all other opening nights.

The 1926 Vanities opened on February 23 at the Earl Carroll Theater. After the show Carroll gave a large opening night party on the stage which Cobb attended. Carroll had arranged as the highlight of that evening for a model named Joyce Hawley to come out after the party was well underway, disrobe, and seat herself nude in a bathtub filled with a potable liquid whose nature became the subject of much debate. Hawley got stage-fright very soon after her appearance and began to cry as guests lined up to drink from the bath, so Carroll had the bathtub moved off stage. Carroll, furious at her behavior, refused to pay her the agreed upon $1,000, and Hawley went to the authorities to report that Carroll was serving alcohol. An investigation was started by the Federal Grand Jury to which Cobb was called as a witness. Cobb said he arrived early, left early, saw no nude girl and no alcohol. Carroll made the foolish mistake of denying Hawley's story entirely, so that Carroll was brought to trial in May, not for serving alcohol (that was never proved) but for perjury.

Cobb, called as the first witness, stated that "measured by the accepted standards of Broadway, the party seemed to me to be perfectly proper." Cobb claimed to have drunk only two glasses of near-beer and one of White Rock at the party, although he admitted that, at other times, "I drink a cocktail when I am reasonably certain that the effect will not be immediately fatal." After he was dismissed Cobb went over and shook Earl Carroll's hand.[3] A later witness, Walter Winchell, disagreed with Cobb's first statement. When asked, "Was it a regular Broadway party?" he answered, "Well, no, there were too many Senators present." He was immediately dismissed from the stand.[4]

Carroll was convicted of perjury and sentenced to a year and a day in the Federal Penitentiary in Atlanta. His appeal kept him out until March of 1926, when Cobb joined in a last minute move to petition the judge for a suspended sentence. He wrote several of his friends, including Bob Davis, who complied as a favor to Cobb, but wrote Cobb, "Personally, I think Earl ought to take his medicine" like so many others arrested under the Volstead Act.[5] The petition failed, and Carroll went to Atlanta to serve his sentence.

What Cobb most needed that summer he was fifty was a project that would enhance his reputation as a serious writer. If his novels and short stories were coming under increasingly patronizing scrutiny, then perhaps the answer was a new field, even one the critics ignored but the public saw as the art of the future. Cobb was jubilant when he received a letter from Irving Thalberg at MGM in Hollywood. Thalberg was trying to make an epic film about the building of the Panama Canal in the tradition of MGM's movie about the World War, *The Big Parade.* Fourteen notable authors had tried and failed to produce a suitable scenario. Would Cobb come give it a try? Cobb took the earliest possible train west.

Thalberg had sent along research material and the fourteen earlier scripts for Cobb to read on his way out. Cobb's first notion had been to base the story on the love affair of an American official and some native woman, perhaps one in the pay of a foreign power. He was rather chagrinned to discover that seven of the rejected scripts had a similar plot; the other seven also dealt with an attempt to overthrow the American plans, but on a larger, less romantic scale, with sinister spies representing a secret but powerful international crime league. Later in conference, Thalberg and Cobb came up with a much better conflict for the movie:

> In that one fleeting flash both of us realized that the only plausible and the most nearly perfect villain of the piece would be the tropics—jungle, fevers, heat, insects, snakes, muck, native superstitions, diseases, death. Here was not just one enemy. Here were a dozen enemies, just made to order.[6]

It was in many ways a perfect vehicle for Cobb. He had been trying to capture the foreboding dangers of gloomy swamps in his fiction for years; he was familiar with the cruel but often necessary rigors of military discipline; he knew the difference between false heroics and the true heroism of the deaths that come slowly and painfully to those trying to do their job against overwhelming odds. And perhaps in Irving Thalberg Cobb had found what he had needed all his life—an editor that would force him out of the security of a well-made plot, that would make him depend on the evocative quality of his situations and the strength of his characters.

Cobb finished the script rapidly—and wrote two more that he sold to Cecil B. deMille for good measure. (One of these, *Turkish Delight,* was made and released in 1927; the other never came to production.) Cobb's MGM script, entitled *The Big Ditch,* was received enthusiastically by the MGM management. This was what they were looking for; it would go into production immediately, with King Vidor as director. Perhaps they would make it the chief release of the coming winter. Cobb would receive the check promised for a successful script, but they wanted him to remain with the production on a weekly salary, to help Vidor with any necessary adjustments in the scenario and to prepare the subtitles.

Cobb would have liked nothing better, but unfortunately he had family obligations. Frank and Buff Chapman had moved to Italy in order to promote Frank's opera career, and Buff was expecting a baby in September. Cobb's passage was booked on August 18. He agreed, however, to return from Italy as soon as possible to join the production staff. Calls followed his train across the country to seek his approval of various casting choices. Cobb was frantic for news in Italy, as they all awaited the birth of Patrizia Cobb Chapman, who delayed her arrival until November 1. As soon as Buff was out of the hospital, the Cobbs caught the next boat home to—silence.

Cobb never heard from MGM again about *The Big Ditch*. Calls to Irvin Thalberg indicated that Thalberg was out of town; his staff revealed a total ignorance of any Panama Canal project. Apparently shortly after Cobb left the country MGM realized that public interest in the Panama Canal had waned and dropped the project. Cobb continued to take movie projects in the years that followed, but was never able to take any as seriously again as *The Big Ditch*.

If Cobb was not yet aware of the fickleness of movie producers, he had a lot more to brood upon as he prepared to go to Italy in the summer of 1926. The country, which he had in the mid-teens thought so noble, so uncorrupted, and above all, so dedicated to individual freedom was, ten years later, a supreme disappointment. In an interview with journalist Marjory Warden earlier that year, he had complained, "All over the country there is a wave of licentiousness running counter to a wave of ultra-Puritanism." Then he had been most concerned with the effects of Puritanism, as shown in Prohibition, the Ku Klux Klan, and the anti-evolutionists:

> And they do it in the name of Scripture!... But the Old Testament, and it's my favorite book, is a mixture of allegory, fiction, burning beauty and sheer brutality. The anti-evolutionists are taking the word for its face value—especially in the story of Creation. You see the Bible says that God made this infinitesimal little world in five or six days—and with a sweep of his hand made the rest of the mighty universe. In relation to which the globe is a tiny speck. Looks to me a lot like God wasted the first week.[7]

The licentiousness that this Purtanism seemed paradoxically to spawn Cobb saw in its full bloom in Hollywood. 1926 was a peak year for what Cobb calls "Babylonian excesses" in Hollywood: extravagant living, bacchanalian parties, divorces, murders, overnight successes and failures. As he travelled back to New York from Hollywood, the country seemed to Cobb to be destroying itself, careening out of control toward anarchy on the one hand and a meddling Puritanism on the other. Cobb, who in the teens had thought the United States superior to any European country and had feared that American entry into the war would corrupt the soldiers involved, ten years later was willing to concede that perhaps a European had the answer to America's problems.

Cobb was not alone among Americans in the mid-twenties in his admiration for Benito Mussolini. American newspaper accounts of Mussolini's rise to power were quite favorable, and soon many Americans were repeating the sentiment that a man who got the beggars off the streets and made the trains run on time was the kind of man needed in the United States. Will Rogers reminded Americans that every successful business had a dictator at the top, and Abe Martin reported, "Nearly ever' buddy I talk to would like t' borrow Mussolini fer a day or two. . . ."[8]

The Chapmans, who had been living in Italy for two years, were far less enthusiastic about Mussolini's supposed benefits, but Cobb didn't listen, and he and Bob Davis, who with Mrs. Davis accompanied the Cobbs to Florence, turned their departure into a forum on what was wrong with America and right with Mussolini.

At shipside Davis displayed to reporters 4,000 newspaper clippings of positive responses to the premier's recent message to the United States and said he planned to show them personally to Mussolini. Cobb also announced his intention to meet with Mussolini if possible, and declared,

> I am searching for personal liberty, and if I can find a country where the people are still free, I will stay there. Of course, if I pick up a quantity of liberty over there and have some left over, I may try to bring some to the United States, but I doubt if I'd be allowed to bring it into the country.[9]

It was a new tone for a public pronouncement from Cobb: shrill, frustrated, out of control. It was, unfortunately, a tone that was to be heard more frequently in succeeding years.

The visit was not a particularly pleasant one. Elisabeth Cobb claims that Cobb and Davis spent most of their time in the

American Express Office waiting for mail from home. Cobb's tone-deafness made the frequent performances of Frank Chapman's musical friends a torture for him, and he disliked touring the art museums with his wife almost as much. But mostly they argued about Mussolini. Cobb and Davis got their forty-minute interview and were bowled over. "He has a remarkably vivid personality," Cobb told reporters on his return. "Mussolini has done wonders in Italy."[10] The reservations of the Chapmans made no impression: in Buff's words, "they roared us down as young malcontents; ignorant and subversive children who did not know what we were talking about."[11]

As Cobb and Davis waited in Florence for a message from Hollywood that never came and a baby that did finally come, but six weeks late, the American Express Office delivered an unexpected and unwanted message: Charley Russell had died on October 24. Cobb was named an honorary pallbearer, but he was unable to get back to the funeral. Eight days later the baby, called Pat as a child, was born, and Cobb became a grandfather. It was a role he enjoyed, one that brought him a lot of happiness. Even arriving as she did, as inconveniently as possible in a time of great stress for Cobb, the grandchild managed to lighten Cobb's spirits. Bob Davis wrote Manie Cobb a few months after their return, "Between you and me, I think the youngster has given him a brand new lease on life."[12]

As usual, Cobb's travels seemed to have no diminishing effect on his publication. *Cosmopolitan,* a monthly magazine, perhaps made fewer demands on Cobb than the weekly *Post* had, but the stories and articles continued to pour out, published both in *Cosmopolitan* and in other magazines. In 1923 Cobb had begun a series of humorous sketches of various states in the union; in 1924 these were published in separate brochures, one each for sixteen states, called *Cobb's American Guyed Books.* In 1926 Doran brought out a volume called *Some United States* that combined the *American Guyed Books* into one. Cobb dedicated it to Charles Russell.

Although Cobb was occasionally pontifical, his main concerns in *Some United States* were humor and aptness of description. Since the writing is from 1923 and 1924, the tone is usually milder than that of his Mussolini proclamations. His biases of course reveal themselves; Kentucky gets a much more favorable portrait than New York. Cities take a beating both for their myopia and their filth:

> Here a curious paradox intrudes: Having no civic pride in the

Top: Back Home viewed from the garden.
Bottom: The Cobbs in their back yard about 1923. On the ground, from left, are Laura Cobb, Pat Chapman, Cobbie Brody, and Elisabeth Cobb Brody. In back, from left, are Laura's father, Marcus S. Baker, Irvin Cobb, and Alton Brody.
Photo reprinted by permission of Mrs. Catherine Adams

> sense that other men in other populous communities have it, nor yet any enthusiasm for the achievements of his individual fellow-townsmen, [the New Yorker] nevertheless holds to the belief that anything worthwhile must originate, must develop, must come to pass in New York or Great Britain or Italy or Germany or Russia; otherwise it might as well not have happened at all, for it doesn't count.
>
> * * *
>
> A city is like unto the dromedary of the Arabian fable—let her but poke her nose under the door flap and presently she has filled the whole tent with her bulk and her fleas and her stinks and her spraddling arrogant presumptions. When a camel grows active it begins to smell bad; where it rises up it blots out the landscape; where it stretches itself the terrain is polluted and disturbed. You may say the same for a city....[13]

On his return to the United States Irvin Cobb, that reluctant New Yorker, started looking for another country house. As Laura Cobb later told a reporter, "He liked to surprise me. He would come home and say 'I've bought you a house.' And he was restless. Every seven years he wanted to move, and we did."[14] The house he bought in 1927, at East Hampton on Long Island, proved to be Laura's favorite, with windows to the floor in the main rooms looking out over the hills. They named it "Back Home." Cobb took a larger, front upstairs room for his study, although he insisted on calling it his "workshop," the name he had given to the made-over out-building at Rebel Ridge. He filled the room with spears, rugs, and costumes from his Indian collection. But over his writing table he hung, not one of his many Russell western scenes, but a painting by Walter Sies of the riverfront of Paducah as it looked in 1884. Under his feet was a bear rug he had shot himself, and he even convinced Laura to hang a moose head in the drawing room. She was preoccupied with planting another garden.

Although he planned to retain the Park Avenue apartment for the time being, Cobb saw "Back Home" as an eventual retirement home. He was slowly reevaluating the ups and downs of his career, becoming used to his position as a grandfather in his fifties who had not become a second Mark Twain after all but who was still one of the highest paid writers in the country. In April of 1927 Elisabeth Chapman published her first novel, *Falling Seeds,* to mostly enthusiastic reviews, and Cobb was prouder of her accomplishment than he had been of his own. He began to talk to friends and family of slowing down, of not renewing his *Cosmopolitan* contract, of fishing more. He even learned to play golf with his East Hampton neighbors. (Bob Davis wrote Manie Cobb in mock complaint that

October, "I have seen very little of him this year. Society at East Hampton almost swallowed him up." Actually he had visited Cobb several times that year, going up in October while Buff and the baby were visiting to make his special lamb curry.)

*Prose and Cons* was the last book Cobb published with Doran; beginning with *Ladies and Gentlemen* in February of 1927, Cobb's books were published by the Cosmopolitan Book Corporation, a subsidiary of the magazine. Apparently the parting was amicable; Doran has nothing but praise for Cobb in his 1935 autobiography, and of course the Doran Company continued to receive a substantial income from the earlier Cobb books they had published. Cosmopolitan also found him an extremely profitable author; although the first two Cobb books they brought out were given the harshest reviews he had ever received (*Saturday Review* found *Ladies and Gentlemen* exaggerated, obvious, and lacking in artistry;[17] *Booklist* said it was unfortunate that Cobb was serious in the novel *Chivalry Peak,* for it would have made a good burlesque of tasteless mediocrity,[18]) sales for those and all Cobb books continued high. Doran in the twenties had continued his earlier pattern of seeking out unestablished talent in this country and in Britain: Aldous Huxley, Michael Arlen, Max Beerbohm, and Frank Harris all published with Doran, and he tried for and just missed Joseph Conrad and D. H. Lawrence. Doran continued to entertain his cohorts and to introduce them to each other whenever possible. Although Cobb had spent less and less time in Doran's company as the decade passed, the break with Doran was still a significant break, Cobb's last one, with the world of literature. By 1927 Cobb was no longer one of Doran's distinguished authors; he was a popular writer for a low-brow magazine and its equally low-brow book-publishing arm.

## Notes

[1]July 25, 1926; clipping, Louisville Free Public Library.

[2]E. Cobb, *Wayward Parent,* p. 176.

[3]New York *Times,* May 26, 1926, 1:2.

[4]Charles Fisher, *The Columnists: A Clinical Survey* (New York: Howell-Soskin Company, 1944), p. 111.

[5]Robert H. Davis to Irvin S. Cobb, March 25, 1927; Davis Collection, New York Public Library.

[6]Cobb, *Exit Laughing,* pp. 477-479.

[7]Louisville *Herald-Post,* March 21, 1926; clipping, Louisville Free Public Library.

[8]Yates, p. 122.

[9]New York *Times,* August 19, 1926, 13:3.
[10]New York *Times,* November 9, 1926, 29:2.
[11]E. Cobb, *Wayward Parent, p. 161.*
[12]Robert H. Davis to Manie S. Cobb, April 4, 1927, Davis Collection, New York Public Library.
[13]Cobb, *Some United States,* p. 303.
[14]Sutton, *Courier-Journal,* April 26, 1964.
[15]Robert H. Davis to Manie S. Cobb, November 22, 1927; Davis Collection, New York Public Library.
[16]Robert H. Davis to "Lolly" (Laura B. Cobb), October, 1927; Davis Collection, New York Public Library.
[17]*Saturday Review of Literature* (April 23, 1927), III, 766.
[18]*Booklist* (December, 1927), XXIV:118.

# Chapter Twenty-Two

As the name of his East Hampton estate perhaps suggests, Cobb in the late twenties began to be more and more nostalgic about the Kentucky of his youth. His later Kentucky stories and novels lack the toughness and social awareness of those he wrote in the teens. Earlier he had protested the magnolia-blossom school of Southern fiction, insisting on the spareness and occasional grimness of life in a community where economics determined behavior more frequently than chivalry. In his later work this earlier intention is blurred; his characters are more genteel, their problems mainly romantic, and their world comfortable and attractive.

The title of *All Aboard: A Saga of the Romantic River,* a novel Cobb published in 1927, suggests this change. The "romantic river" is the Tennessee, and its romance for Cobb is the steamboats that travelled it in his boyhood. The theme of *All Aboard* is reconciliation, specifically of the North and the South. This theme is not new to Cobb, of course; old Confederate and Union soldiers march through many of his early stories, sometimes in conflict, but usually arm in arm by the end of the story. But the tone of those stories had been one of hope; the reconciliation was seen as a solution, a civilizing factor, a way toward the twentieth century.

In *All Aboard* the civilization praised is that of the nineteenth century. The three veterans of the book, one Union, one Confederate, and Major Todd, a Southerner who served with the Union, are commissioners at the Shiloh Battleground. Major Todd helps the children of the other two to elope on a steamboat, where they are married by an A.M.E. minister. The fathers set out in pursuit, thus providing for a steamboat race, but are brought around. Robert A. Lively, who has written about Civil War novels, points out that such a North-South romance is the most frequently used plot of such books, and that, as in *All Aboard,* the man is always from the North, the bride is a Southern belle. When such books deal with the war itself, myth becomes more important than history, and the battles seem as bloodless and polite as cricket matches.[1] In *All Aboard* when the bride's father accuses Major Todd of having fought to free the slaves, he responds,

> I have just this to say for you, suh: You may have fought, among other reasons, to keep that race in servitude. Some may have fought to free it. But, suh, no trivial side-issues for me. I fought only to preserve the Union.[2]

Earlier Cobb (and Judge Priest) had found the "trivial side-issues" to be of great importance. By 1927 nostalgia had taken over.

There is no doubt that one of the things that Cobb was nostalgic for was a time when a man could drink his bourbon in peace, and so in late 1927, with hopes of spurring the end of Prohibition, Cobb decided to write a novel about the Kentucky bourbon industry in the late nineteenth century. He planned a research trip to get background material and wrote John Wilson Townsend in Lexington, asking his help in lining up sources.

Townsend was a Kentucky promoter who had taken Kentucky writers as his special province. Townsend worked in Lexington as a librarian and a newspaper reporter until 1916, when he became the manager of Graceland Farms. But he lived for his spare time, when he corresponded with and wrote about Kentucky authors.[3]

Townsends' early idol was James Lane Allen. He first heard of Cobb when he saw one of Cobb's *Sunday World* columns in 1910. In 1912 he went to New York to meet both Allen and Cobb. Townsend fancied himself a Boswell; if he lacked Boswell's writing style, his social style was frequently similar, as was his unselfconsciousness about revealing himself in print. Allen, a prim and proper gentleman of the old school, barely tolerated Townsend's intrusions. Cobb, as might be expected, welcomed his friendship and encouraged his demands.

The behavior of the three men is shown in Townsend's account of his 1912 New York trip in a biography he wrote of Allen. Townsend had just met Cobb and perhaps was more enthusiastic in describing his work in a later interview with Allen than was agreeable to the more established writer. (The Allen book was dedicated to Cobb.) But Allen praised the Cobb stories that he had read in the *Post* and said he'd have to purchased some of Cobb's books. In a typical gesture, Townsend jumped up and offered to have his friend Cobb send Allen the books. Allen refused; he had no desire to send his books to other people, and he didn't want theirs sent to him. Townsend apparently did not take this rebuff seriously; a few pages after his description of this episode, he printed a letter from Cobb which included the news that he had sent his books to Allen as Townsend had requested.[4]

Townsend and Cobb corresponded for the rest of Cobb's life, although sometimes the length and frequency of Townsend's letters, full of questions, requests, and calls for comment, were too much for Cobb, and he merely scribbled answers in the margins of the original letter and sent it back. Most of their correspondence in the early twenties was related to the biography Townsend was writing of Cobb for the *Library of Southern Literature,* published in 1923. Townsend then decided to expand that biography to book length, a project Cobb discouraged but cooperated with. (Cobb's attitude was the same toward Fred Neuman's biography, published in Paducah in 1924). Townsend's letters are thus full of requests for information and, as the manuscript took shape, of plans for getting it published. Townsend wrote Doran several times about it, and at the time of Cobb's Lexington trip in January and February, 1928, the manuscript was at the Doran offices in New York. They later turned it down, and Cobb had to assure Townsend that he had not himself blocked publication.[5]

However tiresome Townsend must have been at times, Cobb had a warm affection for him and was glad for his help with the research for *Red Likker.* Cobb was quite sensitive to the difference between the blue grass region where the book was set and the region he had grown up in, westward beyond the Tennessee, and he wanted to get the details right.

*Red Likker,* which was published in the summer of 1929, got better reviews than many of Cobb's other books of that period. Even the London *Times,* reviewing the book after its release in Britain, called it "an eminently readable book, full of historical and social interest."[6] The novel traces the Kentucky history of the Bird family, from the earlier settler through the Civil War (in which Birds fought on both sides, displaying and encountering nobility in equal measures) and the subsequent founding of the "Bird and Son" distillery, up to the time of Prohibition, the destruction of the distillery by fire and the final transformation of the family into crossroads grocers. Like *All Aboard,* the book is flawed by the sentimental haze that had settled over Cobb's memories of Kentucky. The Bird family only produces one less than perfect son, Isham Bird III, who is a cliche himself: a dashing seducer killed in a duel by his victim's brother.

Cobb composing, 1932. If the pose is staged, the costume is not. Cobb preferred to work in smocks that he had made to order. They reached to the knee and were worn with knee socks.
Photo reprinted by permission of Louisville Courier Journal and Times

*Red Likker* has many fine passages. Its strengths are those of Cobb's short stories: description of the countryside, details of familiar home scenes, background narrative, felicitious language. But Cobb never developed other skills important to the novel writer: believable dialogue, appropriate pace, consistent point of view, the unification of purpose and plot. Perhaps he might have developed these skills with earlier practice and encouragement; perhaps the novel was always a genre unsuited to his talents. All of *Red Likker* is told at the breakneck speed of exposition: Cobb covers one hundred and twenty-five years in 300 pages without ever really slowing down. Yet conversations when they do occur are ponderous. Cobb may have had difficulty with dialogue because he seldom participated in give-and-take conversations himself: his daughter says sessions with Cobb and his cronies involved each taking the floor in succession to tell a long tale or develop a theme. Seldom do characters reveal themselves through their conversations, only their opinions, which are conveniently Cobb's own. The most unwieldy passages in the book are those in which Cobb develops his anti-Prohibition theme most pointedly. Colonel Bird, the founder of the distillery, argues with his widowed sister, a teetotaler and Prohibitionist, at great length, each allowing the other to make points with the politeness of a public debater. (The colonel, of course, triumphs: when the Volstead Act reduces the alcohol content of her favorite nostrum, the teetotaler is shown to be an alcoholic.) *Red Likker* was obviously a labor of love for Cobb, his last in novel form, for the novels he wrote after it were merely pot-boilers. He himself was disappointed with it; he wrote Bob Davis later that it had probably been a "mistake."[7]

Soon after Cobb returned to New York he and Al Smith were the featured speakers at the national convention of the Child Welfare Committee of America. During his speech Cobb announced that he was supporting Smith for president.[8] Cobb had met Smith twenty years earlier and counted him a friend for a long time. When Smith got the nomination, Cobb campaigned for him and helped form the Actors', Authors' and Artists' League for Smith. He was particularly enraged by the anti-Catholic sentiments he encountered; Smith, Cobb declared, was "the object of an un-American campaign of slander" with "intolerance thundering at him from the Christian pulpits."[9] In October he took the Smith campaign to Paducah, where Democratic Party workers were having an uneasy time pushing their candidate. Although Smith finally carried the district, in Cobb's words, "it did have rather a close call from going Baptist." One of those votes for Smith was cast by Cobb's mother, who had grown so feeble that she had to be carried to the polls but who felt the need to strike back at the prejudice she recognized around her.

Shortly after Hoover's victory over Smith, on December 15, 1928, Cobb, Will Hogg, and Dean Palmer (the son of Cobb's friend Charles Palmer and junior partner in his newspaper brokerage firm) left for an extended tour of South America. Hoover was in South America himself at the time, returning just before his inauguration. The role of the United States in Latin American affairs was a matter of increasing interest. At the Havana Conference the previous January a proposed resolution, blocked by the American delegation, had declared that "no state has the right to intervene in the internal affairs of another."[10] Cobb was on assignment from *Cosmopolitan* magazine to report on current conditions in Latin America and the appropriateness of maintaining the Monroe Doctrine. Hogg and Palmer went along to keep Cobb company.

It was an interesting trio. Each of the three weighed over 200 pounds. Cobb said Dean Palmer "looked like Dickens' somnambulant fat boy and sometimes, but not in business hours, behaved like him." In contrast to Palmer's sleepy calmness, Hogg displayed exuberant animation. He was the linguist of the trio, and, although the Spanish vocabulary he had picked up as a boy in Texas contained fewer than one hundred words, he used them with such verve and gesticulation that they sufficed.[11]

The trio went on ship from New Orleans to Havana and Panama. They spent Christmas Day on Barro Colorado Island, a government preserve on a lake near Panama City. From Panama they sailed down the West Coast to Peru and Chile, then across the Andes to Argentina, and on another ship to Uruguay and Brazil, where the official tour ended in February. Palmer apparently returned to New York at that point, but Cobb and Hogg crossed the Atlantic to meet Laura, who had been spending the months of their trip in Europe with the Chapmans.

The five articles based on Cobb's trip were published in *Cosmopolitan* between October, 1929, and February, 1930. They were later collected along with some unrelated sketches in the 1930 volume *Both Sides of the Street*. Cobb was very impressed with the South Americans and the potential benefits to the United States of increased good will:

It is to South America rather than to Europe or Asia and other

> main divisions of the earth's surface that, in succeeding years, we must look for the best market for Yankee-made goods and find the choicest playgrounds for Yankee-born pleasure seekers. Because South America is the land of the future.

The average South American was polite and non-judgmental:

> In short, he doesn't set himself up to be his brother's keeper, and that, I think, is a beautiful virtue common in his land and, by contrast, exceedingly rare in a certain land I might mention.

Cobb found the cities clean and beautiful; Buenos Aires was "the single city familiar to me where man has neither marred nor destroyed the natural gorgeousness of the setting." Cobb took note of some imperfections in Latin America:

> There are things which ought to be changed—and some of them are being changed. There are primitive things, pitiable things, deplorable things—evidences of ignorance and of dire poverty cheek by jowl with signs and portents of enlightenment and prosperity.[12]

But the greatest cause of South American problems was the patronizing ignorance of the United States. At a luncheon in Sao Paulo he called for discarding the Monroe Doctrine, declaring the South American nations as self-sufficient as France and Spain.

Cobb's views were by no means in opposition to those of Herbert Hoover. Cobb sent Hoover a telegram from Brazil, congratulating him on the wisdom of his trip and the good will it had created. In spite of his strong campaign effort for Al Smith and his disappointment at Hoover's support for Prohibition, Cobb was an admiring acquaintance of Herbert Hoover. In August, 1928, Cobb, Ray Long, the editor of *Cosmopolitan*, and Hoover were seated together at a party at the Bohemian Grove, an exclusive wilderness club north of San Francisco, when someone brought Hoover a telegram informing him of Coolidge's decision not to run for a second term. After Cobb's return in April, 1929, he went to Washington to brief Hoover on his trip. It was Cobb's last opportunity to advise a president.

Cobb continued his campaign against Prohibition. In July, 1929, he accepted the chairmanship of the Authors and Artists Committee of the Association Against the Prohibition Amendment. The committee included 361 members, among them Bob Davis, Stephen Vincent Benet, Rex Beach, and Emily Post. Cobb released a statement to the press blaming Prohibition for increased crime, alcoholism, and disrespect for the law. "If Prohibition is a noble experiment," he said, "then the San Francisco fire and the Galveston flood should be listed among the noble experiments of our national history."[13]

Cobb may have pointed with horror to the wild parties and riotous living of the youth of his day while campaigning against Prohibition, but at other times he exhibited an unexpected complacency about his daughter's generation. In a newspaper interview headlined "Irvin Cobb Votes 'Yes' For Our Revolting Youth," he states:

> My daughter was a regular flapper. She flapped.... As soon as she got married, she turned right-about-face.... Many people think that one of the infallible signs that this is an age of moral decadence is that we are so obsessed with sex.... Yet I can't see that there is anything shameful or disgraceful about it.... [It is equally destructive] to deny its existence as they did in my boyhood. A girl of eighteen then had no understanding of the facts of life, and when she married, unlike the modern girl, she generally knew no more about the physical aspects of marriage than a child. I believe that while [modern youth] may be somewhat overeducated in sex, it is better and far safer, than no education at all.

In this interview Cobb stressed his continuing belief in the importance of careers for women:

> One of the things I admire most about the young girl of today is her desire to do something in the world. No longer does she view child-bearing and keeping house as her only functions in the world....[14]

Cobb was quite aware of the difficulties women faced in abandoning traditional roles and made it the theme of a short story he wrote that year which became the title story of the volume *This Man's World.* Two sisters, Annie and Anita, work in a department store, "doing practically the same tasks that men and half-grown men were doing not so deftly as they, [but receiving] considerably less in wages than the contemporary men earned." Unable to support themselves this way, "Annie got herself a husband, Anita got herself a man." But Annie's husband accuses her of adultery without cause and Anita's lover leaves after she develops an unsightly goiter. The story ends with her saying to her sister, "You go straight and I go crooked and the best either one of us gets is the worst of it. Sis, what the hell's wrong with this rotten world, anyway?"[15] Critics found faults not only with the mechanical presentation of theme, but with the theme itself.[16]

Early 1929 was in many ways a pleasant period for Cobb, however. Still beaming with the confidence his trip to South America and conference with President Hoover gave him, he travelled to Paducah for an honor of another sort: the opening of the Irvin Cobb Hotel on April 30, 1929.

In what is surely a unique gesture to a living writer, Adolph Weil, a Paducah businessman and childhood friend of Cobb, asked his permission to use his name for the hotel he was building. The Irvin Cobb was the largest hotel in far western Kentucky, with eight floors containing large public rooms, a roof garden, and 200 bedrooms, each with a bath. The decor was Old English with half-timbered gables on the outside and beams and gargoyles within. Cobb spoke at the opening ceremonies and presented the hotel with the portrait of himself done by James Montgomery Flagg fourteen years earlier.[17] Later a bridge across the Ohio River at Paducah was named for Cobb, joining a list of Cobb namesakes which also included, as tabulated in a New York *Times* article, "a cigar, a dahlia, a Missouri corncob pipe, a race horse, a bass bait, a hunting shirt, an Oregon canyon, a Texas street, and a pointer dog."[18]

## Notes

[1]Robert A. Lively, *Fiction Fights the Civil War: An Unfinished Chapter in the Literary History of the American People* (Westport, Conn.: Greenwood Press, 1957), p. 57.

[2]All Aboard, (New York: Cosmopolitan Book Corp, 1927), p. 69.

[3]Dorothy Edwards Townsend, *The Life and Works of John Wilson Townsend: Kentucky Author and Historian 1885-1968* (Lexington: Keystone Printery, 1972), passim.

[4]John Wilson Townsend, *James Lane Allen* (Louisville: *Courier Journal* Job Printing Company, 1927), p. 91; p. 97.

[5]letters in Eastern Kentucky Library; specifically, Irvin S. Cobb to John Wilson Townsend, April 24, 1927.

[6]London *Times Literary Supplement,* April 10, 1930; clipping in Louisville Free Public Library.

[7]Irvin S. Cobb to Robert H. Davis, Davis collection, New York Public Library.

[8]New York *Times*, 2 February 1928, 3:3.

[9]*Paducah News Democrat*, 17 October 1928.

[10]Richard B. Morris, *Encyclopedia of American History* (New York: Harper and Brothers, 1953), p. 323.

[11]Irvin S. Cobb, *Both Sides of the Street* (New York: Cosmopolitan Book Corp., 1930), pp. 5; 54.

[12]*Both Sides,* p. 4, p. 20; pp. 22-23.

[13]New York *Times,* 30 July 1929, 21:1.

[14]Louisville Courier Journal, 10 June, 1928.

[15]Irvin S. Cobb, *This Man's World* (New York: Cosmopolitan Book Corporation, 1929), p. 2; p. 28.

[16]*Saturday Review of Literature*, 6 April 1929, clipping, Louisville Free Public Library.

[17]Irvin S. Cobb to John Wilson Townsend, 30 December 1929, Eastern Kentucky University Library. The hotel has recently been restored and converted to apartments.

[18]New York *Times*, 30 July 1929, III, 4:6.

# Chapter Twenty-three

By the fall of 1929, on paper at least, Cobb was close to being a millionaire. His cautious nature had led him to save or invest as much of his income as possible. His happy talk about retirement in the second half of the decade was based on his faith that, however untrustworthy praise and popularity might be, a fortune couldn't go away. If Cobb was beginning to doubt the integrity of the American character, he still believed those who said that "the only way to lose money on Wall Street was to stay out of Wall Street."

Buff, who had brought her daughter back to her parents' house in East Hampton after her marriage had fallen apart, describes the effect of the Crash on her father:

> I remember one gloomy Sunday in November when he and I were taking a walk together. The last mile. That's what we felt that promenade to be. A doomed processional. In the morning the tumbrils would be pulling up at our door....
>
> The day before he had heard of the failure of the great investment house of Goldman Saks...he was greatly involved. He walked silently for many miles. Finally he turned to me and said, "Well, this year I pay no income tax.... Thank you Mr. Goldman—thank you Mr. Sax!"[1]

Although Cobb lost a lot of money, his actual financial situation after the Crash was far from hopeless. There was never any serious consideration given to selling Back Home or giving up the apartment; he still had his *Cosmopolitan* contract, with several articles and stories in the planning stages, and his syndicated column. But his carefully nurtured self-confidence and sense of security were gone. In his boyhood he had acquired the notion that laziness led to poverty and shame, and he had worked incredibly hard all his life to avoid such a fate. The levelling effects of the Crash seemed to call his principle of hard work into question: suddenly it seemed that nothing made any difference at all.

Buff's marital difficulties contributed to his sense of a world turned upside down. Years of associating with Broadway hedonists had never shaken Cobb's firm belief in faithful monogamy, and

Buff's decision to divorce Frank Chapman caused him a lot of pain. It also took her comforting presence away from him right after the Crash, for she left in early December to establish a three month residency in Reno, Nevada, taking Pat with her. Laura joined them for Christmas; Cobb traveled to his mother's and Reubie's home in Paducah where, for the time being at least, everything seemed the same. Buff's divorce was final in March, 1930. The following September she married Alton Brody, a war veteran in the real estate business. They moved into the Park Avenue apartment; the Cobbs stayed in East Hampton for the time being.

Soon Cobb was following the work ethic again, although his goal had changed from providing for retirement to paying off his debts. After the Crash Cobb appeared on the radio much more frequently. Several times in 1930 he appeared as Grantland Rice's guest on the Coca-Cola Programme to talk about sports. In December he became a regular on the Armour Hour. Like Will Rogers, Herb Shriner, and Robert Benchley, he became a perennial guest on various variety shows and talk shows. In April of 1933 he signed a contract with Gulf Oil for a series that lasted the rest of that year. In October he wrote John Wilson Townsend:

> I like radio work, more or less, but shall quit it November 24 after thirty weeks of two shows a week to rest up. I'll go back on the air after Christmas probably.
>
> I'm making some money at it—and applying the money mostly to my debts which are still large and hungry....
>
> I'm fairly well but awfully tired.[2]

Cobb's literary output after the Crash was also steady, if not as profuse as earlier. A new series of Judge Priest tales, begun before the Crash and published in *Cosmopolitan* in 1930 and 1931, brought in several thousand letters welcoming the old boy back.[3] The stories were collected in 1932 as *Down Yonder with Judge Priest and Irvin S. Cobb,* published by a new firm started by Ray Long, who had left Cosmopolitan that year. Long was beginning to develop the emotional problems that led to his suicide a few years later, and his instability showed in several unfortunate career decisions he made in the early thirties. Many of his friends simply dismissed him, but Cobb stuck with him in friendship even when, in the mid-thirties, he sued Cobb over the rights to a movie property.

Cobb helped rescue Long from an explosive situation in 1931. Long gave a dinner for Boris Pilnyak, a visiting Russian novelist. Long thought it would be a nice gesture to invite Sinclair Lewis, who had just been awarded the Nobel Prize for Literature. Also, Long's aide William Lengel convinced him to invite Theodore Dreiser, in spite of tales that Dreiser was jealous of Lewis' award and that Lewis had accused Dreiser of plagiarizing from Dorothy Thompson's book on Russia. Other guests at the March 19, 1931, dinner at the Metropolitan Club included Cobb, Heywood Broun, Arthur Brisbane and Burton Rascoe. Lewis became quite drunk before Dreiser arrived, and answered Dresier's congratulations with a rude sound. When called upon to speak, Lewis stood up and accused Dresier of being a plagiarist and two critics present (he probably meant Brown and Brisbane) of criticizing the Nobel Committee choice. Long quickly jumped to his feet and introduced Cobb, who started telling funny stories as fast as he could. In the lobby after the other speeches were over, Lewis continued his accusations and Dreiser slapped him until pulled off.[4] The situation was a humiliating one for Cobb; he had known both Dreiser and Lewis when he was more famous than they, and now he was serving as comic relief to their struggle for recognition as the best writer in America.

Cobb had another brush with Dreiser that November. Dreiser, touring the coal mining areas of eastern Kentucky, expressed horror to the press at the poverty and misery he found there. Cobb found his tone patronizing and his shock misplaced; he issued an icy comment on the universality of poverty and misery. "I know Dreiser pretty well," he said, "and I don't want to doubt the purity of his altruism but New York is known to have shocking conditions too." [5]

Some of Cobb's writing during the early thirties involved techniques or genres new to his work. Some of this experimentation seems based on genuine interest; most of it, however, is probably an attempt to write what would sell best. One of his most successful experiments is the essay in fictionalized history; perhaps a better description of Cobb's work is anachronistic reporting. His volume *Incredible Truth,* published in 1931, recreates thirty famous situations or events, most told from the specific point of view of a participant. The subjects range from the Forty-niners to Nero's crimes, from Joan of Arc to Pepys on the London fire. The nostalgia that had led Cobb to impose an excess of nobility on nineteenth century Kentucky is here contained; Cobb picks subjects suitable to the heroics he wishes to display.

Cobb's attempt to enter the lucrative murder mystery field was not nearly as successful. *Murder Day by Day* (1933) is interesting only because no one seems to have objected to his using the same

Cobb mugging the camera during a fishing trip in April, 1936.
Photo reprinted by permission of Louisville Courier Journal and Times

device that had created such a stir several years earlier in Agatha Christie's *Murder of Roger Ackroyd:* the presumably trustworthy narrator who turns out to be the murderer. *Judge Priest Turns Detective,* 1936, is even more painfully inept. Cobb had lost his facility for fiction. He realized this and made no attempt to renew his *Cosmopolitan* contract after Long left. After the middle of the decade, he wrote no more fiction.

Many of Cobb's trips during the early thirties were sad ones, or interrupted by bad news. In September, 1930, Cobb was on a hunting trip to the Bob White Lodge in North Carolina when he received word of the sudden death of Will Hogg. He returned immediately to New York and the McIntyres' apartment, where all were overcome by tears. Cobb soon insisted that they stop: "You know what old Bill would say to this? He'd say I don't want any of you so-and-so's sniveling over me." Cobb, the McIntyres, and three other New York friends accompanied the body to Houston for the burial, and Cobb told jokes and kept the conversation light all the way. McIntyre remembers, "Bleeding inwardly, he made us laugh and he laughed himself."[6]

Bob Davis did not join the group of mourners; he was off on a trip to Germany. After Frank Munsey's death in 1925 (and without the inheritance that Munsey had always promised him) Davis had become a columnist on the New York *Sun.* Some early experiments there with writing about his travels proved very popular, so Davis had made that his speciality, both in his column and in numerous books that described trips to destinations both exotic and familiar. Although he and Cobb perhaps saw each other less in the early thirties than they had in the twenties, they kept up a regular correspondence, much of it concerned with plans for (and not infrequent cancellations of) hunting and fishing trips.[7]

Cobb joined a large group of writers and editors, including Dreiser, Ray Long, Jesse Lasky, Rube Goldberg, and Bugs Baer, in paying tribute to Davis in June of 1931 at a luncheon at the Hotel Ritz Tower. The immediate occasion was the publication of Davis' book on O. Henry, but his friends welcomed the opportunity to honor this modest, generous man whom the New York *Times* called "the most lovable figure in American literature today."[8]

Davis continued his correspondence with Cobb's mother, sending her a telegram on February 14, 1930, that asked "Will you on this your birthday be my Valentine." Her acceptance was signed "Your Kentucky mother." In February, 1931, he wrote her,

> Well, I saw all the Cobbs in the world the other night. We rounced

> up at the Norris teas [apparently Charles and Kathleen Norris].
> Frankly, I'd rather sit in your parlor with you and Miss Reubie than be one of a mob of tea drinkers. Everybody looked his best—Manie, Hewett, Irvin, Buff, and Lollie.[9]

A year later Cobb's mother died. She had fractured two ribs in a fall, but Reubie had decided that it was not serious enough for Cobb and Manie Howland to come down from New York. They hurried down for the funeral and were still in town when Reubie suddenly decided to marry Richard Rudy, local businessman and banker and her beau of forty years. Cobb made no attempt to understand his sister's behavior; their intense rivalry had cooled down as they aged, and they had grown quite fond of one another. Cobb appreciated the care Reubie devoted to their mother and the hero's welcome she prepared for him when he returned. As Elizabeth Cobb explains,

> She nursed, cooked, cosseted, worked like a Trojan, laughed all the time, was always funny, and dainty as a rose tree.... It is very hard to stay angry with a woman who makes you laugh, and feeds you.[10]

Cobb was still grieving for his mother ten years later when he wrote *Exit Laughing.* He made two more sad trips to Paducah in 1933; first for Richard Rudy's funeral, then, in October, for Reubie's.[11] Bob Davis wrote to express his grief: "she had just begun to live." Cobb did not return to Paducah for eight years.

Cobb made these trips to Paducah alone, as he had usually done. Laura had gone at least once to see her mother-in-law during her final years, but at the time of her death she stayed in New York with Buff and her new grandson. Irvin Cobb Brody, called Cobbie, had been born in 1931. Buff's second marriage was no more successful than her first, and she and the two children during most of their childhood made their home with her parents. Cobb welcomed a boy into the family and spent a lot of time with his namesake, but repeated the same pattern with his grandchildren that he had found so painful as a boy: Pat was coddled and spoiled, but Cobbie was expected to toe the mark and behave like a man. He rebelled against this treatment and several years later demanded that his name be changed: he was was tired of being treated like a junior edition of his grandfather. His choice for a name was Tom Sawyer; he became "Tom," but in compromise his legal name became Thomas Cobb Brody. Pat also later changed her name; when she became an actress she adopted her mother's nickname, becoming "Buff Cobb" professionally.

Cobb's connection with the anti-Prohibition movement brought him a lot of attention when Repeal came in 1934. The Waldorf-Astoria reprinted an earlier Cobb tribute to drink called "Here's How!" to distribute at the re-opening of the Waldorf Bar.[12] The Frankfort Distilleries brought out *Irvin S. Cobb's Own Recipe Book,* with a long essay by Cobb glorifying Kentucky bourbon and the various things one could do with it. One of the stories he incorporates in it provides him with a delightful oportunity to revenge himself on Wall Street financiers, as he describes the effect on one such man of several Creole mint juleps:

> You should have witnessed what a magic transformation it was that stole over that man. At the outset he seemed but poor material to work on, too. For he was a typical Wall Street investment banker—had an eye in his head like an undertaker's night bell, and a jaw like a clamped wolftrap, and...thought of the future only in terms of thirty, sixty, and ninety days....
>
> After his first helping of julep he...said that although he came of Old Puritan stock from up in the interior of Massachusetts,... his people always had been very strong Southern sympathizers.... Following the next replenishment, he requested that somebody be so kind as to take him riding in a barouche along the old bayou so he could harken to the mocking bird warbling in the magnolia tree.... His mood changed [after the third julep], and when I left he had just offered to whip any damn-Yankee in the house.[13]

## Notes

[1]E. Cobb, *Wayward Parent,* p. 181.

[2]Irvin S. Cobb to John Wilson Townsend, October 18, 1933; University of Kentucky Library.

[3]Logsdon, p. 26.

[4]Swann, pp. 372-373.

[5]Louisville *Herald-Post,* November 4, 1931; clipping, Louisville Free Public Library.

[6]1O. O. McIntyre, introduction to Neuman *Cobb* (1934), p. 15.

[20]Davis Collection, New York Public Library.

[8]New York *Times,* October 12, 1942; 17:1.

[9]Robert H. Davis to Manie S. Cobb, February 11, 1931; Davis Collection, New York Public Library.

[10]E. Cobb, *Wayward Parent,* p. 35.

[11]Robert H. Davis to Irvin S. Cobb, October 17, 1933; Davis Collection, New York Public Library.

[12]Cobb collection, University of Kentucky.

[13]*Irvin S. Cobb's Own Recipe Book* (Louisville and Baltimore: Frankfort Distilleries, Inc., 1934), pp. 22-23.

# Chapter Twenty-Four

In 1934, at age 58, Cobb found a new career; he became a movie actor. His last Hollywood writing assignment had been *Turkish Delight,* 1927, a silent movie, and the advent of talkies had made him apprehensive about seeking any new movie work. In 1933 he was one of "ten well-known authors" who supplied the story for *The Woman Accused,* but Bayard Veiller wrote the actual screenplay.[1] Will Rogers, however, was enthusiastic about the new medium. In silent films Rogers' performances had been a disappointment both to himself and his audiences, but his early talkies established him as a star. In early 1934 Rogers was slated to film *Judge Priest,* based on Cobb's Kentucky stories, and he invited Cobb to come out and advise the production.[2] Buff was anxious to go: she had sold movie rights of her third novel, *She Was a Lady,* to Twentieth-Century Fox, and she wanted to watch the filming.

Cobb had not yet made up his mind to go when the clincher arrived: a telegram from Hal Roach, whom Cobb had met on his earlier Hollywood trips, which read:

> If you feel like doing a series of shorts for this shop, why not come on out here at my expense and talk it over?[3]

They went, and as Elisabeth Cobb puts it, "We were absolutely delighted with everything. Sunshine, palm trees... people, architecture, the movie business, the Pacific ocean...." Many of their old New York friends were there, writing for or acting in the movies; many of the Hollywood crowd whom Cobb had met earlier were glad to see him back. They were invited to dinners and parties. To honor their arrival Hal Roach threw a costume party with a prison theme. All guests were provided with prison uniforms, balls and chains, and a mugging and finger printing routine. Everyone was amused except Louis B. Mayer, who departed in a huff.[4]

Part of Cobb's new exuberance came from his discovery that Hal Roach had not asked him out to write comedy sketches, but to act in them. Putting radio comedians into movies was hardly an original idea; Will Rogers was a big success, and Robert Benchley starred in several successful shorts. But Cobb was flabbergasted. The more he protested, however, the more Roach insisted, and the more pleased Cobb became at the prospect.

Will Rogers' presence was also a good tonic for Cobb. Elisabeth Cobb remembers:

> Dad took me to the Rogers ranch when we made that first trip together. It was a most glorious blue and gold spring day, and when Will came out to meet us, grinning that wonderful, inimitable grin of his,... I felt that he was giving us a welcome as big as he was, and there isn't anything bigger than that, and that here was a man as good as bread and butter and as rare as golden wine. I don't suppose there was anyone who ever met Will Rogers who didn't feel that way about him.[5]

Rogers' guests that day also included the McIntyres, on a visit from New York, the Will Hays, and Billie Burke Ziegfeld, newly widowed. For entertainment Rogers decided to take them up to the top of the mountain trail in a wagon drawn by mules. On the way down, the brake on the wagon broke, and the group was in considerable danger until a ranch employee on horseback managed to get the mules under control. Rogers made light of the incident in his column the next week, which was mostly devoted to Cobb's reactions and comments on the affair. The younger women decided to walk down the mountain afterwards, and Cobb, who had been terrified, offered to join them, saying "he didn't mind staying in, but he didn't like to see the ladies walk down the hill alone as no telling what leading man might attack them."[6]

Cobb was so pleased with the opportunities in Hollywood that he sent for Laura to join him when Buff left after six weeks to rejoin her family. Perhaps, he suggested, they might settle out West if she liked it; getting out of New York had already done wonders for him. As soon as Laura arrived, she started looking for a house to rent. Cobb insisted that they buy no houses: they required too much investment and were too hard to sell. He also had very strict requirements in a house: absolute privacy, no mountain roads, space without pretentiousness ("I don't want a house that looks like it had been built by a collaboration between Grover Cleveland and a Mexican day laborer.") Laura searched for most of the summer without finding anything suitable. When she finally found something she liked, it was for sale, not for rent. She intended to pass it by, but Cobb got interested and demanded a tour. The next morning, without waking Laura or telling her his plans, he went down to the real estate office and bought the house.[7]

It was located on San Vincente Boulevard in Santa Monica, a section settled mostly by movie people. Earlier owners of the house included Miriam Hopkins, Bette Davis, and Greta Garbo. The privacy Cobb wanted was provided by the high walls and hedges that totally surrounded the property; a visitor passed down a long drive bordered by tall cedars to another high wall surrounding the entrance courtyard. A huge oak tree shaded the flagstone patio where the Cobbs liked to sit, with a view of mountains, canyons, and, through them, the Pacific Ocean a mile away. Although they did not give up Back Home and the Manhattan apartment for several more years, the Santa Monica house served as their main residence until Cobb's final illness. By that time Laura had the garden in beautiful shape, with specimen shrubs, tropical flowers and a waterlily pool.

The movie shorts Hal Roach had in mind, however, proved unsuitable to Cobb's talents. Roach's speciality was farce, highly physical humor. His was the genius behind Mack Sennett's famous pie-throwing routines. Although Cobb frequently made jokes about his bulk, his humor was verbal, not physical, and his attempts to be a comedian in the Roach tradition were agonizing for both of them. After four films they agreed the experiment had not been a success. Cobb became very discouraged; before a trip to New York in October he wrote Bob Davis, "I miss you and a few others like hell out here. They have plenty of climate but in spots are short on human beings who talk my language."

Cobb's spirits were lifted somewhat by the arrival of his daughter, who had left Brody for good and who moved in with her two children. Although she married again in 1938, she lived until 1943 in her father's house in Santa Monica, and it is the house Cobb's grandchildren remember most clearly as their childhood home.

In that winter of 1934-35 Cobb soon found other Hollywood opportunities. Paramount was filming a movie entitled *Mississippi*, starring Bing Crosby, Joan Bennett, and W. C. Fields. As a publicity gimmick, the studio hired Cobb as a "Dixie expert." Cobb passed no judgments on the story, loosely based on Booth Tarkington's "Magnolia," although its story of an eastern singer (Crosby) who is denied the hand of a Kentucky belle because he refuses to fight a

Irvin Cobb, his daughter, and his two grandchildren outside their Santa Monica home, about 1934.
Photo reprinted by permission of Louisville Courier Journal and Times

duel to defend his supposedly besmirched honor would certainly have offended his standards in the days of his *Back Home* preface. Nor is the continuation of the plot in keeping with his boyhood knowledge of Kentucky: Crosby escapes to become a singer on Fields' showboat, where he is pursued by his fiancee's younger sister (Joan Bennett), with the inevitable happy ending. Cobb's suggestions for authenticity were unconnected with the plot: he advised the director about the appropriate hounds for a hunt scene, the amount of mint in a julep, the restriction of "you-all" to the plural, and the correct material for wrapping cotton bales (jute, not burlap).[9] If Cobb had not thoroughly incorporated the Southern myth into his own memories at this point, he certainly no longer made the destruction of that myth an important goal.

In February, 1935, Cobb was asked to serve as Master of Ceremonies at the Academy Awards ceremony. 1935 was the first year that one movie swept the top awards and Cobb played upon this unprecedented situation. As the Los Angeles *Herald Express* explained.

> Irvin S. Cobb, incomparable humorist, tried, like any good master of ceremonies, to keep his audience keyed to the mood of surprise.... But after [the third or fourth envelope] "You guessed it," he shouted over the loudspeakers. "It is something that..." "Happened One Night!" vociferated the audience.

The Los Angeles *Post-Record* described the presentation to Claudette Colbert, the leading lady of *It Happened One Night:*

> There was a taxi waiting and a great mixup of men briskly clearing each other aside to provide an aisle as she, dressed in traveling clothes, accepted the award from Irvin S. Cobb and kissed him and tripped out, gold statuette in hand like a kewpie doll she won at a carnival, to catch a train....[10]

Cobb got another kiss that evening from Shirley Temple, who received a special award.

Cobb's most exciting opportunity in early 1935, however, was a new movie contract. Darryl F. Zanuck at Twentieth-Century Fox decided that Cobb had possibilities as a character actor, especially when teamed with his good friend Will Rogers. The first part Fox offered him was that of a river captain in *Steamboat Round the Bend.* Cobb describes the offer from Zanuck's lieutenant Sol Wartzel:

"It's not much of a part, Cobb, you understand that."

"Well," I told him, "I'm not much of an actor."

"Never mind that," he said. "You know how Bill [Rogers] is. He'll go out of his way—yes, fade into the background himself—to give you a chance."[11]

Filming *Steamboat* with Rogers was one of the great larks of Cobb's life. Rogers was famous for ad-libbing on sets, and he and Cobb played off each other until the director, John Ford, was forced to call them down. Here is Cobb's account:

"Gentlemen," said Ford, with just a whiff of sarcasm in his tones, "I don't suppose either of you has gone so far as to read the script for this production?"

"Who, me?" said Will, in pretended surprise. "When did I ever read one of those fool things? I been too busy roping calves and romancing around."

"How about you, Mr. Cobb?" inquired Ford, formally.

"Oh, I took one glance at it," I said, taking cue from Will. "And then I quit. I could write a better script than that with one hand and Eugene O'Neill tied behind my back."

"Permit me to explain—if I'm not boring you?" said Ford. "In the opening sequence you, Mr. Cobb, are in the pilothouse of your boat *Pride of Paducah.* Will comes butting in to tell you he's just bought the *Claremore Queen* which is a little old wreck of a condemned ferryboat. So you start twitting him about being stung on the deal. And so on and on, back and forth for about four minutes. Now then, I might suggest that you rehearse the routine along that general line, just ad libbing as you go."

"Listen, Cobb," said Will, "let's humor the poor mick. But to keep down heartburning and ill feelings, I'll make up all your speeches for you and you make up all my speeches for me. . . ."

So for twenty minutes, while a large and expensive cast and a technical crew seventy-odd strong fidgeted about, and several hundred extras in costumes simmered pleasantly under the ardent sun of a California midsummer, we raked each other with cross fires; at the end of which time Ford held up his hand.

"That's fine," he explained," that's certainly mightly fine dialogue. This show is supposed to be laid along back about eighteen-ninety and so you've brought in the New Deal and Madame Perkins and Aimee Semple McPherson and Mae West and Dizzy Dean and a lot of other interesting topics, for all of which I'm naturally grateful. Please though, do me one small favor. Just once in a while mention the plot, won't you? With your gifts I'm sure you can work it into the conversation naturally and casually." His voice changed from a soothing Celtic monotone to the sharp-cornered accents of the Maine coast where he was born and fetched up: "And now, you two crooks, you'll play this scene and play it right or I'll have you thrown into the river—and I hope neither one of you can swim."

Even so, a good many of the lines that percolated into the sound tracks of that picture did not come out of the book.[12]

The movie was filmed in June and July of 1935. On the last day of filming Rogers invited Cobb to go back up to the ranch with him for some horseback riding. Cobb turned him down, thinking that Rogers was probably anxious to do some real riding, not trailing along after a tenderfoot. As he turned to go, Rogers said, "Better change your mind, old-timer. I may not be seeing you again for quite a spell." Cobb never saw him again; Rogers was killed in a plane crash that August.[13]

*Steamboat Round the Bend* was released the month after Rogers' death, which made it a sentimental favorite with critics and audiences both. Cobb's performance was also praised, however.[14] He was already at work on the Fox film *Everybody's Old Man;* in April, 1936, he was given a contract for two more films. Cobb wrote articles and gave interviews in 1936 about the pleasure he took in acting:

> Writing is a lonely, thankless job. When you're an actor, you're with people. There's a heap of fun connected with the work. I wish I'd started forty years ago.[15]

In another article:

> I can still read my newspaper and write my daily stint between scenes, and get a lot more honest variety of reactions to my stuff on the set than I would shut up in my room.... I never expect to win the Academy Prize. I've got too many hunting trophies around the house now, and Mrs. Cobb thinks I ought to pay more attention to the garden. Yes, Sir, acting is a swell job.[16]

Cobb is always careful to emphasize his low estimation of his acting talent and to make jokes about the exasperation he sometimes caused in production crews:

> When on one of the stages one day about three separate individuals approached me and whispered in my furry ear that it would be very wise to act natural, I stopped all acting long enough to say "the next sucker who tells me to be natural will get a bust in his ear!"

Cobb summed up his delight, "I am like a small boy with a brand new toy."[17]

The reviews Cobb got in 1936 justified his delight. In March the New York *Times* said of his latest performance:

> Of course folks applauded the efforts of one Irvin S. Cobb as the

> Cap'n Eli of the late Will Rogers' *Steamboat Round the Bend* and there were naturally chuckles at the humor of the whimsical if portly first citizen of Paducah (or is it Paris?), Kentucky, in a few cinema shorts some years back. But after a glance at *Everybody's Old Man* at the Center Theater it becomes difficult to understand why Hollywood has failed to star the noted humorist long before this.[18]

Cobb was right, of course, about not being an actor, but his attempts at "acting natural" were quite successful. In his movies he exploited the comic potential of his facial expressions, his unique modulation and his instinct for timing and delivery to create an impressive comic screen presence. He had been doing this for years in private and public, of course; the proprietor of a Paducah clothing once tried to explain the charm of his delivery:

> He had very thick lips, and I claim his diction and voice were a little different from anybody else. His voice commanded your attention. Here's an example of what I mean: Cobb came in here one time in 1940, saw a tie he liked, and said, "I'll buy that damn tie!" His voice—it sounded like music.[19]

Cobb also got his own radio show in 1936, broadcast from Hollywood. It was called "Paducah Plantation," although Western Kentucky was definitely outside of plantation country, but Cobb apparently never objected to the name or to the role of the comic Southerner he was expected to play. Success felt very good after failure, and Cobb was determined to enjoy it. The program ran for six months.

Rogers' death was a blow to Cobb, and he worked as a member of the commission to establish the Rogers Memorial in Claremore, Oklahoma. But he found other cronies in California, many of them former Rogers friends: the former vaudevillian Fred Stone, the actor Leo Carillo, the artist Ed Borein. Buff, who was working as a scenario writer, filled the house with younger Hollywood people, such as Scott Fitzgerald and Sheilah Graham, but Cobb often found the conversation of her friends too brittle and artistic for his taste.[20] He did make an exception of Clare Booth Luce, who had remained a good friend of Buff from their school days together and a great favorite of Cobb. She brought her new husband, Harry Luce, out for a visit to meet the Cobbs in 1935. Lonely for the Broadway clubs, Cobb joined in the formation of a Los Angeles club, The Authors, and agreed to be its first president. He also made a pilgrimage to the Bohemian Grove in San Francisco whenever possible, meeting Bob Davis there for a joint vacation in July, 1936.[21]

NBC publicity photograph for "Paducah Plantation," 1937.
Photo reprinted by permission of Louisville Courier Journal and Times

Cobb also made frequent trips back to New York, although not frequent enough to justify the house and apartment there. Both went up for sale in 1936. That year he was elected to the Advisory Board of the Chemical Bank and Trust Company of New York. He was a friend of the President, Percy H. Johnston. Cobb saw his chief role on the Board, like his chief role at any gathering, to entertain everyone else. According to Frank Case, also an Advisory Board member, he succeeded admirably. At the first meeting he assured the company that he took his membership seriously and that he had a proposal. In Case's version of Cobb's words, the proposal was "that owah bank confine itself to two signs only. Ovah the receivin' tellah's window a sign readin' 'Yes' and ovah the payin' telluh's window a sing readin' 'No'."[22]

Cobb's delight in California did not last. By 1937 the warm welcome he had received was being extended to more recent newcomers, and he felt he knew only a few people he could call friends. Cobb found the stiff competition in Hollywood, the snubs given to those whose reputations slipped, very hard to deal with. Writing in 1941, Leo Rosten explained, "In the movie colony, there are few places for the ego to rest in peace, except at the very top—and the top in Hollywood is very high."[23] Part of Cobb's initial reaction had been relief at getting away from a competitive situation in which he no longer felt he could win. Hollywood proved to be no easier on his ego.

Cobb's professional problems were just beginning to be evident in 1937. His movie career was still going fairly well. *Pepper,* in which he starred with Jane Withers, was released in 1936. He and Jane got better reviews than the movie itself did. There was a long delay in filming the second movie of that contract, however. It was released as *Hawaii Calls* in early 1938 with Cobb playing the minor role of a ship's captain. Cobb also had only small roles in the last two movies in which he acted, *The Young in Heart* and *The Arkansas Traveler,* both released in 1938.

Cobb's increasing discontent was also affected by health problems. The ulcers that had hemorrhaged in Boston in 1922 continued to plague him, and Cobb insisted on highly spiced food and a lot of it. Doctors put him on diets, his wife and daughter planned simple meals, and then Cobb added the pickles, sauces, and pepper. Under such a strain not only his digestion but his general health deteriorated. At some time in the thirties he was diagnosed a diabetic and eventually required an insulin shot every day.[24] The condition of his teeth deteriorated and they finally had to be pulled.

He became increasingly weak and uncomfortable, and by the late thirties was in almost constant pain.[25]

Cobb's daughter attributes the growing conservatism of his political views in his last years to his poor health. Not only did his pain make him less tolerant and more anxious about his own situation, she feels, but his various ailments may have affected his mind as well.[26] Certainly, many of the public statements Cobb made in the late thirties and forties seem to have little connection with his earlier passionate concern with human freedom and equality.

Sanity about politics was a rare commodity in the Hollywood of the thirties. The liberal and conservative camps were both rabidly extreme, and there was very little middle ground. Cobb moved to California the year that Upton Sinclair was the Democratic candidate for governor against Frank Merriam, the Republican. Sinclair's followers talked of him and his movement as though he were a messiah; the Republicans pictured him as a devil. Power and the press were on the side of Merriam, and he won a lopsided victory, but Sinclair's followers, which included many of the younger movie people, were by no means silenced. The conservatives, who included most of the studio executives and producers, frequently accused the liberal organizations, such as the Anti-Nazi League of 1936 (Cobb's friends Rupert Hughes and Eddie Cantor were members) of being communist front organizations. In 1939 Congressman Dies' accusations that many Hollywood figures were communists further increased the tension.

Cobb sided with the conservatives. Even though he had become more and more disappointed with Hoover's performance, he had never warmed to Franklin Roosevelt, and the changes of the New Deal frightened him. The possibility of involvement in another war frightened him even more.

Cobb's last job for the movies was an attempt in 1939 to present a possible compromise between the uncompromising positions of the radicals and reactionaries around him in California: tolerance, good sense, and the willingness to give a little. Cobb merely provided the story for the film *Our Leading Citizen;* someone else wrote the screenplay, but it is doubtful that it would have been better received had he written the script. In the movie an outside agitator stirs up a strike at a factory, and the factory owner refuses to give the demanded raise. The citizen of the title has such winning rhetoric, however, that he not only convinces everyone at the factory to give a little for the common good but also brings together a pair of lovers in his spare time.

20th Century Fox publicity photography for "Pepper." 1936. With Cobb are Slim Summerville and Jane Withers.
Photo reprinted by Louisville Courier Journal and Times

Most reviewers treated the movie with derision. This, from the New York *Times,* is not atypical:

> When a genial, tolerant, and folksy old humorist like Irvin S. Cobb snuggles close to his desk, or as close as nature allows, and decides to clarify the capital-labor situation, there isn't much any of us can do, we suppose, but be grim and bear it. For Mr. Cobb. . . presents the appalling spectacle of a man who is not merely beyond his depth but insists on showing off as he goes down for the third time. . . . [It is] an affront to intelligence and good taste. . . nothing so synthetic, so confused and so full of balderdash has come this way in months.[27]

Cobb never wrote for or acted in the movies again.

When Cobb had planned to spend his final years in comfortable retirement, he had set the writing of his memoirs as one of his goals for that period. In 1938 he started on that project, working in the morning before the rest of his household awoke. He did not want to write a continuous story, with strict attention to chronology and completeness, but to speak conversationally to the reader, moving at random from one topic to another. The memoirs became the volume *Exit Laughing,* published in 1941.

## Notes

[1]New York *Times*, March 13, 1933, 18:2.

[2]David Shipman, *The Great Movie Stars: The Golden Years* (New York: Crown Publ. Co., 1970), p. 476.

[3]Irvin S. Cobb, "Hal Roach: The Cosmopolitan of the Month," *Cosmopolitan* (April, 1940), p. 11.

[4]Louisville *Courier-Journal,* May 17, 1934; clipping, Louisville Free Public Library.

[5]E. Cobb, *Wayward Parent,* pp. 201-202.

[6]Rogers, *Autobiography,* p. 333.

[7]E. Cobb, *Wayward Parent,* pp. 186-187.

[8]Irvin S. Cobb to Robert H. Davis, October 8, 1934; Davis Collection, New York Public Library.

[9]New York *Times,* February 10, 1935, VIII, 4:1.

[10]Frank Capra, *The Name Above the Title: An Autobiography* (New York: The MacMillan Co., 1971), p. 171; p. 172.

[11]New York *Times,* August 22, 1935, 17:6.

[12]Cobb, *Exit Laughing,* pp. 404-405.

[13]New York *Times*, August 22, 1935; 17:6.

[14]New York *Times,* September 20, 1935, 17:2 *Time Magazine* (September 2, 1935), 26:40; *Newsweek* (September 14, 1945), 6:28.

[15]Louisville *Courier-Journal,* March 11, 1936; clipping, Louisville Free Public Library.

[16]Louisville *Times,* October 1, 1936; clipping, Louisville Free Public Library.

[17]Louisville *Herald-Post*, May 9, 1936; clipping Louisville Free Public Library.

[18]New York *Times*, October 1, 1936; clipping, Louisville Free Public Library.

[19]Burkhalter, p. 55.

[20]Sheilah Graham, *The Real F. Scott Fitzgerald: Thirty-Five Years Later* (New York: Warner Books, Inc., 1976), p. 230.

[21]Irvin S. Cobb to Robert H. Davis, July 7, 1936; Davis Collection, New York Public Library.

[22]Case, *Do Not Disturb, p. 181.*

[23]Leo C. Rosten, *Hollywood: The Movie Colony, The Movie Makers* (New York: Harcourt, Brace & Co., 1941), p. 40.

[24]Irvin S. Cobb to Charlie Heddon, May 30, 1940; Davis Collection, New York Public Library.

[25]Irvin S. Cobb to John Wilson Townsend, June 20, 1935, University of Kentucky Library.

[26]E. Cobb, *Wayward Parent,* p. 217.

[27]New York *Times,* August 24, 1939, 17:1.

# Chapter Twenty-five

In July, 1939, during a brief vacation at the Bohemian Grove Cobb was struck with a sudden gastric hemorrhage like the one he had suffered in Boston in 1922. He was rushed to the University of California Hospital, where he remained for three weeks. He had a typical comment for reporters on his release: "It isn't often that a man can boast he has had fifteen doctors and lived."[1]

By early 1940 Cobb had recovered enough to take on some speaking engagements. He was worried about the state of the world, and, as he had done twenty-five years earlier, he set out to tell the country what ought to be done. That he had lost his earlier authority is shown by a news account of a speech he made in St. Louis that February: Cobb had been "hired to be funny," it said, but he "got off on communism."[2] Many Americans had forgotten or never known the Cobb who reported from the first World War; his public image in 1940 was the movie personality and the humorist whose joke columns with their stories about Southern "darkies" and Broadway personalities of the twenties were becoming more and more dated. For such a man to be lecturing on world affairs must have seemed strange indeed.

Cobb had reluctantly voted for Roosevelt the first two times, but he could stomach neither the idea of a third term nor the prospect of Henry Wallace as vice-president.[3] (In the spring of 1940 he wrote an article suggesting Alben Barkely for vice president.)[4] Although he had never before supported a Republican, he joined the Wilkie bandwagon, salving his conscience by calling himself a Democrat for Wilkie and by proclaiming that Wilkie himself was really a Democrat who just happened to be nominated by a Republican convention. Cobb wrote news releases, gave lectures, and made radio speeches for Wilkie that summer and fall. Cobb enjoyed the campaign, and its energizing quality seemed to control his paranoia about communists somewhat. He was criticized several times, however, for the "unedifying and uncharitable" remarks he made about FDR's family life and for his tendency to compare Roosevelt to Hitler and Mussolini.[5] After the election Wallace seemed his biggest worry. He wrote Bob Davis in January, 1941, "God keep our president—because think what would happen if...the well-known star-gazer Mr. Wallace succeeded to the throne!"[6]

Cobb also worried about involvement in another war. In 1939 he had joined the America First Committee (he resigned after Pearl Harbor), and in August, 1941, he and fourteen Republicans (including Alf Landon and Herbert Hoover) joined in an appeal to Congress to stop preparations for war. "Freedom in America does not depend on the outcome of struggles for material power by other nations," they said.[7]

Cobb's public pronouncements were interrupted in March, 1941, by the publication of *Exit Laughing.* The book got, and deserved, a warm reception. The growing bitterness of Cobb's last years shows up only occasionally. As he writes of early friends and experiences his warmth and human sympathy returns. Although he occasionally becomes verbose, his style is more often like that of his prime. Some sections, such as the chapter on the celebration at the black Paducah church which was reprinted separately that same year, are as good as anything he ever wrote.

Noteworthy among the many reviews was one in the *Saturday Review* by William Allen White. White praises Cobb for having brought "something precious and lovable into American life and letters" and calls him "a real man, a hard-working man, a conscientious man, tremendously impressed by the dignity and nobility of his profession." White sums up, "I know of no book published in recent years which is so American as *Exit Laughing.*"[8]

Cobb was gratified by the book's success, and not just for the lift it gave his spirits. He wrote John Wilson Townsend in April, "The book is selling well, thank God! I'll need the money." It was five years since *Judge Priest Turns Detective;* in the meantime he had written only two children's books, *Azam* and *Four Useful Pups,* which had not been very profitable.[9]

Cobb had other pleasures in the early forties. During a lecture trip on the Wilkie campaign he made his first visit to Paducah in eight years. He was disturbed by the memories of his mother and sister—"I found myself walking through a town of ghosts," he wrote Bob Davis[10]—but he enjoyed the suite at the Irvin Cobb Hotel his friends arranged for him. He was shown his latest namesakes, a

Irvin Cobb and his Paducah friend George Goodman at the Pendennis Club, Lexington, Kentucky, 1942.
Photo reprinted by permission of Louisville Courier Journal and Times

park and a tugboat, and met with old friends. George Goodman, then serving as Kentucky WPA administrator, went down from Louisville to see him. Cobb went to Kentucky again in 1942 and visited Paducah before going to the University of Kentucky to receive an honorary degree. John Wilson Townsend and George Goodman joined him in Lexington for a dinner of "turnip greens and hog jowl."[11]

Cobb was most like his earlier self when he was surrounded by a group of old friends or when he could help someone in trouble. Scott Fitzgerald and Sheilah Graham were as open to charges of being "pink" as anyone in Hollywood: they had "flirted" with communism, supported the Spanish Civil War, and voted for Roosevelt. Although Cobb tolerated them as he tolerated all of Buff's friends, he must have been upset by their radicalism. When Fitzgerald died suddenly of a heart attack in December, 1940, immediately after the election, Buff was one of the first persons Sheilah called. Buff came and took Sheilah home with her, to her father's house. Cobb's welcome was warm. Sheilah Graham remembers, "It was a few days before Christmas, and Mr. Cobb insisted that I stay with them until it was over. I loved them for their kindness...."[12]

More and more, however, it was Cobb who needed taking care of. Laura was more equal to the task than her tiny frame indicated. Her politics, when she expressed any, were closer to those of her daughter than those of her husband. Pearl Harbor didn't scare her any more than communism did, and even Cobb was surprised the night she thanked him kindly for checking on her after a loud blast of anti-aircraft fire broke the stillness, but said she'd just as soon sleep. Cobb came to lean on her, both emotionally and even physically, during the forties.[13]

Cobb lost another source of strength, Bob Davis, who died in October, 1942, in a hospital in Montreal. Their correspondence had dwindled toward the end, as the fishing and hunting trips they loved to plan became less and less possible. O. O. McIntyre had died in 1938; except for the Kentucky contingent, Cobb outlived all of his closest friends.

The biggest blow, however, the one that Elisabeth Cobb thinks her father felt most keenly, was the cancellation of his syndicated column. Cobb's joke column had been running fairly steadily since 1922. At first it was called "Laugh a Day," then "Just a Minute," then "Laughing Around the World." By 1941 several newspapers no longer found it profitable, and the syndicate wrote Cobb that it would be discontinued. Only later did someone send him a copy of the announcement dispatched to the newspapers that bought it: it was short, blunt, and insulting.[14] The column was Cobb's last sure income; he was sick and probably dying and the comfortable inheritance he'd always wanted to leave his wife and daughter seemed out of reach.

Cobb corresponded with various publishers about bringing out collections of his works. World Publishing Company brought out *Faith, Hope, and Charity,* a collection of works previously published only in magazines, in 1942 and *Cobb's Cavalcade,* a selection of Cobb's most popular short works, in 1944. Cobb's last published work was *Roll Call,* 1942, a sentimental melange of poetry and prose with a Vachel Lindsey flavor. It praises various traditional American heroes—Daniel Boone, Stonewall Jackson, Davey Crockett—with the refrain, "Uncle Sam needn't be ashamed of his seed." *Exit Laughing* had been dedicated to his granddaughter; *Roll Call* was for his grandson.

During his last years Cobb worked on another set of reminiscences which he entitled *Curtain Call.* He had written about 20,000 words when he died.[15] Elisabeth Cobb tells of searching for the manuscript after his death and of her disappointment in it. There was too much that was bitter, too many more references to enemies than friends, too little of the Irvin Cobb she loved.[16] Her children believe that she must have destroyed the manuscript.

In 1943 Cobb felt well enough to take a trip with Buff and a few other friends to Arizona and New Mexico. The fiery pastels of the Southwest had fascinated him since he had first seen them thirty years earlier, and on the trip he seemd to be stronger and more relaxed than he had been in years. They visited old friends and Cobb told stories and relaxed as he had in earlier times. He even managed to ride on horseback through some of the spectacular scenery that he loved so much.

After the New Mexico trip the Cobbs decided to move back to New York City for the time being. Cobb's only professional activities at the time were better pursued on the east coast, and the war in the Pacific made California an uneasy place to be. Buff and her children went first, to locate and furnish a hotel apartment. Cobb, pleased with the success of his New Mexico trip, made ambitious plans for a hunting trip, so Laura traveled cross-country alone without him, arriving in New York ill herself. Cobb, alone in California, became suddenly worse and was forced to cancel his hunting trip and enter the hospital. The women in New York were helpless to come to his aid; in 1943 tickets from the east coast to the west coast were unavailable. After two weeks Cobb came east alone; when Buff picked him up at the station she found a "slow-moving, stooped, shambling, thin, old man." He went to bed as soon as they reached the apartment and never got up again. In addition to the debilitating diseases already plaguing him he became a victim of dropsy, and the swelling of his body, complicated by his weakness, made movement impossible.[17]

Cobb delighted in visitors that last winter of his life, and, as always, he strove to entertain them. B. D. Zevin, the editor of *Cobb's Cavalcade,* remarked on the contrast between his feeble, wasted appearance and the energy with which he greeted old friends and called up stories and memories.[18]

One old friend who visited Cobb that winter was Kent Cooper, whom he had known since his Louisville days and who was then head of the Associated Press. Earlier in mock seriousness (Cooper had professed amazement at his ability to find humor in grim situations) Cobb had vowed to write a humorous letter for Cooper from his deathbed. After an operation in October his condition grew steadily worse, and in December of 1943 he decided that the time had come to write the letter. Mrs. Cobb gave Cooper permission to print it. The letter itself was typical Cobb humor with jokes about doctors, undertakers, and the dropsy. He closes it "Merry symptoms and a tappy new year." Had Cooper published only the body of the letter at the time, as he did later in his autobiography,[19] it would have been greeted as the brave and fairly successful attempt of a very sick man to be funny. Unfortunately, Cobb had added a postscript which indicated the irrational bitterness of his final days, and Cooper chose to print it also. In it Cobb supports General Patton, then being criticized for slapping a soldier suffering from battle fatigue, and nominates him as the ideal manager of the Tula Lake Relocation Center, where Californians of Japanese descent had been incarcerated. If Patton were to deal with the "slimy, scaly, shark-toothed yellow-bellied concentrates," he feels, it would "look as though somebody had been cleaning fish—gills, gore, and guts all over the place." In the last months of his life Cobb was attacked in the press for his remarks; C. G. Paudling called him a "disgusting old man."[20]

Cobb lingered, the pain and weariness increasing, for three more months. After a two week coma he died on March 10, 1944. Two days after his death his friends in Paducah released the text of another letter he had written that last December, this one setting down his wishes for his funeral and, in passing, summing up his feelings about organized religion. The letter was reprinted, attacked, applauded, and dissected that spring in waves of editorials and letters to the editors.

In the letter Cobb asks that his funeral be simple, natural, and cheerful. He sketches plans for a graveside ceremony in Paducah with all his friends present. He requests that his ashes be scattered on the roots of a dogwood tree while a Negro choir sings spirituals.[21]

The tone of Cobb's funeral letter is far gentler than that of his letter to Cooper, and instead of the hatred seen there it reveals a controlled amusement at human folly as represented by traditional funeral practices. Many of the readers were not amused, however, by what they took to be his blasphemous treatment of religion.[22] In requesting the Twenty-third Psalm as an acceptable Bible selection, Cobb says,

> it contains no charnal words, no morbid mouthings about corruption and decay and, being mercifully without creed or dogma, carries no threat of eternal hell-fire for those parties we do not like, no direct promise of a heaven which, if one may judge by the people who are surest of going there, must be a powerfully dull place, populated to a considerable degree by prigs, time-servers and unpleasantly aggressive individuals. Hell may have a worse climate but undoubtedly the company is sprightlier.

Cobb goes on to praise Jesus Christ, but only as "the greatest gentleman who ever lived," and to compare Hitler and Stalin to the Jehovah of the Old Testament. "One advantage of dying" he admits, "is that it affords a fellow opportunity to say a lot of things that have been curdling in his system all these years. Frankly, I'm enjoying myself." He ends the letter with thanks to the people of Paducah for having been so good to him.

Most of Cobb's wishes were carried out. A simple memorial service was held in New York that March. Cobb's body was cremated, and the Paducah burial service was delayed until the following October because of Mrs. Cobb's health. A far larger crowd than Cobb had envisioned gathered to watch Cobb's wife, sister, daughter, and granddaughter shovel dirt on the dogwood tree planted over his ashes. Later, in keeping with the suggestions in his letter, a rough-hewn granite boulder, carved with his name and dates and the inscription "Back Home," was placed over his grave.

At Cobb's funeral in 1944, Cobb's granddaughter, then Mrs. Gregson Bautzer, presents flowers to Mattie Copeland.
Photo reprinted by permission of Louisville Courier Journal and Times

Whatever Cobb's precise intentions in writing the funeral letter, it had one result that would have delighted him: editorialists and citizens commenting on his death were forced to deal with his opinions, not merely with his jokes. The articles and letters which praised him soon outnumbered those which criticized him, and they used such phrases to describe him as "deliberate individualist" and "humorous philosopher."[23] William Rose Benet wrote in the *Saturday Review* that Cobb "stands somewhere between Mark Twain and Joel Chandler Harris in the American Pantheon."[24] Other writers recalled with praise his skill with words and his evocation of Western Kentucky. All seemed to agree in praising the uniqueness of his talents and the industry with which he applied them; in the words of Paducahan Tom Waller at his funeral, "he had the touch, and he used it."[25]

## Notes

[1]New York *Times,* August 12, 1939, 16:3.

[2]Burkhalter, p. 56.

[3]Louisville *Courier-Journal,* July 20, 1940; clipping Louisville Free Public Library.

[4]Barkley, p. 69.

[5]Louisville *Times,* November 1, 1940; *Courier-Journal,* November 3, 1940; clippings, Louisville Free Public Library.

[6]Davis Collection, New York Public Library.

[7]Louisville *Courier-Journal,* August 6, 1941; clipping, Louisville Free Public Library.

[8]William Allen White, "The Humor of the Self-Kidder," *Saturday Review of Literature,* March 22, 1941; clipping, Kentucky Library, Western Kentucky University.

[9]Note on letter, John Wilson Townsend to Irvin S. Cobb, April 5, 1941, University of Kentucky.

[10]Irvin S. Cobb to Robert H. Davis, March 5, 1940, Davis Collection, New York Public Libary.

[11]John Wilson Townsend to Irvin S. Cobb, April 4, 1929; University of Kentucky Library.

[12]Graham, p. 243.

[13]Gene Buck to Elisabeth Cobb, December 4, 1945, Brody collection.

[14]E. Cobb, *Wayward Parent,* p. 204.

[15]Pittsburgh, Kansas, *Headlight,* March 13, 1944; clipping, Brody collection.

[16]E. Cobb, *Wayward Parent,* p. 20.

[17]E. Cobb, *Wayward Parent,* pp. 245-246.

[18]Cobb's Cavalcade, p. 12.

[19]Kent Cooper, *Kent Cooper and Associated Press: An Autobiography* (New York: Random House), pp. 285-286.

[20]C. G. Paulding, "On All Fours," *Commonweal* (December 24, 1943), XXXIX, 10, 245-246.

[21]The letter is reprinted in E. Cobb, *Wayward Parent,* pp. 249-255.

[22]Baltimore *Evening Sun,* March 23, 1944; Erie, Pennsylvania, *Dispatch Herald,* March 27, 1944; and other clippings, Brody collection.

[23]Washington *Evening Star,* March 11, 1944; clipping, Paducah Public Library.

[24]William Rose Benet, "Mortality in Writing," *Saturday Review of Literature,* March 18, 1944, p. 14.

[25]Paducah *Sun-Democrat,* March 14, 1944; clipping, Paducah Public Library.

# Bibliography

Adams, Samuel Hopkins. *Alexander Woolcott: His Life and His World.* New York: Reynal and Hitchcock, 1945.

Alley, James P. *Hambone's Meditations.* Louisville, The Standard Printing Co., 1934.

Ashford, Daisy. *Daisy Ashford: Her Book.* New York: G. H. Doran and Co., 1920.

Barkley, Alben. *That Reminds Me.* Garden City, New York: Doubleday and Co., 1954.

Battle, J.H., *et al. Kentucky: A History of the State.* Louisville: FA Bulley Publishing Co., 1885, Part II.

Bennett, Arnold. *Your United States.* New York: G. H. Doran and Co., 1912.

Bleyer, Willard Grosvenor. *Main Currents in the History of American Journalism.* Boston: Houghton, Mifflin, 1927.

Bode, Carl, ed. *The New H. L. Mencken Letters.* New York: Dial Press, 1977.

Browning, Sister Mary Carmel, O.S.O. *Kentucky Authors: A History of Kentucky Literature.* Evansville, Ind.: Keller Crescent Co., 1968.

Burkhalter, Betty K. *A Rhetorical Study of Irvin S. Cobb.* Unpublished thesis, Murray State University, 1967.

Buxton, Frank, and Bill Owen. *The Big Broadcast: 1920-1950.* New York: Viking Press, 1972.

Case, Frank. *Do Not Disturb.* New York: Frederick A. Stokes, Co., 1940.

Case, Frank. *Tales of a Wayside Inn.* New York: Frederick A. Stokes Co., 1938.

Chapin, Charles F. *Charles E. Chapin's Story.* New York: Putnam's, 1920.

Cobb, Elisabeth. *My Wayward Parent.* Indianapolis: Bobbs-Merrill. 1945.

Connelly, Marc. *Voices Offstage. A Book of Memoirs.* New York: Holt, Rinehart and Winston, 1968.

Cooper, Kent. *Kent Cooper and the Associated Press: An Autobiography.* New York: Random House, 1959.

Correll, Charles J. and Freeman F. Gosden. *Here They Are—Amos and Andy.* New York: Ray Long and Rich R. Smith, Inc., 1931.

Crozier, Emmet. *American Reporters on the Western Front, 1914-1918.* New York: Oxford University Press, 1959.

Davies, Marion. *The Times We Had: Life with William Randolph Hearst.* New York: Ballantine Books, 1977.

Daviess, Maria Thompson. *Seven Times Seven: An Autobiography.* New York: Dodd Mead and Co., 1924.

Davis, Richard Harding, *Ransom's Folly.* New York: Charles Scribner's Sons, 1917.

Davis, Robert H. *Irvin S. Cobb: Storyteller.* New York: George H. Doron Co., 1924.

Davis, Robert H. *On Home Soil With Bob Davis.* New York: D. Appleton and Co., 1927.

Davis, Robert H. *Over My Left Shoulder: A Panorama of Men and Events. Burlesques and Tragedies, Cabbages and Kings and*

*Sometimes Wand Y.* D. Appleton and Co., 1926.

Davis, Robert H. *Who's Cobb and Why.* New York: George H. Doran Co., 1927.

De Mille, Cecil. *The Autobiography of Cecil B. De Mille.* Englewood Cliffs, New Jersey: Prentice Hall, 1959.

Drennan, Robert E., Editor. *The Algonquin Wits.* New York: The Citadel Press, 1968.

Doran, George Henry. *Chronicles of Barabbas, 1884-1934.* New York: Harcourt Brace, 1935.

Driscoll, Charles B. *Life of O. O. McIntyre.* New York: Greystone Press, 1938.

Elder, Donald. *Ring Lardner.* Garden City: Doubleday, 1956.

Fisher, Charles. *The Columnists: A Clinical Survey.* New York, 1944.

Fitzgerald, Scott. *Letters to His Daughter.* New York: Charles Scribner's Sons, 1963.

Flint, Charles Panlett. *Memories of an Active Life.* New York: G. P. Putnam Sons, 1923.

Forgue, Guy J., ed. *The Letters of H. L. Mencken.* New York: Alfred A. Knopf, 1961.

Garst, Shannon. *Cowboy-Artist: Charles M. Russell.* New York: George H. Doran, 1918.

Goodman, Ezra. *The Fifty-Year Decline and Fall of Hollywood.* New York: Simon and Schuster, 1961.

Graham, Sheilah. *The Real F. Scott Fitzgerald: Thirty-five Years Later.* New York: Warner Books, Inc., 1976.

Hall, Wade. *The Smiling Phoenix: Southern Humor from 1865 to 1914.* Gainesville: University of Florida Press, 1965.

Hamilton, Cosmo. *People Worth Talking About.* Freeport, New York: Books for Libraries Press, 1970.

Harriman, Margaret Case. *Blessed Are The Debonair.* New York: Rinehart and Co., Inc., 1956.

Harriman, Margaret Case. *The Vicious Circle: The Story of the Algonquin Round Table.* New York: Rinehart and Co., Inc., 1951.

Hawes, G. W. *Commercial Gazetteer and Business Directory of the Ohio River.* Indianapolis: Hawes, 1861.

Henderson, Robert M. *D. W. Griffith: His Life and Work.* New York: Oxford University Press, 1972.

Henry, O. *Complete Works of O. Henry.* Garden City, New York: Doubleday, 1953.

Hopper, Hedda. *From Under My Hat.* Garden City, New York: Doubleday and Co., 1952.

Hurst, Fannie. *Anatomy of Me: A Wanderer in Search of Herself.* Garden City, New York: Doubleday and Co., Inc., 1958.

Jacobs, Lewis. *The Rise of the American Film: A Critical History.* New York: Harcourt Brace and World, 1939.

Jillson, Willard Rouse, Sc.D. *Irvin S. Cobb at Frankfort, KY.* News Democrat Press, Carrollton, Ky., 1944.

Juergens, George. *Joseph Pulitzer and the New York World.* Princeton: Princeton University Press, 1966.

Keller, Bruce. *Carl Van Vechten and the Irreverent Decades.* Norman: University of Oklahoma Press, 1968.
Kemler, Edgar. *The Irreverent Mr. Mencken.* New York: Little, Brown & Co., 1950.
Ketchum, Richard M. *Will Rogers: His Life and Times.* New York: American Heritage Publishing Co., Inc., 1973.
Klotter, James C. *William Goebel: The Politics of Wrath.* Lexington: The University Press of Kentucky, 1977.
Knightly, Phillip. *The First Casualty: From the Crimean War to Vietnam: The War Correspondent as Hero, Propagandist, and Myth Maker.* New York: Harcourt Brace, Jovanovich, 1975.
Lively, Robert A. *Fiction Fights The Civil War: An Unfinished Chapter in the Literary History of the American People.* Westport, Conn.: Greenwood Press, 1957.
Logsdon, Katherine. *Irvin S. Cobb and the Judge Priest Stories.* Unpublished thesis, Western Kentucky University, 1936.
Marx, Arthur. *Goldwyn: A Biography of the Man Behind the Myth.* New York: Ballantine Books, 1976.
Mason, Walt. *Walt Mason: His Book.* New York: Books for Libraries Press, 1920.
McCracken, Harold. *The Charles M. Russell Book: The Life and Work of the Cowboy Artist.* Garden City: Doubleday, 1957.
Mencken, H. L. *The Bathtub Hoax and Other Blasts and Bravos from the Chicago Tribune.* New York: A. A. Knopf, 1958.
Mencken, H. L. *A Gang of Pecksniffs: And Other Comments on Newspaper Publishers, Editors, and Reporters.* New Rochelle, New York: Arlington House, 1975.
Mencken, H. L. *Prejudices: First Series.* New York: Alfred A. Knopf, 1919.
Meredith, Scott. *George S. Kaufman and His Friends.* Garden City, New York: Doubleday, 1974.
Meyer, Susan E. *James Montgomery Flagg.* New York: Watson Guptell Publications, 1974.
Montague, James T. *More Truth than Poetry.* New York: George H. Doran, Co. 1920.
Morris, Richard B. *Encyclopedia of American History.* New York: Harper & Brothers, 1953.
Mott, Frank Luther. *American Journalism: A History, 1690-1960.* New York: Macmillan, 1962.
Neuman, Fred Gus. *Irvin S. Cobb.* Paducah: Young, 1924.
Neuman, Fred Gus. *Irvin S. Cobb: His Life and Achievements.* Paducah: Young, 1934.
Neuman, Fred Gus. *Paducahans in History.* Paducah: Young, 1922.
Neuman, Fred Gus. *The Story of Paducah.* Paducah: Young, 1927.
O'Brien, Frank. *The Story of the Sun: New York: 1833-1928.* New York: Greenwood Press, 1968.
O'Connor, Richard. *Heywood Broun: A Bibliography.* New York: G. P. Putnam's Sons, 1975.
Overton, Grant. *Cargoes for Crusoes.* New York: George H. Doran, 1924.
Overton, Grant. *When Winter Comes to Main Street.* New York: George H.

Doran, 1922.
Pickett, Calder M. *Ed Howe: Country Town Philosopher.* Lawrence, Kansas: University Press of Kansas, 1968.
Pound, Reginald. *Arnold Bennett: A Biography.* London: William Heinemann Ltd., 1952.
Rascoe, Burton. *We Were Interrupted.* Garden City: Doubleday and Co., Inc., 1942.
Read, Opie. *I Remember.* New York: Richard R. Smith, Inc., 1930.
Revell, Nellie. *Right Off the Chest.* New York: George H. Doran, 1923.
Rinehart, Mary Roberts. *Mary Roberts Rinehart.* Chicago: E. M. Hale and Co., 1931.
Robinson, Edward G. *All My Yesterdays: An Autobiography.* New York: Hawthorne Books, Inc., 1973.
Roger, Will. *The Autobiography of Will Rogers.* New York: Avon Books, 1975.
Rosten, Leo C. *Holywood: The Movie Colony, The Movie Makers.* New York: Harcourt, Brace and Co., 1941.
Russell, Charles Marion. *Good Medicine: The Illustrated Letters of Charles M. Russell.* Garden City: Doubleday, 1929.
Schorer, Mark. *Sinclair Lewis: An American Life.* New York: McGraw-Hill Book Co., Inc., 1961.
Shadegg, Stephen. *Clare Boothe Luce.* New York: Simon and Schuster. 1970.
Sheaffer, Louis. *O'Neill, Son and Playwright.* Boston: Little Brown and Co., 1968.
Shipman, David. *The Great Movie Stars: The Golden Years.* New York: Crown Publ. Co., 1970.
Slate, Sam J. and Joe Cook. *It Sounds Impossible.* New York: Macmillan, 1963.
Smith, H. Allen. *To Hell in a Handbasket.* Garden City: Doubleday, 1962.
Stenerson, Douglas C. *H. L. Menken.* Chicago: Univ. of Chicago Press, 1971.
Swanberg, W. A. *Dreiser.* New York: Charles Scribner's Sons, 1965.
Swing, Raymond. *Good Evening.: A Professional Memoir.* New York: Harcourt Brace, and World, 1964.
Taylor, Deims. *A Pictorial History of the Movies.* New York: Simon and Schuster, 1943.
Thompson, Lawrence S. *Kentucky Tradition.* Hamden, Conn.: Shoe String Press, 1956.
Townsend, Dorothy Edwards. *The Life and Works of John Wilson Townsend: Kentucky Author and Historian, 1885-1968.* Lexington, Ky.: Keystone Printery, 1972.
Townsend, John Wilson. *Concerning Irvin S. Cobb (1876-1922) Paducah—Louisville—New York-Europe.* Unpublished manuscript University of Kentucky Library, 1931.
Townsend, John Wilson. *Irvin S. Cobb.* Atlanta, Ga.: The Martin and Hoyt Co., 1923.
Townsend, John Wilson. *James Lane Allen.* Louisville, Ky.: Courier-Journal Job Printing Co., 1927.
Townsend, John Wilson. *Kentucky in American Letters.* Cedar Rapids.

Iowa, 1913.
Truitt, Evelyn Mack. *Who's Who on Screen.* New York: R. R. Bowker Co., 1974.
Weiner, Ed. *The Damon Runyon Story.* New York: Longmans, Green and Co., 1948.
White, Walter. *A Man Called White: The Autobiography of Walter White.* New York: Viking Press, 1948.
Williams, Blanche Colton. *Our Short Story Writers.* New York, 1920.
Woodson, Urey. *The First New Dealer: William Goebel: His Origin, Ambition, Achievements: His Assassination: Loss to the State and Nation: The Story of a Great Crime.* Louisville, Ky.: The Standard Press, 1939.
Yates, Morris W. *The American Humorists: Conscience of The Twentieth Century.* Ames, Iowa: Iowa University Press, 1964.
Yates, Norris W. *Robert Benchley.* New York: Twayne Publishers, 1968.

# Index